Apache Solr 4 Cookbook

Over 100 recipes to make Apache Solr faster,
more reliable, and return better results

Rafał Kuć

BIRMINGHAM - MUMBAI

Apache Solr 4 Cookbook

First published: July 2011

Second edition: January 2013

Production Reference: 1150113

Published by Packt Publishing Ltd.
Livery Place
35 Livery Street
Birmingham B3 2PB, UK.

ISBN 978-1-78216-132-5

www.packtpub.com

Cover Image by J. Blaminsky (milak6@wp.pl)

Credits

Author

Rafał Kuć

Reviewers

Ravindra Bharathi

Marcelo Ochoa

Vijayakumar Ramdoss

Acquisition Editor

Andrew Duckworth

Lead Technical Editor

Arun Nadar

Technical Editors

Jalasha D'costa

Charmaine Pereira

Lubna Shaikh

Project Coordinator

Anurag Banerjee

Proofreaders

Maria Gould

Aaron Nash

Indexer

Tejal Soni

Production Coordinators

Manu Joseph

Nitesh Thakur

Cover Work

Nitesh Thakur

About the Author

Rafał Kuć is a born team leader and software developer. Currently working as a Consultant and a Software Engineer at Sematext Inc, where he concentrates on open source technologies such as Apache Lucene and Solr, ElasticSearch, and Hadoop stack. He has more than 10 years of experience in various software branches, from banking software to e-commerce products. He is mainly focused on Java, but open to every tool and programming language that will make the achievement of his goal easier and faster. Rafał is also one of the founders of the `solr.pl` site, where he tries to share his knowledge and help people with their problems with Solr and Lucene. He is also a speaker for various conferences around the world such as Lucene Eurocon, Berlin Buzzwords, and ApacheCon.

Rafał began his journey with Lucene in 2002 and it wasn't love at first sight. When he came back to Lucene later in 2003, he revised his thoughts about the framework and saw the potential in search technologies. Then Solr came and that was it. From then on, Rafał has concentrated on search technologies and data analysis. Right now Lucene, Solr, and ElasticSearch are his main points of interest.

Acknowledgement

This book is an update to the first cookbook for Solr that was released almost two year ago now. What was at the beginning an update turned out to be a rewrite of almost all the recipes in the book, because we wanted to not only bring you an update to the already existing recipes, but also give you whole new recipes that will help you with common situations when using Apache Solr 4.0. I hope that the book you are holding in your hands (or reading on a computer or reader screen) will be useful to you.

Although I would go the same way if I could get back in time, the time of writing this book was not easy for my family. Among the ones who suffered the most were my wife Agnes and our two great kids, our son Philip and daughter Susanna. Without their patience and understanding, the writing of this book wouldn't have been possible. I would also like to thank my parents and Agnes' parents for their support and help.

I would like to thank all the people involved in creating, developing, and maintaining Lucene and Solr projects for their work and passion. Without them this book wouldn't have been written.

Once again, thank you.

About the Reviewers

Ravindra Bharathi has worked in the software industry for over a decade in various domains such as education, digital media marketing/advertising, enterprise search, and energy management systems. He has a keen interest in search-based applications that involve data visualization, mashups, and dashboards. He blogs at `http://ravindrabharathi.blogspot.com`.

Marcelo Ochoa works at the System Laboratory of Facultad de Ciencias Exactas of the Universidad Nacional del Centro de la Provincia de Buenos Aires, and is the CTO at `Scotas.com`, a company specialized in near real time search solutions using Apache Solr and Oracle. He divides his time between University jobs and external projects related to Oracle, and big data technologies. He has worked in several Oracle related projects such as translation of Oracle manuals and multimedia CBTs. His background is in database, network, web, and Java technologies. In the XML world, he is known as the developer of the DB Generator for the Apache Cocoon project, the open source projects DBPrism and DBPrism CMS, the Lucene-Oracle integration by using Oracle JVM Directory implementation, and the Restlet.org project – the Oracle XDB Restlet Adapter, an alternative to writing native REST web services inside the database resident JVM.

Since 2006, he has been a part of the Oracle ACE program. Oracle ACEs are known for their strong credentials as Oracle community enthusiasts and advocates, with candidates nominated by ACEs in the Oracle Technology and Applications communities.

He is the author of *Chapter 17* of the book *Oracle Database Programming using Java and Web Services, Kuassi Mensah, Digital Press* and *Chapter 21* of the book *Professional XML Databases, Kevin Williams, Wrox Press*.

www.PacktPub.com

Support files, eBooks, discount offers and more

You might want to visit www.PacktPub.com for support files and downloads related to your book.

Did you know that Packt offers eBook versions of every book published, with PDF and ePub files available? You can upgrade to the eBook version at www.PacktPub.com and as a print book customer, you are entitled to a discount on the eBook copy. Get in touch with us at service@packtpub.com for more details.

At www.PacktPub.com, you can also read a collection of free technical articles, sign up for a range of free newsletters and receive exclusive discounts and offers on Packt books and eBooks.

 PACKTLiB®

http://PacktLib.PacktPub.com

Do you need instant solutions to your IT questions? PacktLib is Packt's online digital book library. Here, you can access, read and search across Packt's entire library of books.

Why Subscribe?

- ▶ Fully searchable across every book published by Packt
- ▶ Copy and paste, print and bookmark content
- ▶ On demand and accessible via web browser

Free Access for Packt account holders

If you have an account with Packt at www.PacktPub.com, you can use this to access PacktLib today and view nine entirely free books. Simply use your login credentials for immediate access.

Table of Contents

Preface

Welcome to the Solr Cookbook for Apache Solr 4.0. You will be taken on a tour through the most common problems when dealing with Apache Solr. You will learn how to deal with the problems in Solr configuration and setup, how to handle common querying problems, how to fine-tune Solr instances, how to set up and use SolrCloud, how to use faceting and grouping, fight common problems, and many more things. Every recipe is based on real-life problems, and each recipe includes solutions along with detailed descriptions of the configuration and code that was used.

What this book covers

Chapter 1, Apache Solr Configuration, covers Solr configuration recipes, different servlet container usage with Solr, and setting up Apache ZooKeeper and Apache Nutch.

Chapter 2, Indexing Your Data, explains data indexing such as binary file indexing, using Data Import Handler, language detection, updating a single field of document, and much more.

Chapter 3, Analyzing Your Text Data, concentrates on common problems when analyzing your data such as stemming, geographical location indexing, or using synonyms.

Chapter 4, Querying Solr, describes querying Apache Solr such as nesting queries, affecting scoring of documents, phrase search, or using the parent-child relationship.

Chapter 5, Using the Faceting Mechanism, is dedicated to the faceting mechanism in which you can find the information needed to overcome some of the situations that you can encounter during your work with Solr and faceting.

Chapter 6, Improving Solr Performance, is dedicated to improving your Apache Solr cluster performance with information such as cache configuration, indexing speed up, and much more.

Chapter 7, In the Cloud, covers the new feature in Solr 4.0, the SolrCloud, and the setting up of collections, replica configuration, distributed indexing and searching, and understanding Solr administration.

Chapter 8, Using Additional Solr Functionalities, explains documents highlighting, sorting results on the basis of function value, checking user spelling mistakes, and using the grouping functionality.

Chapter 9, Dealing with Problems, is a small chapter dedicated to the most common situations such as memory problems, reducing your index size, and similar issues.

Appendix, Real Life Situations, describes how to handle real-life situations such as implementing different autocomplete functionalities, using near real-time search, or improving query relevance.

What you need for this book

In order to be able to run most of the examples in the book, you will need the Java Runtime Environment 1.6 or newer, and of course the 4.0 version of the Apache Solr search server.

A few chapters in this book require additional software such as Apache ZooKeeper 3.4.3, Apache Nutch 1.5.1, Apache Tomcat, or Jetty.

Who this book is for

This book is for users working with Apache Solr or developers that use Apache Solr to build their own software that would like to know how to combat common problems. Knowledge of Apache Lucene would be a bonus, but is not required.

Conventions

In this book, you will find a number of styles of text that distinguish between different kinds of information. Here are some examples of these styles, and an explanation of their meaning.

Code words in text are shown as follows: "The `lib` entry in the `solrconfig.xml` file tells Solr to look for all the JAR files from the `../../langid` directory".

A block of code is set as follows:

```
<field name="id" type="string" indexed="true" stored="true"
required="true" multiValued="false" />
<field name="name" type="text_general" indexed="true" stored="true"/>
<field name="description" type="text_general" indexed="true"
stored="true" />
<field name="langId" type="string" indexed="true" stored="true" />
```

When we wish to draw your attention to a particular part of a code block, the relevant lines or items are set in bold:

```
<updateRequestProcessorChain name="langid">
  <processor class="org.apache.solr.update.processor.
  TikaLanguageIdentifierUpdateProcessorFactory">
    <str name="langid.fl">name,description</str>
    <str name="langid.langField">langId</str>
    <str name="langid.fallback">en</str>
  </processor>
```

Any command-line input or output is written as follows:

```
curl 'localhost:8983/solr/update?commit=true' -H 'Content-
type:application/json' -d '[{"id":"1","file":{"set":"New file name"}}]'
```

New terms and **important words** are shown in bold. Words that you see on the screen, in menus or dialog boxes for example, appear in the text like this: "clicking the **Next** button moves you to the next screen".

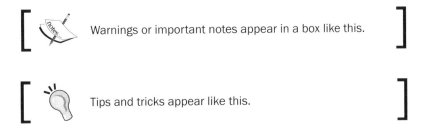

> Warnings or important notes appear in a box like this.

> Tips and tricks appear like this.

Reader feedback

Feedback from our readers is always welcome. Let us know what you think about this book—what you liked or may have disliked. Reader feedback is important for us to develop titles that you really get the most out of.

To send us general feedback, simply send an e-mail to feedback@packtpub.com, and mention the book title through the subject of your message.

If there is a topic that you have expertise in and you are interested in either writing or contributing to a book, see our author guide on www.packtpub.com/authors.

Customer support

Now that you are the proud owner of a Packt book, we have a number of things to help you to get the most from your purchase.

Downloading the example code

You can download the example code files for all Packt books you have purchased from your account at `http://www.packtpub.com`. If you purchased this book elsewhere, you can visit `http://www.packtpub.com/support` and register to have the files e-mailed directly to you.

Errata

Although we have taken every care to ensure the accuracy of our content, mistakes do happen. If you find a mistake in one of our books—maybe a mistake in the text or the code—we would be grateful if you would report this to us. By doing so, you can save other readers from frustration and help us improve subsequent versions of this book. If you find any errata, please report them by visiting `http://www.packtpub.com/support`, selecting your book, clicking on the **errata submission form** link, and entering the details of your errata. Once your errata are verified, your submission will be accepted and the errata will be uploaded to our website, or added to any list of existing errata, under the Errata section of that title.

Piracy

Piracy of copyright material on the Internet is an ongoing problem across all media. At Packt, we take the protection of our copyright and licenses very seriously. If you come across any illegal copies of our works, in any form, on the Internet, please provide us with the location address or website name immediately so that we can pursue a remedy.

Please contact us at `copyright@packtpub.com` with a link to the suspected pirated material.

We appreciate your help in protecting our authors, and our ability to bring you valuable content.

Questions

You can contact us at `questions@packtpub.com` if you are having a problem with any aspect of the book, and we will do our best to address it.

1
Apache Solr Configuration

In this chapter we will cover:

- ► Running Solr on Jetty
- ► Running Solr on Apache Tomcat
- ► Installing a standalone ZooKeeper
- ► Clustering your data
- ► Choosing the right directory implementation
- ► Configuring spellchecker to not use its own index
- ► Solr cache configuration
- ► How to fetch and index web pages
- ► How to set up the extracting request handler
- ► Changing the default similarity implementation

Introduction

Setting up an example Solr instance is not a hard task, at least when setting up the simplest configuration. The simplest way is to run the example provided with the Solr distribution, that shows how to use the embedded Jetty servlet container.

If you don't have any experience with Apache Solr, please refer to the Apache Solr tutorial which can be found at: `http://lucene.apache.org/solr/tutorial.html` before reading this book.

During the writing of this chapter, I used Solr version 4.0 and Jetty version 8.1.5, and those versions are covered in the tips of the following chapter. If another version of Solr is mandatory for a feature to run, then it will be mentioned.

We have a simple configuration, simple index structure described by the schema.xml file, and we can run indexing.

In this chapter you'll see how to configure and use the more advanced Solr modules; you'll see how to run Solr in different containers and how to prepare your configuration to different requirements. You will also learn how to set up a new SolrCloud cluster and migrate your current configuration to the one supporting all the features of SolrCloud. Finally, you will learn how to configure Solr cache to meet your needs and how to pre-sort your Solr indexes to be able to use early query termination techniques efficiently.

Running Solr on Jetty

The simplest way to run Apache Solr on a Jetty servlet container is to run the provided example configuration based on embedded Jetty. But it's not the case here. In this recipe, I would like to show you how to configure and run Solr on a standalone Jetty container.

Getting ready

First of all you need to download the Jetty servlet container for your platform. You can get your download package from an automatic installer (such as, apt-get), or you can download it yourself from http://jetty.codehaus.org/jetty/.

How to do it...

The first thing is to install the Jetty servlet container, which is beyond the scope of this book, so we will assume that you have Jetty installed in the /usr/share/jetty directory or you copied the Jetty files to that directory.

Let's start by copying the solr.war file to the webapps directory of the Jetty installation (so the whole path would be /usr/share/jetty/webapps). In addition to that we need to create a temporary directory in Jetty installation, so let's create the temp directory in the Jetty installation directory.

Next we need to copy and adjust the solr.xml file from the context directory of the Solr example distribution to the context directory of the Jetty installation. The final file contents should look like the following code:

```
<?xml version="1.0"?>
<!DOCTYPE Configure PUBLIC "-//Jetty//Configure//EN" "http://www.
eclipse.org/jetty/configure.dtd">
<Configure class="org.eclipse.jetty.webapp.WebAppContext">
  <Set name="contextPath">/solr</Set>
  <Set name="war"><SystemProperty name="jetty.home"/>/webapps/solr.
war</Set>
  <Set name="defaultsDescriptor"><SystemProperty name="jetty.home"/>/
etc/webdefault.xml</Set>
  <Set name="tempDirectory"><Property name="jetty.home" default="."/>/
temp</Set>
</Configure>
```

Downloading the example code

You can download the example code files for all Packt books you have purchased from your account at http://www.packtpub.com. If you purchased this book elsewhere, you can visit http://www.packtpub.com/support and register to have the files e-mailed directly to you.

Now we need to copy the jetty.xml, webdefault.xml, and logging.properties files from the etc directory of the Solr distribution to the configuration directory of Jetty, so in our case to the /usr/share/jetty/etc directory.

The next step is to copy the Solr configuration files to the appropriate directory. I'm talking about files such as schema.xml, solrconfig.xml, solr.xml, and so on. Those files should be in the directory specified by the solr.solr.home system variable (in my case this was the /usr/share/solr directory). Please remember to preserve the directory structure you'll see in the example deployment, so for example, the /usr/share/solr directory should contain the solr.xml (and in addition zoo.cfg in case you want to use SolrCloud) file with the contents like so:

```
<?xml version="1.0" encoding="UTF-8" ?>
<solr persistent="true">
  <cores adminPath="/admin/cores" defaultCoreName="collection1">
    <core name="collection1" instanceDir="collection1" />
  </cores>
</solr>
```

All the other configuration files should go to the /usr/share/solr/collection1/conf directory (place the schema.xml and solrconfig.xml files there along with any additional configuration files your deployment needs). Your cores may have other names than the default collection1, so please be aware of that.

The last thing about the configuration is to update the `/etc/default/jetty` file and add `-Dsolr.solr.home=/usr/share/solr` to the `JAVA_OPTIONS` variable of that file. The whole line with that variable could look like the following:

```
JAVA_OPTIONS="-Xmx256m -Djava.awt.headless=true -Dsolr.solr.home=/usr/
share/solr/"
```

If you didn't install Jetty with `apt-get` or a similar software, you may not have the `/etc/default/jetty` file. In that case, add the `-Dsolr.solr.home=/usr/share/solr` parameter to the Jetty startup.

We can now run Jetty to see if everything is ok. To start Jetty, that was installed, for example, using the `apt-get` command, use the following command:

`/etc/init.d/jetty start`

You can also run Jetty with a `java` command. Run the following command in the Jetty installation directory:

`java -Dsolr.solr.home=/usr/share/solr -jar start.jar`

If there were no exceptions during the startup, we have a running Jetty with Solr deployed and configured. To check if Solr is running, try going to the following address with your web browser: `http://localhost:8983/solr/`.

You should see the Solr front page with cores, or a single core, mentioned. Congratulations! You just successfully installed, configured, and ran the Jetty servlet container with Solr deployed.

How it works...

For the purpose of this recipe, I assumed that we needed a single core installation with only `schema.xml` and `solrconfig.xml` configuration files. Multicore installation is very similar – it differs only in terms of the Solr configuration files.

The first thing we did was copy the `solr.war` file and create the `temp` directory. The WAR file is the actual Solr web application. The `temp` directory will be used by Jetty to unpack the WAR file.

The `solr.xml` file we placed in the `context` directory enables Jetty to define the context for the Solr web application. As you can see in its contents, we set the context to be `/solr`, so our Solr application will be available under `http://localhost:8983/solr/`. We also specified where Jetty should look for the WAR file (the `war` property), where the web application descriptor file (the `defaultsDescriptor` property) is, and finally where the temporary directory will be located (the `tempDirectory` property).

The next step is to provide configuration files for the Solr web application. Those files should be in the directory specified by the system `solr.solr.home` variable. I decided to use the `/usr/share/solr` directory to ensure that I'll be able to update Jetty without the need of overriding or deleting the Solr configuration files. When copying the Solr configuration files, you should remember to include all the files and the exact directory structure that Solr needs. So in the directory specified by the `solr.solr.home` variable, the `solr.xml` file should be available – the one that describes the cores of your system.

The `solr.xml` file is pretty simple – there should be the root element called `solr`. Inside it there should be a `cores` tag (with the `adminPath` variable set to the address where Solr's cores administration API is available and the `defaultCoreName` attribute that says which is the default core). The `cores` tag is a parent for cores definition – each core should have its own `cores` tag with `name` attribute specifying the core name and the `instanceDir` attribute specifying the directory where the core specific files will be available (such as the `conf` directory).

If you installed Jetty with the `apt-get` command or similar, you will need to update the `/etc/default/jetty` file to include the `solr.solr.home` variable for Solr to be able to see its configuration directory.

After all those steps we are ready to launch Jetty. If you installed Jetty with `apt-get` or a similar software, you can run Jetty with the first command shown in the example. Otherwise you can run Jetty with a `java` command from the Jetty installation directory.

After running the example query in your web browser you should see the Solr front page as a single core. Congratulations! You just successfully configured and ran the Jetty servlet container with Solr deployed.

There's more...

There are a few tasks you can do to counter some problems when running Solr within the Jetty servlet container. Here are the most common ones that I encountered during my work.

I want Jetty to run on a different port

Sometimes it's necessary to run Jetty on a different port other than the default one. We have two ways to achieve that:

- Adding an additional startup parameter, `jetty.port`. The startup command would look like the following command:

  ```
  java -Djetty.port=9999 -jar start.jar
  ```

▶ Changing the `jetty.xml` file – to do that you need to change the following line:

```
<Set name="port"><SystemProperty name="jetty.port"
default="8983"/></Set>
```

To:

```
<Set name="port"><SystemProperty name="jetty.port"
default="9999"/></Set>
```

Buffer size is too small

Buffer overflow is a common problem when our queries are getting too long and too complex, – for example, when we use many logical operators or long phrases. When the standard *head* buffer is not enough you can resize it to meet your needs. To do that, you add the following line to the Jetty connector in the `jetty.xml` file. Of course the value shown in the example can be changed to the one that you need:

```
<Set name="headerBufferSize">32768</Set>
```

After adding the value, the connector definition should look more or less like the following snippet:

```
<Call name="addConnector">
<Arg>
<New class="org.mortbay.jetty.bio.SocketConnector">
<Set name="port"><SystemProperty name="jetty.port" default="8080"/></Set>
<Set name="maxIdleTime">50000</Set>
<Set name="lowResourceMaxIdleTime">1500</Set>
<Set name="headerBufferSize">32768</Set>
</New>
</Arg>
</Call>
```

Running Solr on Apache Tomcat

Sometimes you need to choose a servlet container other than Jetty. Maybe because your client has other applications running on another servlet container, maybe because you just don't like Jetty. Whatever your requirements are that put Jetty out of the scope of your interest, the first thing that comes to mind is a popular and powerful servlet container – Apache Tomcat. This recipe will give you an idea of how to properly set up and run Solr in the Apache Tomcat environment.

Getting ready

First of all we need an Apache Tomcat servlet container. It can be found at the Apache Tomcat website – `http://tomcat.apache.org`. I concentrated on the Tomcat Version 7.x because at the time of writing of this book it was mature and stable. The version that I used during the writing of this recipe was Apache Tomcat 7.0.29, which was the newest one at the time.

How to do it...

To run Solr on Apache Tomcat we need to follow these simple steps:

1. Firstly, you need to install Apache Tomcat. The Tomcat installation is beyond the scope of this book so we will assume that you have already installed this servlet container in the directory specified by the `$TOMCAT_HOME` system variable.

2. The second step is preparing the Apache Tomcat configuration files. To do that we need to add the following inscription to the connector definition in the `server.xml` configuration file:

    ```
    URIEncoding="UTF-8"
    ```

    The portion of the modified `server.xml` file should look like the following code snippet:

    ```
    <Connector port="8080" protocol="HTTP/1.1"
                connectionTimeout="20000"
                redirectPort="8443"
                URIEncoding="UTF-8" />
    ```

3. The third step is to create a proper context file. To do that, create a `solr.xml` file in the `$TOMCAT_HOME/conf/Catalina/localhost` directory. The contents of the file should look like the following code:

    ```
    <Context path="/solr" docBase="/usr/share/tomcat/webapps/solr.war"
    debug="0" crossContext="true">
        <Environment name="solr/home" type="java.lang.String" value="/
    usr/share/solr/" override="true"/>
    </Context>
    ```

4. The next thing is the Solr deployment. To do that we need the `apache-solr-4.0.0.war` file that contains the necessary files and libraries to run Solr that is to be copied to the Tomcat `webapps` directory and renamed `solr.war`.

5. The one last thing we need to do is add the Solr configuration files. The files that you need to copy are files such as `schema.xml`, `solrconfig.xml`, and so on. Those files should be placed in the directory specified by the `solr/home` variable (in our case `/usr/share/solr/`). Please don't forget that you need to ensure the proper directory structure. If you are not familiar with the Solr directory structure please take a look at the example deployment that is provided with the standard Solr package.

6. Please remember to preserve the directory structure you'll see in the example deployment, so for example, the `/usr/share/solr` directory should contain the `solr.xml` (and in addition `zoo.cfg` in case you want to use SolrCloud) file with the contents like so:

```
<?xml version="1.0" encoding="UTF-8" ?>
<solr persistent="true">
  <cores adminPath="/admin/cores" defaultCoreName="collection1">
    <core name="collection1" instanceDir="collection1" />
  </cores>
</solr>
```

7. All the other configuration files should go to the `/usr/share/solr/collection1/conf` directory (place the `schema.xml` and `solrconfig.xml` files there along with any additional configuration files your deployment needs). Your cores may have other names than the default `collection1`, so please be aware of that.

8. Now we can start the servlet container, by running the following command:

   `bin/catalina.sh start`

9. In the log file you should see a message like this:

   `Info: Server startup in 3097 ms`

10. To ensure that Solr is running properly, you can run a browser and point it to an address where Solr should be visible, like the following:

    `http://localhost:8080/solr/`

If you see the page with links to administration pages of each of the cores defined, that means that your Solr is up and running.

How it works...

Let's start from the second step as the installation part is beyond the scope of this book. As you probably know, Solr uses UTF-8 file encoding. That means that we need to ensure that Apache Tomcat will be informed that all requests and responses made should use that encoding. To do that, we modified the `server.xml` file in the way shown in the example.

The **Catalina context** file (called `solr.xml` in our example) says that our Solr application will be available under the `/solr` context (the `path` attribute). We also specified the WAR file location (the `docBase` attribute). We also said that we are not using debug (the `debug` attribute), and we allowed Solr to access other context manipulation methods. The last thing is to specify the directory where Solr should look for the configuration files. We do that by adding the `solr/home` environment variable with the `value` attribute set to the path to the directory where we have put the configuration files.

The `solr.xml` file is pretty simple – there should be the root element called `solr`. Inside it there should be the `cores` tag (with the `adminPath` variable set to the address where the Solr cores administration API is available and the `defaultCoreName` attribute describing which is the default core). The `cores` tag is a parent for cores definition – each core should have its own `core` tag with a `name` attribute specifying the core name and the `instanceDir` attribute specifying the directory where the core-specific files will be available (such as the `conf` directory).

The shell command that is shown starts Apache Tomcat. There are some other options of the `catalina.sh` (or `catalina.bat`) script; the descriptions of these options are as follows:

- ▶ `stop`: This stops Apache Tomcat
- ▶ `restart`: This restarts Apache Tomcat
- ▶ `debug`: This start Apache Tomcat in debug mode
- ▶ `run`: This runs Apache Tomcat in the current window, so you can see the output on the console from which you run Tomcat.

After running the example address in the web browser, you should see a Solr front page with a core (or cores if you have a multicore deployment). Congratulations! You just successfully configured and ran the Apache Tomcat servlet container with Solr deployed.

There's more...

There are some other tasks that are common problems when running Solr on Apache Tomcat.

Changing the port on which we see Solr running on Tomcat

Sometimes it is necessary to run Apache Tomcat on a different port other than 8080, which is the default one. To do that, you need to modify the `port` variable of the connector definition in the `server.xml` file located in the `$TOMCAT_HOME/conf` directory. If you would like your Tomcat to run on port 9999, this definition should look like the following code snippet:

```
<Connector port="9999" protocol="HTTP/1.1"
           connectionTimeout="20000"
           redirectPort="8443"
           URIEncoding="UTF-8" />
```

While the original definition looks like the following snippet:

```
<Connector port="8080" protocol="HTTP/1.1"
           connectionTimeout="20000"
           redirectPort="8443"
           URIEncoding="UTF-8" />
```

Installing a standalone ZooKeeper

You may know that in order to run SolrCloud—the distributed Solr installation—you need to have **Apache ZooKeeper** installed. Zookeeper is a centralized service for maintaining configurations, naming, and provisioning service synchronization. SolrCloud uses ZooKeeper to synchronize configuration and cluster states (such as elected shard leaders), and that's why it is crucial to have a highly available and fault tolerant ZooKeeper installation. If you have a single ZooKeeper instance and it fails then your SolrCloud cluster will crash too. So, this recipe will show you how to install ZooKeeper so that it's not a single point of failure in your cluster configuration.

Getting ready

The installation instruction in this recipe contains information about installing ZooKeeper Version 3.4.3, but it should be useable for any minor release changes of Apache ZooKeeper. To download ZooKeeper please go to `http://zookeeper.apache.org/releases.html`. This recipe will show you how to install ZooKeeper in a Linux-based environment. You also need Java installed.

How to do it...

Let's assume that we decided to install ZooKeeper in the `/usr/share/zookeeper` directory of our server and we want to have three servers (with IP addresses `192.168.1.1`, `192.168.1.2`, and `192.168.1.3`) hosting the distributed ZooKeeper installation.

1. After downloading the ZooKeeper installation, we create the necessary directory:

   ```
   sudo mkdir /usr/share/zookeeper
   ```

2. Then we unpack the downloaded archive to the newly created directory. We do that on three servers.

3. Next we need to change our ZooKeeper configuration file and specify the servers that will form the ZooKeeper quorum, so we edit the `/usr/share/zookeeper/conf/zoo.cfg` file and we add the following entries:

   ```
   clientPort=2181
   dataDir=/usr/share/zookeeper/data
   tickTime=2000
   initLimit=10
   syncLimit=5
   server.1=192.168.1.1:2888:3888
   server.2=192.168.1.2:2888:3888
   server.3=192.168.1.3:2888:3888
   ```

4. And now, we can start the ZooKeeper servers with the following command:

   `/usr/share/zookeeper/bin/zkServer.sh start`

5. If everything went well you should see something like the following:

   `JMX enabled by default`

   `Using config: /usr/share/zookeeper/bin/../conf/zoo.cfg`

   `Starting zookeeper ... STARTED`

And that's all. Of course you can also add the ZooKeeper service to start automatically during your operating system startup, but that's beyond the scope of the recipe and the book itself.

How it works...

Let's skip the first part, because creating the directory and unpacking the ZooKeeper server there is quite simple. What I would like to concentrate on are the configuration values of the ZooKeeper server. The `clientPort` property specifies the port on which our SolrCloud servers should connect to ZooKeeper. The `dataDir` property specifies the directory where ZooKeeper will hold its data. So far, so good right ? So now, the more advanced properties; the `tickTime` property specified in milliseconds is the basic time unit for ZooKeeper. The `initLimit` property specifies how many ticks the initial synchronization phase can take. Finally, the `syncLimit` property specifies how many ticks can pass between sending the request and receiving an acknowledgement.

There are also three additional properties present, `server.1`, `server.2`, and `server.3`. These three properties define the addresses of the ZooKeeper instances that will form the quorum. However, there are three values separated by a colon character. The first part is the IP address of the ZooKeeper server, and the second and third parts are the ports used by ZooKeeper instances to communicate with each other.

Clustering your data

After the release of Apache Solr 4.0, many users will want to leverage SolrCloud distributed indexing and querying capabilities. It's not hard to upgrade your current cluster to SolrCloud, but there are some things you need to take care of. With the help of the following recipe you will be able to easily upgrade your cluster.

Getting ready

Before continuing further it is advised to read the *Installing a standalone ZooKeeper* recipe in this chapter. It shows how to set up a ZooKeeper cluster in order to be ready for production use.

How to do it...

In order to use your old index structure with SolrCloud, you will need to add the following field to your fields definition (add the following fragment to the `schema.xml` file, to its `fields` section):

```
<field name="_version_" type="long" indexed="true" stored="true"
multiValued="false"/>
```

Now let's switch to the `solrconfig.xml` file – starting with the replication handlers. First, you need to ensure that you have the replication handler set up. Remember that you shouldn't add master or slave specific configurations to it. So the replication handlers' configuration should look like the following code:

```
<requestHandler name="/replication" class="solr.ReplicationHandler" />
```

In addition to that, you will need to have the administration panel handlers present, so the following configuration entry should be present in your `solrconfig.xml` file:

```
<requestHandler name="/admin/" class="solr.admin.AdminHandlers" />
```

The last request handler that should be present is the real-time `get` handler, which should be defined as follows (the following should also be added to the `solrconfig.xml` file):

```
<requestHandler name="/get" class="solr.RealTimeGetHandler">
  <lst name="defaults">
    <str name="omitHeader">true</str>
  </lst>
</requestHandler>
```

The next thing SolrCloud needs in order to properly operate is the transaction log configuration. The following fragment should be added to the `solrconfig.xml` file:

```
<updateLog>
  <str name="dir">${solr.data.dir:}</str>
</updateLog>
```

The last thing is the `solr.xml` file. It should be pointing to the default cores administration address – the `cores` tag should have the `adminPath` property set to the `/admin/cores` value. The example `solr.xml` file could look like the following code:

```
<solr persistent="true">
  <cores adminPath="/admin/cores" defaultCoreName="collection1"
host="localhost" hostPort="8983" zkClientTimeout="15000">
    <core name="collection1" instanceDir="collection1" />
  </cores>
</solr>
```

And that's all, your Solr instances configuration files are now ready to be used with SolrCloud.

How it works...

So now let's see why all those changes are needed in order to use our old configuration files with SolrCloud.

The `_version_` field is used by Solr to enable documents versioning and optimistic locking, which ensures that you won't have the newest version of your document overwritten by mistake. Because of that, SolrCloud requires the `_version_` field to be present in your index structure. Adding that field is simple – you just need to place another field definition that is stored and indexed, and based on the `long` type. That's all.

As for the replication handler, you should remember not to add slave or master specific configuration, only the simple request handler definition, as shown in the previous example. The same applies to the administration panel handlers: they need to be available under the default URL address.

The real-time `get` handler is responsible for getting the updated documents right away, even if no commit or the `softCommit` command is executed. This handler allows Solr (and also you) to retrieve the latest version of the document without the need for re-opening the searcher, and thus even if the document is not yet visible during usual search operations. The configuration is very similar to the usual request handler configuration – you need to add a new handler with the `name` property set to `/get` and the `class` property set to `solr.RealTimeGetHandler`. In addition to that, we want the handler to be omitting response headers (the `omitHeader` property set to `true`).

One of the last things that is needed by SolrCloud is the transaction log, which enables real-time `get` operations to be functional. The transaction log keeps track of all the uncommitted changes and enables a real-time `get` handler to retrieve those. In order to turn on transaction log usage, one should add the `updateLog` tag to the `solrconfig.xml` file and specify the directory where the transaction log directory should be created (by adding the `dir` property as shown in the example). In the configuration previously shown, we tell Solr that we want to use the Solr data directory as the place to store the transaction log directory.

Finally, Solr needs you to keep the default address for the core administrative interface, so you should remember to have the `adminPath` property set to the value shown in the example (in the `solr.xml` file). This is needed in order for Solr to be able to manipulate cores.

Choosing the right directory implementation

One of the most crucial properties of Apache Lucene, and thus Solr, is the **Lucene directory implementation**. The directory interface provides an abstraction layer for Lucene on all the I/O operations. Although choosing the right directory implementation seems simple, it can affect the performance of your Solr setup in a drastic way. This recipe will show you how to choose the right directory implementation.

How to do it...

In order to use the desired directory, all you need to do is choose the right directory factory implementation and inform Solr about it. Let's assume that you would like to use `NRTCachingDirectory` as your directory implementation. In order to do that, you need to place (or replace if it is already present) the following fragment in your `solrconfig.xml` file:

```
<directoryFactory name="DirectoryFactory" class="solr.
NRTCachingDirectoryFactory" />
```

And that's all. The setup is quite simple, but what directory factories are available to use? When this book was written, the following directory factories were available:

- ▶ `solr.StandardDirectoryFactory`
- ▶ `solr.SimpleFSDirectoryFactory`
- ▶ `solr.NIOFSDirectoryFactory`
- ▶ `solr.MMapDirectoryFactory`
- ▶ `solr.NRTCachingDirectoryFactory`
- ▶ `solr.RAMDirectoryFactory`

So now let's see what each of those factories provide.

How it works...

Before we get into the details of each of the presented directory factories, I would like to comment on the directory factory configuration parameter. All you need to remember is that the `name` attribute of the `directoryFactory` tag should be set to `DirectoryFactory` and the `class` attribute should be set to the directory factory implementation of your choice.

If you want Solr to make the decision for you, you should use `solr.StandardDirectoryFactory`. This is a filesystem-based directory factory that tries to choose the best implementation based on your current operating system and Java virtual machine used. If you are implementing a small application, which won't use many threads, you can use `solr.SimpleFSDirectoryFactory` which stores the index file on your local filesystem, but it doesn't scale well with a high number of threads. `solr.NIOFSDirectoryFactory` scales well with many threads, but it doesn't work well on Microsoft Windows platforms (it's much slower), because of the JVM bug, so you should remember that.

`solr.MMapDirectoryFactory` was the default directory factory for Solr for the 64-bit Linux systems from Solr 3.1 till 4.0. This directory implementation uses virtual memory and a kernel feature called mmap to access index files stored on disk. This allows Lucene (and thus Solr) to directly access the I/O cache. This is desirable and you should stick to that directory if near real-time searching is not needed.

If you need near real-time indexing and searching, you should use `solr.NRTCachingDirectoryFactory`. It is designed to store some parts of the index in memory (small chunks) and thus speed up some near real-time operations greatly.

The last directory factory, `solr.RAMDirectoryFactory`, is the only one that is not persistent. The whole index is stored in the RAM memory and thus you'll lose your index after restart or server crash. Also you should remember that replication won't work when using `solr.RAMDirectoryFactory`. One would ask, why should I use that factory? Imagine a volatile index for an autocomplete functionality or for unit tests of your queries' relevancy. Just anything you can think of, when you don't need to have persistent and replicated data. However, please remember that this directory is not designed to hold large amounts of data.

Configuring spellchecker to not use its own index

If you are used to the way spellchecker worked in the previous Solr versions, you may remember that it required its own index to give you spelling corrections. That approach had some disadvantages, such as the need for rebuilding the index, and replication between master and slave servers. With the Solr Version 4.0, a new spellchecker implementation was introduced – `solr.DirectSolrSpellchecker`. It allowed you to use your main index to provide spelling suggestions and didn't need to be rebuilt after every commit. So now, let's see how to use that new spellchecker implementation in Solr.

How to do it...

First of all, let's assume we have a field in the index called `title`, in which we hold titles of our documents. What's more, we don't want the spellchecker to have its own index and we would like to use that `title` field to provide spelling suggestions. In addition to that, we would like to decide when we want a spelling suggestion. In order to do that, we need to do two things:

1. First, we need to edit our `solrconfig.xml` file and add the spellchecking component, whose definition may look like the following code:

```
<searchComponent name="spellcheck" class="solr.
SpellCheckComponent">
  <str name="queryAnalyzerFieldType">title</str>
  <lst name="spellchecker">
    <str name="name">direct</str>
    <str name="field">title</str>
    <str name="classname">solr.DirectSolrSpellChecker</str>
    <str name="distanceMeasure">internal</str>
    <float name="accuracy">0.8</float>
    <int name="maxEdits">1</int>
```

```
      <int name="minPrefix">1</int>
      <int name="maxInspections">5</int>
      <int name="minQueryLength">3</int>
      <float name="maxQueryFrequency">0.01</float>
  </lst>
</searchComponent>
```

2. Now we need to add a proper request handler configuration that will use the previously mentioned search component. To do that, we need to add the following section to the `solrconfig.xml` file:

```
<requestHandler name="/spell" class="solr.SearchHandler"
startup="lazy">
  <lst name="defaults">
    <str name="df">title</str>
    <str name="spellcheck.dictionary">direct</str>
    <str name="spellcheck">on</str>
    <str name="spellcheck.extendedResults">true</str>
    <str name="spellcheck.count">5</str>
    <str name="spellcheck.collate">true</str>
    <str name="spellcheck.collateExtendedResults">true</str>
  </lst>
  <arr name="last-components">
    <str>spellcheck</str>
  </arr>
</requestHandler>
```

3. And that's all. In order to get spelling suggestions, we need to run the following query:

```
/spell?q=disa
```

4. In response we will get something like the following code:

```
<?xml version="1.0" encoding="UTF-8"?>
<response>
<lst name="responseHeader">
  <int name="status">0</int>
  <int name="QTime">5</int>
</lst>
<result name="response" numFound="0" start="0">
</result>
<lst name="spellcheck">
  <lst name="suggestions">
    <lst name="disa">
      <int name="numFound">1</int>
      <int name="startOffset">0</int>
      <int name="endOffset">4</int>
      <int name="origFreq">0</int>
      <arr name="suggestion">
        <lst>
          <str name="word">data</str>
          <int name="freq">1</int>
```

```
        </lst>
      </arr>
    </lst>
    <bool name="correctlySpelled">false</bool>
    <lst name="collation">
      <str name="collationQuery">data</str>
      <int name="hits">1</int>
      <lst name="misspellingsAndCorrections">
        <str name="disa">data</str>
      </lst>
    </lst>
  </lst>
 </lst>
</lst>
</response>
```

If you check your data folder you will see that there is not a single directory responsible for holding the spellchecker index. So, now let's see how that works.

How it works...

Now let's get into some specifics about how the previous configuration works, starting from the search component configuration. The `queryAnalyzerFieldType` property tells Solr which field configuration should be used to analyze the query passed to the spellchecker. The `name` property sets the name of the spellchecker which will be used in the handler configuration later. The `field` property specifies which field should be used as the source for the data used to build spelling suggestions. As you probably figured out, the `classname` property specifies the implementation class, which in our case is `solr.DirectSolrSpellChecker`, enabling us to omit having a separate spellchecker index. The next parameters visible in the configuration specify how the Solr spellchecker should behave and that is beyond the scope of this recipe (however, if you would like to read more about them, please go to the following URL address: `http://wiki.apache.org/solr/SpellCheckComponent`).

The last thing is the request handler configuration. Let's concentrate on all the properties that start with the `spellcheck` prefix. First we have `spellcheck.dictionary`, which in our case specifies the name of the spellchecking component we want to use (please note that the value of the property matches the value of the `name` property in the search component configuration). We tell Solr that we want the spellchecking results to be present (the `spellcheck` property with the value set to `on`), and we also tell Solr that we want to see the extended results format (`spellcheck.extendedResults` set to `true`). In addition to the mentioned configuration properties, we also said that we want to have a maximum of five suggestions (the `spellcheck.count` property), and we want to see the collation and its extended results (`spellcheck.collate` and `spellcheck.collateExtendedResults` both set to `true`).

There's more...

Let's see one more thing – the ability to have more than one spellchecker defined in a request handler.

More than one spellchecker

If you would like to have more than one spellchecker handling your spelling suggestions you can configure your handler to use multiple search components. For example, if you would like to use search components (spellchecking ones) named `word` and `better` (you have to have them configured), you could add multiple `spellcheck.dictionary` parameters to your request handler. This is how your request handler configuration would look:

```
<requestHandler name="/spell" class="solr.SearchHandler"
startup="lazy">
  <lst name="defaults">
    <str name="df">title</str>
    <str name="spellcheck.dictionary">direct</str>
    <str name="spellcheck.dictionary">word</str>
    <str name="spellcheck.dictionary">better</str>
    <str name="spellcheck">on</str>
    <str name="spellcheck.extendedResults">true</str>
    <str name="spellcheck.count">5</str>
    <str name="spellcheck.collate">true</str>
    <str name="spellcheck.collateExtendedResults">true</str>
  </lst>
  <arr name="last-components">
    <str>spellcheck</str>
  </arr>
</requestHandler>
```

Solr cache configuration

As you may already know, caches play a major role in a Solr deployment. And I'm not talking about some exterior cache – I'm talking about the three Solr caches:

- **Filter cache**: This is used for storing filter (query parameter `fq`) results and mainly `enum` type facets

- **Document cache**: This is used for storing Lucene documents which hold stored fields

- **Query result cache**: This is used for storing results of queries

There is a fourth cache – **Lucene's internal cache** – which is a field cache, but you can't control its behavior. It is managed by Lucene and created when it is first used by the `Searcher` object.

With the help of these caches we can tune the behavior of the Solr searcher instance. In this task we will focus on how to configure your Solr caches to suit most needs. There is one thing to remember – Solr cache sizes should be tuned to the number of documents in the index, the queries, and the number of results you usually get from Solr.

Getting ready

Before you start tuning Solr caches you should get some information about your Solr instance. That information is as follows:

- Number of documents in your index
- Number of queries per second made to that index
- Number of unique filter (the `fq` parameter) values in your queries
- Maximum number of documents returned in a single query
- Number of different queries and different sorts

All these numbers can be derived from Solr logs.

How to do it...

For the purpose of this task I assumed the following numbers:

- Number of documents in the index: `1.000.000`
- Number of queries per second: `100`
- Number of unique filters: `200`
- Maximum number of documents returned in a single query: `100`
- Number of different queries and different sorts: `500`

Let's open the `solrconfig.xml` file and tune our caches. All the changes should be made in the query section of the file (the section between `<query>` and `</query>` XML tags).

1. First goes the filter cache:

```
<filterCache
    class="solr.FastLRUCache"
    size="200"
    initialSize="200"
    autowarmCount="100"/>
```

2. Second goes the query result cache:

```
<queryResultCache
    class="solr.FastLRUCache"
    size="500"
    initialSize="500"
autowarmCount="250"/>
```

3. Third we have the document cache:

```
<documentCache
    class="solr.FastLRUCache"
    size="11000"
    initialSize="11000" />
```

Of course the above configuration is based on the example values.

4. Further let's set our result window to match our needs – we sometimes need to get 20–30 more results than we need during query execution. So we change the appropriate value in the `solrconfig.xml` file to something like this:

```
<queryResultWindowSize>200</queryResultWindowSize>
```

And that's all!

How it works...

Let's start with a little bit of explanation. First of all we use the `solr.FastLRUCache` implementation instead of `solr.LRUCache`. So the called `FastLRUCache` tends to be faster when Solr puts less into caches and gets more. This is the opposite to `LRUCache` which tends to be more efficient when there are more `puts` than `gets` operations. That's why we use it.

This colud be the first time you see cache configuration, so I'll explain what cache configuration parameters mean:

- ▸ `class`: You probably figured that out by now. Yes, this is the class implementing the cache.

- ▸ `size`: This is the maximum size that the cache can have.

- ▸ `initialSize`: This is the initial size that the cache will have.

- ▸ `autowarmCount`: This is the number of cache entries that will be copied to the new instance of the same cache when Solr invalidates the `Searcher` object – for example, during a commit operation.

As you can see, I tend to use the same number of entries for `size` and `initialSize`, and half of those values for `autowarmCount`. The `size` and `initialSize` properties can be set to the same size in order to avoid the underlying Java object resizing, which consumes additional processing time.

There is one thing you should be aware of. Some of the Solr caches (`documentCache` actually) operate on internal identifiers called `docid`. Those caches cannot be automatically warmed. That's because `docid` is changing after every commit operation and thus copying `docid` is useless.

Please keep in mind that the settings for the size of the caches is usually good for the moment you set them. But during the life cycle of your application your data may change, your queries may change, and your user's behavior may, and probably will change. That's why you should keep track of the cache usage with the use of Solr administration pages, JMX, or a specialized software such as Scalable Performance Monitoring from Sematext (see more at `http://sematext.com/spm/index.html`), and see how the utilization of each of the caches changes in time and makes proper changes to the configuration.

There's more...

There are a few additional things that you should know when configuring your caches.

Using a filter cache with faceting

If you use the term enumeration faceting method (parameter `facet.method=enum`) Solr will use the filter cache to check each term. Remember that if you use this method, your filter cache size should have at least the size of the number of unique facet values in all your faceted fields. This is crucial and you may experience performance loss if this cache is not configured the right way.

When we have no cache hits

When your Solr instance has a low cache hit ratio you should consider not using caches at all (to see the hit ratio you can use the administration pages of Solr). Cache insertion is not free – it costs CPU time and resources. So if you see that you have a very low cache hit ratio, you should consider turning your caches off – it may speed up your Solr instance. Before you turn off the caches please ensure that you have the right cache setup – a small hit ratio can be a result of bad cache configuration.

When we have more "puts" than "gets"

When your Solr instance uses put operations more than get operations you should consider using the `solr.LRUCache` implementation. It's confirmed that this implementation behaves better when there are more insertions into the cache than lookups.

Filter cache

This cache is responsible for holding information about the filters and the documents that match the filter. Actually this cache holds an unordered set of document IDs that match the filter. If you don't use the faceting mechanism with a filter cache, you should at least set its size to the number of unique filters that are present in your queries. This way it will be possible for Solr to store all the unique filters with their matching document IDs and this will speed up the queries that use filters.

Query result cache

The query result cache holds the ordered set of internal IDs of documents that match the given query and the sort specified. That's why if you use caches you should add as many filters as you can and keep your query (the q parameter) as clean as possible. For example, pass only the search box content of your search application to the query parameter. If the same query will be run more than once and the cache has enough capacity to hold the entry, it will be used to give the IDs of the documents that match the query, thus a no Lucene (Solr uses Lucene to index and query data that is indexed) query will be made saving the precious I/O operation for the queries that are not in the cache – this will boost up your Solr instance performance.

The maximum size of this cache that I tend to set is the number of unique queries and their sorts that are handled by my Solr in the time between the `Searcher` object's invalidation. This tends to be enough in most cases.

Document cache

The document cache holds the Lucene documents that were fetched from the index. Basically, this cache holds the stored fields of all the documents that are gathered from the Solr index. The size of this cache should always be greater than the number of concurrent queries multiplied by the maximum results you get from Solr. This cache can't be automatically warmed – that is because every commit is changing the internal IDs of the documents. Remember that the cache can be memory consuming in case you have many stored fields, so there will be times when you just have to live with evictions.

Query result window

The last thing is the query result window. This parameter tells Solr how many documents to fetch from the index in a single Lucene query. This is a kind of super set of documents fetched. In our example, we tell Solr that we want the maximum of one hundred documents as a result of a single query. Our query result window tells Solr to always gather two hundred documents. Then when we need some more documents that follow the first hundred they will be fetched from the cache, and therefore we will be saving our resources. The size of the query result window is mostly dependent on the application and how it is using Solr. If you tend to do a lot of paging, you should consider using a higher query result window value.

You should remember that the size of caches shown in this task is not final, and you should adapt them to your application needs. The values and the method of their calculation should only be taken as a starting point to further observation and optimization of the process. Also, please remember to monitor your Solr instance memory usage as using caches will affect the memory that is used by the JVM.

See also

There is another way to warm your caches if you know the most common queries that are sent to your Solr instance – auto-warming queries. Please refer to the *Improving Solr performance right after a startup or commit operation* recipe in *Chapter 6, Improving Solr Performance*. For information on how to cache whole pages of results please refer to the *Caching whole result pages* recipe in *Chapter 6, Improving Solr Performance*.

How to fetch and index web pages

There are many ways to index web pages. We could download them, parse them, and index them with the use of Lucene and Solr. The indexing part is not a problem, at least in most cases. But there is another problem – how to fetch them? We could possibly create our own software to do that, but that takes time and resources. That's why this recipe will cover how to fetch and index web pages using Apache Nutch.

Getting ready

For the purpose of this task we will be using Version 1.5.1 of Apache Nutch. To download the binary package of Apache Nutch, please go to the download section of `http://nutch.apache.org`.

How to do it...

Let's assume that the website we want to fetch and index is `http://lucene.apache.org`.

1. First of all we need to install Apache Nutch. To do that we just need to extract the downloaded archive to the directory of our choice; for example, I installed it in the directory `/usr/share/nutch`. Of course this is a single server installation and it doesn't include the Hadoop filesystem, but for the purpose of the recipe it will be enough. This directory will be referred to as $NUTCH_HOME.

2. Then we'll open the file `$NUTCH_HOME/conf/nutch-default.xml` and set the value `http.agent.name` to the desired name of your crawler (we've taken `SolrCookbookCrawler` as a name). It should look like the following code:

```
<property>
<name>http.agent.name</name>
<value>SolrCookbookCrawler</value>
<description>HTTP 'User-Agent' request header.</description>
</property>
```

3. Now let's create empty directories called `crawl` and `urls` in the `$NUTCH_HOME` directory. After that we need to create the `seed.txt` file inside the created `urls` directory with the following contents:

   ```
   http://lucene.apache.org
   ```

4. Now we need to edit the `$NUTCH_HOME/conf/crawl-urlfilter.txt` file. Replace the `+.` at the bottom of the file with `+^http://([a-z0-9]*\.)*lucene.apache.org/`. So the appropriate entry should look like the following code:

   ```
   +^http://([a-z0-9]*\.)*lucene.apache.org/
   ```

   One last thing before fetching the data is Solr configuration.

5. We start with copying the index structure definition file (called `schema-solr4.xml`) from the `$NUTCH_HOME/conf/` directory to your Solr installation configuration directory (which in my case was `/usr/share/solr/collection1/conf/`). We also rename the copied file to `schema.xml`.

We also create an empty `stopwords_en.txt` file or we use the one provided with Solr if you want stop words removal.

Now we need to make two corrections to the `schema.xml` file we've copied:

▶ The first one is the correction of the `version` attribute in the `schema` tag. We need to change its value from `1.5.1` to `1.5`, so the final `schema` tag would look like this:

   ```
   <schema name="nutch" version="1.5.1">
   ```

▶ Then we change the `boost` field type (in the same `schema.xml` file) from `string` to `float`, so the `boost` field definition would look like this:

   ```
   <field name="boost" type="float" stored="true" indexed="false"/>
   ```

Now we can start crawling and indexing by running the following command from the `$NUTCH_HOME` directory:

```
bin/nutch crawl urls -solr http://localhost:8983/solr/ -depth 3 -topN 50
```

Depending on your Internet connection and your machine configuration you should finally see a message similar to the following one:

```
crawl finished: crawl-20120830171434
```

This means that the crawl is completed and the data was indexed to Solr.

How it works...

After installing Nutch and Solr, the first thing we did was set our crawler name. Nutch does not allow empty names so we must choose one. The file `nutch-default.xml` defines more properties than the mentioned ones, but at this time we only need to know about that one.

In the next step, we created two directories; one (`crawl`) which will hold the crawl data and the second one (`urls`) to store the addresses we want to crawl. The contents of the `seed.txt` file we created contains addresses we want to crawl, one address per line.

The `crawl-urlfilter.txt` file contains information about the filters that will be used to check the URLs that Nutch will crawl. In the example, we told Nutch to accept every URL that begins with `http://lucene.apache.org`.

The `schema.xml` file we copied from the Nutch configuration directory is prepared to be used when Solr is used for indexing. But the one for Solr 4.0 is a bit buggy, at least in Nutch 1.5.1 distribution, and that's why we needed to make the changes previously mentioned.

We finally came to the point where we ran the Nutch command. We specified that we wanted to store the crawled data in the `crawl` directory (first parameter), and the addresses to crawl data from are in the `urls` directory (second parameter). The `-solr` switch lets you specify the address of the Solr server that will be responsible for the indexing crawled data and is mandatory if you want to get the data indexed with Solr. We decided to index the data to Solr installed at the same server. The `-depth` parameter specifies how deep to go after the links defined. In our example, we defined that we want a maximum of three links from the main page. The `-topN` parameter specifies how many documents will be retrieved from each level, which we defined as 50.

There's more...

There is one more thing worth knowing when you start a journey in the land of Apache Nutch.

Multiple thread crawling

The `crawl` command of the Nutch command-line utility has another option – it can be configured to run crawling with multiple threads. To achieve that you add the following parameter:

```
-threads N
```

So if you would like to crawl with 20 threads you should run the crawl command like sot:

```
bin/nutch crawl crawl/nutch/site -dir crawl -depth 3 -topN 50 -threads 20
```

See also

If you seek more information about Apache Nutch please refer to the `http://nutch.apache.org` and go to the Wiki section.

How to set up the extracting request handler

Sometimes indexing prepared text files (such as XML, CSV, JSON, and so on) is not enough. There are numerous situations where you need to extract data from binary files. For example, one of my clients wanted to index PDF files – actually their contents. To do that, we either need to parse the data in some external application or set up Solr to use Apache Tika. This task will guide you through the process of setting up Apache Tika with Solr.

How to do it...

In order to set up the extracting request handler, we need to follow these simple steps:

1. First let's edit our Solr instance `solrconfig.xml` and add the following configuration:

   ```
   <requestHandler name="/update/extract" class="solr.extraction.
   ExtractingRequestHandler" >
    <lst name="defaults">
     <str name="fmap.content">text</str>
     <str name="lowernames">true</str>
     <str name="uprefix">attr_</str>
     <str name="captureAttr">true</str>
    </lst>
   </requestHandler>
   ```

2. Next create the `extract` folder anywhere on your system (I created that folder in the directory where Solr is installed), and place the `apache-solr-cell-4.0.0.jar` from the `dist` directory (you can find it in the Solr distribution archive). After that you have to copy all the libraries from the `contrib/extraction/lib/` directory to the `extract` directory you created before.

3. In addition to that, we need the following entries added to the `solrconfig.xml` file:

   ```
   <lib dir="../../extract" regex=".*\.jar" />
   ```

And that's actually all that you need to do in terms of configuration.

To simplify the example, I decided to choose the following index structure (place it in the `fields` section in your `schema.xml` file):

```
<field name="id" type="string" indexed="true" stored="true"
required="true" multiValued="false" />
<field name="text" type="text_general" indexed="true" stored="true"/>
<dynamicField name="attr_*" type="text_general" indexed="true"
stored="true" multiValued="true"/>
```

To test the indexing process, I've created a PDF file `book.pdf` using PDFCreator which contained the following text only: `This is a Solr cookbook`. To index that file, I've used the following command:

```
curl "http://localhost:8983/solr/update/extract?literal.id=1&commit=true"
-F "myfile=@book.pdf"
```

You should see the following response:

```
<?xml version="1.0" encoding="UTF-8"?>
<response>
<lst name="responseHeader">
<int name="status">0</int>
<int name="QTime">578</int>
</lst>
</response>
```

How it works...

Binary file parsing is implemented using the **Apache Tika** framework. Tika is a toolkit for detecting and extracting metadata and structured text from various types of documents, not only binary files but also HTML and XML files. To add a handler that uses Apache Tika, we need to add a handler based on the `solr.extraction.ExtractingRequestHandler` class to our `solrconfig.xml` file as shown in the example.

In addition to the handler definition, we need to specify where Solr should look for the additional libraries we placed in the `extract` directory that we created. The `dir` attribute of the `lib` tag should be pointing to the path of the created directory. The `regex` attribute is the regular expression telling Solr which files to load.

Let's now discuss the default configuration parameters. The `fmap.content` parameter tells Solr what field content of the parsed document should be extracted. In our case, the parsed content will go to the field named `text`. The next parameter `lowernames` is set to `true`; this tells Solr to lower all names that come from Tika and have them lowercased. The next parameter, `uprefix`, is very important. It tells Solr how to handle fields that are not defined in the `schema.xml` file. The name of the field returned from Tika will be added to the value of the parameter and sent to Solr. For example, if Tika returned a field named `creator`, and we don't have such a field in our index, then Solr would try to index it under a field named `attr_creator` which is a dynamic field. The last parameter tells Solr to index Tika XHTML elements into separate fields named after those elements.

Next we have a command that sends a PDF file to Solr. We are sending a file to the `/update/extract` handler with two parameters. First we define a unique identifier. It's useful to be able to do that during document sending because most of the binary document won't have an identifier in its contents. To pass the identifier we use the `literal.id` parameter. The second parameter we send to Solr is the information to perform the commit right after document processing.

See also

To see how to index binary files please refer to the *Indexing PDF files* and *Extracting metadata from binary files* recipes in *Chapter 2, Indexing Your Data*.

Changing the default similarity implementation

Most of the time, the default way of calculating the score of your documents is what you need. But sometimes you need more from Solr; that's just the standard behavior. Let's assume that you would like to change the default behavior and use a different score calculation algorithm for the `description` field of your index. The current version of Solr allows you to do that and this recipe will show you how to leverage this functionality.

Getting ready

Before choosing one of the score calculation algorithms available in Solr, it's good to read a bit about them. The description of all the algorithms is beyond the scope of the recipe and the book, but I would suggest going to the Solr Wiki pages (or look at Javadocs) and read the basic information about available implementations.

How to do it...

For the purpose of the recipe let's assume we have the following index structure (just add the following entries to your `schema.xml` file to the `fields` section):

```
<field name="id" type="string" indexed="true" stored="true"
required="true" />
<field name="name" type="text_general" indexed="true" stored="true"/>
<field name="description" type="text_general_dfr" indexed="true"
stored="true" />
```

The `string` and `text_general` types are available in the default `schema.xml` file provided with the example Solr distribution. But we want `DFRSimilarity` to be used to calculate the score for the `description` field. In order to do that, we introduce a new type, which is defined as follows (just add the following entries to your `schema.xml` file to the `types` section):

```
<fieldType name="text_general_dfr" class="solr.TextField"
positionIncrementGap="100">
 <analyzer type="index">
  <tokenizer class="solr.StandardTokenizerFactory"/>
  <filter class="solr.StopFilterFactory" ignoreCase="true"
words="stopwords.txt" enablePositionIncrements="true" />
  <filter class="solr.LowerCaseFilterFactory"/>
 </analyzer>
 <analyzer type="query">
  <tokenizer class="solr.StandardTokenizerFactory"/>
  <filter class="solr.StopFilterFactory" ignoreCase="true"
words="stopwords.txt" enablePositionIncrements="true" />
  <filter class="solr.SynonymFilterFactory" synonyms="synonyms.txt"
ignoreCase="true" expand="true"/>
  <filter class="solr.LowerCaseFilterFactory"/>
 </analyzer>
 <similarity class="solr.DFRSimilarityFactory">
  <str name="basicModel">P</str>
  <str name="afterEffect">L</str>
  <str name="normalization">H2</str>
  <float name="c">7</float>
 </similarity>
</fieldType>
```

Also, to use per-field similarity we have to add the following entry to your `schema.xml` file:

```
<similarity class="solr.SchemaSimilarityFactory"/>
```

And that's all. Now let's have a look and see how that works.

How it works...

The index structure presented in this recipe is pretty simple as there are only three fields. The one thing we are interested in is that the `description` field uses our own custom field type called `text_general_dfr`.

The thing we are mostly interested in is the new field type definition called `text_general_dfr`. As you can see, apart from the index and query analyzer there is an additional section – `similarity`. It is responsible for specifying which similarity implementation to use to calculate the score for a given field. You are probably used to defining field types, filters, and other things in Solr, so you probably know that the `class` attribute is responsible for specifying the class implementing the desired similarity implementation which in our case is `solr.DFRSimilarityFactory`. Also, if there is a need, you can specify additional parameters that configure the behavior of your chosen similarity class. In the previous example, we've specified four additional parameters: `basicModel`, `afterEffect`, `normalization`, and `c`, which all define the `DFRSimilarity` behavior.

`solr.SchemaSimilarityFactory` is required to be able to specify the similarity for each field.

There's more...

In addition to per-field similarity definition, you can also configure the global similarity:

Changing the global similarity

Apart from specifying the similarity class on a per-field basis, you can choose any other similarity than the default one in a global way. For example, if you would like to use `BM25Similarity` as the default one, you should add the following entry to your `schema.xml` file:

```
<similarity class="solr.BM25SimilarityFactory"/>
```

As well as with the per-field similarity, you need to provide the name of the factory class that is responsible for creating the appropriate similarity class.

2
Indexing Your Data

In this chapter, we will cover:

- ▶ Indexing PDF files
- ▶ Generating unique fields automatically
- ▶ Extracting metadata from binary files
- ▶ How to properly configure Data Import Handler with JDBC
- ▶ Indexing data from a database using Data Import Handler
- ▶ How to import data using Data Import Handler and delta query
- ▶ How to use Data Import Handler with the URL data source
- ▶ How to modify data while importing with Data Import Handler
- ▶ Updating a single field of your document
- ▶ Handling multiple currencies
- ▶ Detecting the document language
- ▶ Optimizing your primary key field indexing

Introduction

Indexing data is one of the most crucial things in every Lucene and Solr deployment. When your data is not indexed properly your search results will be poor. When the search results are poor, it's almost certain the users will not be satisfied with the application that uses Solr. That's why we need our data to be prepared and indexed as well as possible.

On the other hand, preparing data is not an easy task. Nowadays we have more and more data floating around. We need to index multiple formats of data from multiple sources. Do we need to parse the data manually and prepare the data in XML format? The answer is no – we can let Solr do that for us. This chapter will concentrate on the indexing process and data preparation beginning from how to index data that is a binary PDF file, teaching how to use the Data Import Handler to fetch data from database and index it with Apache Solr, and finally describing how we can detect the document's language during indexing.

Indexing PDF files

Imagine that the library on the corner that we used to go to wants to expand its collection and make it available for the wider public though the World Wide Web. It asked its book suppliers to provide sample chapters of all the books in PDF format so they can share it with the online users. With all the samples provided by the supplier came a problem – how to extract data for the search box from more than 900 thousand PDF files. Solr can do it with the use of Apache Tika. This recipe will show you how to handle such a task.

Getting ready

Before you start getting deeper into the task, please refer to the *How to set up the extracting request handler* recipe in *Chapter 1, Apache Solr Configuration*, which will guide you through the process of configuring Solr to use Apache Tika. We will use the same index structure and Solr configuration presented in that recipe, and I assume you already have Solr properly configured (according to the mentioned recipe) and ready to work.

How to do it...

To test the indexing process I've created a PDF file `book.pdf` using PDFCreator (`http://sourceforge.net/projects/pdfcreator/`) which contained the following text only: `This is a Solr cookbook..`. To index that file I've used the following command:

```
curl "http://localhost:8983/solr/update/extract?literal.id=1&commit=true"
-F "myfile=@cookbook.pdf"
```

You should then see the following response:

```
<?xml version="1.0" encoding="UTF-8"?>
  <response>
    <lst name="responseHeader">
      <int name="status">0</int>
      <int name="QTime">578</int>
    </lst>
  </response>
```

To see what was indexed I've run the following within a web browser:

```
http://localhost:8983/solr/select/?q=text:solr
```

In return I've got:

```xml
<?xml version="1.0" encoding="UTF-8"?>
 <response>

  ...
   <result name="response" numFound="1" start="0">
    <doc>
     <arr name="attr_created"><str>Thu Oct 21 16:11:51 CEST 2010</
     str></arr>
     <arr name="attr_creator"><str>PDFCreator Version 1.0.1</str></arr>
     <arr name="attr_producer"><str>GPL Ghostscript 8.71</str></arr>
     <arr name="attr_stream_content_type"><str>application/octet-
     stream</str></arr>
     <arr name="attr_stream_name"><str>cookbook.pdf</str></arr>
     <arr name="attr_stream_size"><str>3209</str></arr>
     <arr name="attr_stream_source_info"><str>myfile</str></arr>
      <str name="author">Gr0</str>
       <arr name="content_type"><str>application/pdf</str></arr>
      <str name="id">1</str>
      <str name="keywords"/>
      <date name="last_modified">2010-10-21T14:11:51Z</date>
      <str name="subject"/>
       <arr name="title"><str>cookbook</str></arr>
    </doc>
   </result>
  </response>
```

How it works...

The `curl` command we used sends a PDF file to Solr. We are sending a file to the `/update/ extract` handler along with two parameters. It's useful to be able to do that during document sending because most of the binary documents won't have an identifier in its contents. To pass the identifier we use the `literal.id` parameter. The second parameter we send asks Solr to perform the commit operation right after document processing.

The test file I've created, for the purpose of the recipe, contained a simple sentence: "This is a Solr cookbook".

Remember the contents of the PDF file I created? It contained the word "Solr". That's why I asked Solr to give me documents which contain the word "Solr" in a field named `text`.

In response, I got one document which matched the given query. To simplify the example, I removed the response header part. As you can see in the response there were a few fields that were indexed dynamically – their names start with `attr_`. Those fields contained information about the file such as the size, the application that created it, and so on. As we can see, we have our identifier indexed as we wished, and some other fields that were present in the `schema.xml` file that Apache Tika could parse and return to Solr.

Generating unique fields automatically

Imagine you have an application that crawls the web and index documents found during that crawl. The problem is that for some particular reason you can't set the document identifier during indexing, and you would like Solr to generate one for you. This recipe will help you, if you faced a similar problem.

How to do it...

The following steps will help you to generate unique fields automatically:

1. First let's create our index structure by adding the following entries to the `schema.xml` fields section:

   ```
   <field name="id" type="uuid" indexed="true" stored="true"
   default="NEW" multiValued="false"/>
   <field name="name" type="text_general" indexed="true"
   stored="true"/>
   <field name="text" type="text_general" indexed="true"
   stored="true"/>
   ```

2. In addition to that, we need to define the `uuid` field type by adding the following entry to the `types` section of our `schema.xml` file:

   ```
   <fieldType name="uuid" class="solr.UUIDField" indexed="true" />
   ```

3. In addition to that, we must remove the unique field definition, because Solr doesn't allow using a unique field with the `default="NEW"` configuration, so the following needs to be removed:

   ```
   <uniqueKey>id</uniqueKey>
   ```

4. And now, let's try to index a document without an `id` field, for example one like this:

   ```
   <add>
    <doc>
     <field name="name">Test name</field>
     <field name="text">Test text contents</field>
    </doc>
   </add>
   ```

In order to see if Solr generated an identifier for the document, let's run the following query:

```
http://localhost:8983/solr/select?q=*:*&indent=true
```

The response will be as follows:

```xml
<?xml version="1.0" encoding="UTF-8"?>
<response>
 <lst name="responseHeader">
  <int name="status">0</int>
  <int name="QTime">1</int>
  <lst name="params">
   <str name="indent">true</str>
   <str name="q">*:*</str>
  </lst>
 </lst>
 <result name="response" numFound="1" start="0">
  <doc>
   <str name="name">Test name</str>
   <str name="text">Test text contents</str>
   <str name="id">b6f17c35-e5ad-4a09-b799-71580ca6be8a</str>
  </doc>
 </result>
</response>
```

As you can see in the response, our document had one additional field we didn't add manually – the id field, which is what we wanted to have.

How it works...

The idea is quite simple – we let Solr generate the id field for us. To do that, we defined the id field to be based on the uuid field type, and to have a default value of new (default="NEW"). By doing this we tell Solr that we want that kind of behavior. If you look at the uuid field type, you can see that it is a simple type definition based on solr.UUIDField. Nothing complicated.

Having your document's identifiers generated automatically is handy in some cases, but it also comes with some restrictions from Solr and its components. One of the issues is that you can't have the unique field defined, and because of that, the elevation component won't work. Of course that's only an example. But if your application doesn't know the identifiers of the documents and can't generate them, then using solr.UUIDField is one of the ways of having document identifiers for your indexed documents.

Extracting metadata from binary files

Suppose that our current client has a video and music store. Not the e-commerce one, just the regular one – just around the corner. And now he wants to expand his business to e-commerce. He wants to sell the products online. But his IT department said that this will be tricky – because they need to hire someone to fill up the database with the product names and their metadata. And that is the place where you come in and tell them that you can extract titles and authors from the MP3 files that are available as samples.Now let's see how that can be achieved.

Getting ready

Before you start getting deeper into the task, please refer to the *How to set up the extracting request handler* recipe in *Chapter 1, Apache Solr Configuration*, which will guide you through the process of configuring Solr to use Apache Tika.

How to do it...

1. Let's start by defining an index structure in the file `schema.xml`. The field definition section should look like the following code:

    ```
    <field name="id" type="string" indexed="true" stored="true"
    required="true"/>
    <field name="author" type="string" indexed="true" stored="true"
    multiValued="true"/>
    <field name="title" type="text" indexed="true" stored="true"/>
    <dynamicField name="ignored_*" type="string" indexed="false"
    stored="false" multiValued="true"/>
    ```

2. Now let's get the `solrconfig.xml` file ready:

    ```
    <requestHandler name="/update/extract" class="solr.extraction.
    ExtractingRequestHandler">
     <lst name="defaults">
      <str name="lowernames">true</str>
      <str name="uprefix">ignored_</str>
      <str name="captureAttr">true</str>
     </lst>
    </requestHandler>
    ```

3. Now we can start sending the documents to Solr. To do that, let's run the following command:

    ```
    curl "http://localhost:8983/solr/update/extract?literal.
    id=1&commit=true" -F "myfile=@sample.mp3"
    ```

4. Let's check how the document was indexed. To do that type a query like the following to your web browser:

```
http://localhost:8983/solr/select/?q=title:207
```

As a result I've got the following document:

```xml
<?xml version="1.0" encoding="UTF-8"?>
 <response>
  <lst name="responseHeader">
   <int name="status">0</int>
   <int name="QTime">0</int>
   <lst name="params">
    <str name="q">title:207</str>
   </lst>
  </lst>
  <result name="response" numFound="1" start="0">
   <doc>
    <str name="author">Armin Van Buuren</str>
    <str name="id">1</str>
    <str name="title">Desiderium 207 (Feat Susana)</str>
   </doc>
  </result>
 </response>
```

So it seems that everything went well.

How it works...

First we define an index structure that will suit our needs. I decided that besides the unique ID, I need to store the title and author name. We also defined a dynamic field called `ignored` to handle the data we don't want to index (not indexed and not stored).

The next step is to define a new request handler to handle our updates, as you already know. We also added a few default parameters to define our handler behavior. In our case the parameter `uprefix` tells Solr to index all unknown fields to the dynamic field whose name begins with `ignored_`, thus the additional data will not be visible in the index. The last parameter tells Solr to index Tika XHTML elements into separate fields named after those elements.

Next we have a command that sends an MP3 file to Solr. We are sending a file to the `/update/extract` handler with two parameters. First we define a unique identifier and pass that identifier to Solr using the `literal.id` parameter. The second parameter we send to Solr is information to perform a commit right after document processing.

The query is a simple one, so I'll skip commenting on this part.

The last listing is an XML with Solr response. As you can see, there are only fields that are explicitly defined in `schema.xml` – no dynamic fields. Solr and Tika managed to extract the name and author of the file.

See also

> ▸ If you want to index other types of binary files please refer to the *Indexing PDF files* recipe in this chapter.

How to properly configure Data Import Handler with JDBC

One of our clients is having a problem. His database of users grew to such size that even the simple SQL select statement is taking too much time, and he seeks how to improve the search time. Of course he heard about Solr but he doesn't want to generate XML or any other data format and push it to Solr; he would like the data to be fetched. What can we do about it? Well there is one thing – we can use one of the contribute modules of Solr, **Data Import Handler**. This task will show you how to configure the basic setup of Data Import Handler and how to use it.

How to do it...

1. First of all, copy the appropriate libraries that are required to use Data Import Handler. So, let's create the `dih` folder anywhere on your system (I created it in the directory where Solr is installed), and place `apache-solr-dataimporthandler-4.0.0.jar` and `apache-solr-dataimporthandler-extras-4.0.0.jar` from the Solr distribution `dist` directory in the folder. In addition to that, we need the following entry to be added to the `solrconfig.xml` file:

   ```
   <lib dir="../../dih" regex=".*\.jar" />
   ```

2. Next we need to modify the `solrconfig.xml` file. You should add an entry like the following code:

   ```
   <requestHandler name="/dataimport" class="org.apache.solr.handler.
   dataimport.DataImportHandler">
    <lst name="defaults">
     <str name="config">db-data-config.xml</str>
    </lst>
   </requestHandler>
   ```

3. Now we will create the `db-data-config.xml` file that is responsible for the Data Import Handler configuration. It should have contents like the following example:

```
<dataConfig>
 <dataSource driver="org.postgresql.Driver"
 url="jdbc:postgresql://localhost:5432/users" user="users"
 password="secret" />
 <document>
  <entity name="user" query="SELECT user_id, user_name from
  users">
   <field column="user_id" name="id" />
   <field column="user_name" name="name" />
   <entity name="user_desc" query="select desc from users_
   description where user_id=${user.user_id}">
    <field column="description" name="description" />
   </entity>
  </entity>
 </document>
</dataConfig></dataConfig>
```

If you want to use other database engines, please change the `driver`, `url`, and `user` and `password` attributes.

4. Now, let's create a sample index structure. To do that we need to modify the fields section of the `schema.xml` file to something like the following snippet:

```
<field name="id" type="string" indexed="true" stored="true"
required="true"/>
<field name="name" type="text" indexed="true" stored="true" />
<field name="user_desc" type="text" indexed="true" stored="true"/>
<field name="description" type="text" indexed="true"
stored="true"/>
```

5. One more thing before the indexing – you should copy an appropriate JDBC driver to the `lib` directory of your Solr installation or the `dih` directory we created before. You can get the library for PostgreSQL here `http://jdbc.postgresql.org/download.html`.

6. Now we can start indexing. Run the following query to Solr:

```
http://localhost:8983/solr/dataimport?command=full-import
```

As you may know, the HTTP protocol is asynchronous, and thus you won't be updated on how the process of indexing is going. To check the status of the indexing process, you can run the command once again.

And that's how we configure Data Import Handler.

How it works...

First we have a `solrconfig.xml` part which actually defines a new request handler, Data Import Handler, to be used by Solr. The `<str name="config">` XML tag specifies the name of the Data Import Handler configuration file.

The second listing is the actual configuration of Data Import Handler. I used the JDBC source connection sample to illustrate how to configure Data Import Handler. The contents of this configuration file start with the `root` tag named `dataConfig` which is followed by a second tag defining a data source and named `dataSource`. In the example, I used the PostgreSQL database and thus the JDBC driver is `org.postgresql.Driver`. We also define the database connection URL (attribute named `url`), and the database credentials (attributes `user` and `password`).

Next we have a document definition – a tag named `document`. This is the section containing information about the document that will be sent to Solr. The document definition is made of database queries – the **entities**.

The entity is defined by a name (the `name` attribute) and a SQL query (the `query` attribute). The entity name can be used to reference values in sub-queries – you can see an example of such a behavior in the second entity named `user_desc`. As you may already have noticed, entities can be nested to handle sub-queries. The SQL query is there to fetch the data from the database and use it to fill the entity variables which will be indexed.

After the entity comes the mapping definition. There is a single `field` tag for every column returned by a query, but that is not a must – Data Import Handler can guess what the mapping is (for example, where the entity field name matches the column name), but I tend to use mappings because I find it easier to maintain. But let's get back to fields. The `field` tag is defined by two attributes: `column` which is the column name returned by a query, and `name` which is the field to which the data will be written.

Next we have a Solr query to start the indexing process. There are actually five commands that can be run:

- ▶ `/dataimport`: This will return the actual status.
- ▶ `/dataimport?command=full-import`: This command will start the full import process. Remember that the default behavior is to delete the index contents at the beginning.
- ▶ `/dataimport?command=delta-import`: This command will start the incremental indexing process.
- ▶ `/dataimport?command=reload-config`: This command will force a configuration reload.
- ▶ `/dataimport?command=abort`: This command will stop the indexing process.

There's more...

If you don't want to delete the index contents at the start of the full indexing using Data Import Handler, add the `clean=false` parameter to your query. An example query should look like this:

```
http://localhost:8983/solr/data?command=full-import&clean=false
```

Indexing data from a database using Data Import Handler

Let's assume that we want to index the Wikipedia data, and we don't want to parse the whole Wikipedia data and make another XML file. Instead we asked our DB expert to import the data dump information from the PostgreSQL database, so we could fetch that data. Did I say fetch? Yes it is possible – with the use of Data Import Handler and JDBC data source. This task will guide you through how to do it.

Getting ready

Please refer to the *How to properly configure Data Import Handler* recipe in this chapter to get to know the basics about how Data Import Handler is configured. I'll assume that you already have Solr set up according to the instructions available in the mentioned recipe.

How to do it...

The Wikipedia data I used in this example is available under the Wikipedia downloads page at `http://download.wikimedia.org/`.

1. First let's add a sample index structure. To do that we need to modify the fields section of the `schema.xml` file so it looks like the following code:

```
<field name="id" type="string" indexed="true" stored="true"
required="true"/>
<field name="name" type="string" indexed="true" stored="true"/>
<field name="revision_id" type="string" indexed="true"
stored="true"/>
<field name="contents" type="text" indexed="true" stored="true"/>
```

2. The next step is to add the request handler definition to the `solrconfig.xml` file, like so:

```
<requestHandler name="/dataimport" class="org.apache.solr.handler.
dataimport.DataImportHandler">
 <lst name="defaults">
  <str name="config">db-data-config.xml</str>
 </lst>
</requestHandler>
```

3. Now we have to add a `db-data-config.xml` file to the `conf` directory of your Solr instance (or core):

```
<dataConfig>
 <dataSource driver="org.postgresql.Driver"
url="jdbc:postgresql://localhost:5432/wikipedia" user="wikipedia"
password="secret" />
 <document>
  <entity name="page" query="SELECT page_id, page_title from
  page">
   <field column="page_id" name="id" />
   <field column="page_title" name="name" />
   <entity name="revision" query="select rev_id from revision
   where rev_page=${page.page_id}">
    <field column="rev_id" name="revision_id" />
    <entity name="pagecontent" query="select old_text from
    pagecontent where old_id=${revision.rev_id}">
     <field column="old_text" name="contents" />
    </entity>
   </entity>
  </entity>
 </document>
</dataConfig>
```

4. Now let's start indexing. Type the following URL into your browser:

```
http://localhost:8983/solr/dataimport?command=full-import
```

5. Let's check the indexing status during import. To do that we run the following query:

```
http://localhost:8983/solr/dataimport
```

Solr will show us a response like the following reponse:

```
<?xml version="1.0" encoding="UTF-8"?>
 <response>
  <lst name="responseHeader">
   <int name="status">0</int>
   <int name="QTime">0</int>
  </lst>
  <lst name="initArgs">
   <lst name="defaults">
```

```
      <str name="config">db-data-config.xml</str>
      </lst>
    </lst>
    <str name="status">busy</str>
    <str name="importResponse">A command is still running...</str>
    <lst name="statusMessages">
     <str name="Time Elapsed">0:1:15.460</str>
     <str name="Total Requests made to DataSource">39547</str>
     <str name="Total Rows Fetched">59319</str>
     <str name="Total Documents Processed">19772</str>
     <str name="Total Documents Skipped">0</str>
     <str name="Full Dump Started">2010-10-25 14:28:00</str>
    </lst>
    <str name="WARNING">This response format is experimental.
    It is likely to change in the future.</str>
  </response>
```

6. Running the same query after the importing process is done should result in a response like the following:

```
<?xml version="1.0" encoding="UTF-8"?>
  <response>
   <lst name="responseHeader">
    <int name="status">0</int>
    <int name="QTime">0</int>
   </lst>
   <lst name="initArgs">
    <lst name="defaults">
      <str name="config">db-data-config.xml</str>
     </lst>
   </lst>
   <str name="status">idle</str>
   <str name="importResponse"/>
   <lst name="statusMessages">
     <str name="Total Requests made to DataSource">2118645</str>
     <str name="Total Rows Fetched">3177966</str>
     <str name="Total Documents Skipped">0</str>
     <str name="Full Dump Started">2010-10-25 14:28:00</str>
     <str name="">Indexing completed. Added/Updated: 1059322
     documents. Deleted 0 documents.</str>
     <str name="Committed">2010-10-25 14:55:20</str>
     <str name="Optimized">2010-10-25 14:55:20</str>
     <str name="Total Documents Processed">1059322</str>
     <str name="Time taken ">0:27:20.325</str>
   </lst>
   <str name="WARNING">This response format is experimental.
   It is likely to change in the future.</str>
  </response>
```

How it works...

To illustrate how Data Import Handler works, I decided to index the Polish Wikipedia data. I decided to store four fields: page identifier, page name, page revision number, and its contents. The field definition part is fairly simple so I decided to skip commenting on this.

The request handler definition, the Data Import Handler configuration, and command queries were discussed in the *How to properly configure Data Import Handler with JDBC* recipe in this chapter. The portions of interest in this task are in the `db-data-config.xml` file.

As you can see, we have three entities defined. The first entity gathers data from the `page` table and maps two of the columns to the index fields. The next entity is nested inside the first one and gathers the revision identifier from the table `revision` with the appropriate condition. The revision identifier is then mapped to the index field. The last entity is nested inside the second and gathers data from the `pagecontent` table again with the appropriate condition. And again, the returned column is mapped to the index field.

We have the response which shows us that the import is still running (the listing with `<str name="importResponse">A command is still running...</str>`). As you can see there is information about how many data rows were fetched, how many requests to the database were made, how many Solr documents were processed, and how many were deleted. There is also information about the start of the indexing process. One thing you should be aware of: this response can change in the next versions of Solr and Data Import Handler.

The last listing shows us the summary of the indexing process.

How to import data using Data Import Handler and delta query

Do you remember the task with the users import from the recipe named *How to properly configure Data Import Handler*? We imported all the users from our client database but it took ages – about two weeks. Our client is very happy with the results. His database is now not used for searching but only updating. And yes, that is the problem for us – how do we update data in the index? We can't fetch the whole data every time – it took two weeks. What we can do is an incremental import which will modify only the data that has changed since the last import. This task will show you how to do that.

Getting ready

Please refer to the *How to properly configure Data Import Handler* recipe in this chapter to get to know the basics of the Data Import Handler configuration. I assume that Solr is set up according to the description given in the mentioned recipe.

How to do it...

1. The first thing you should do is add an additional column to the tables you use. So in our case let's assume that we added a column named `last_modified` (which should be a timestamp-based column). Now our `db-data-config.xml` will look like the following code:

```
<dataConfig>

 <dataSource driver="org.postgresql.Driver"
 url="jdbc:postgresql://localhost:5432/users" user="users"
 password="secret" />
  <document>
   <entity name="user" query="SELECT user_id, user_name FROM users"
 deltaImportQuery="select user_id, user_name FROM users WHERE user_
 id = '${dataimporter.delta.user_id}'"deltaQuery="select user_id
   FROM users WHERE last_modified &gt; '${dataimporter.last_index_
   time}'">
    <field column="user_id" name="id" />
    <field column="user_name" name="name" />
    <entity name="user_desc" query="select description from
    users_description where user_id=${user.user_id}">
     <field column="description" name="description" />
    </entity>
   </entity>
  </document>
 </dataConfig></dataConfig>
```

2. After that we run a new kind of query to start delta import:

```
http://localhost:8983/solr/dataimport?command=delta-import
```

How it works...

First we modified our database table to include a column named `last_modified`. We need to ensure that the column will be modified at the same time as the table is. Solr will not modify the database, so you have to ensure that your application will do that.

When running a delta import, Data Import Handler will create a file named `dataimport.properties` inside a Solr configuration directory. In that file, the last index time will be stored as a timestamp. This timestamp will be later used to distinguish whether the data was changed or not. It can be used in a query by using a special variable: `${dataimporter.last_index_time}`.

You may have already noticed the two differences – two additional attributes defining an entity named `user` – `deltaQuery` and `deltaImportQuery`. The first one is responsible for getting the information about which users were modified since the last index. Actually it only gets the user's unique identifiers. It uses the `last_modified` field to determine which users were modified since the last import. Then the second query is executed – `deltaImportQuery`. This query gets users with the appropriate unique identifier, to get all the data which we want to index. One thing worth noticing is the way that I used the user identifier in `deltaImportQuery`. I used the `delta` variable with its `user_id` (the same name as the table column name) variable to get it: `${dataimporter.delta.user_id}`.

You may have noticed that I left the `query` attribute in the entity definition. It's left on purpose; you may need to index the entire data once again, so that configuration will be useful for full imports as well as for the partial ones.

Next we have a query that shows how to run the delta import. You may have noticed that compared to the full import, we didn't use the `full-import` command – we've sent the `delta-import` command.

The statuses that are returned by Solr are the same as with the full import, so please refer to the appropriate chapters to see what information they carry.

One more thing – the delta queries are only supported for the default `SqlEntityProcessor` class. This means that you can only use those queries with JDBC data sources.

How to use Data Import Handler with the URL data source

Do you remember the first example with the Wikipedia data? We asked our fellow DB expert to import the data dump into PostgreSQL and we fetched the data from there. But what if our colleague is sick and can't help us, and we need to import that data? We can parse the data and send it to Solr, but that's not an option – we don't have much time to do that. So what to do? Yes, you guessed – we can use Data Import Handler and one of its data sources, **file data source**. This task will show you how to do that.

Getting ready

Please refer to the *How to properly configure Data Import Handler* recipe in this chapter to get to know the basics of the Data Import Handler configuration. I assume that Solr is set up according to the description given in the mentioned recipe.

How to do it...

Let's take a look at our data source. To be consistent, I chose to index the Wikipedia data, which you should already be familiar with.

1. First of all, the index structure. Our field definition part of `schema.xml` should look like the following code:

    ```
    <field name="id" type="string" indexed="true" stored="true"
    required="true"/>
    <field name="name" type="string" indexed="true" stored="true"/>
    <field name="revision_id" type="string" indexed="true"
    stored="true"/>
    <field name="contents" type="text" indexed="true" stored="true"/>
    ```

2. The next step is to define a Data Import Handler request handler (put that definition in the `solrconfig.xml` file):

    ```
    <requestHandler name="/dataimport" class="org.apache.solr.handler.
    dataimport.DataImportHandler">
     <lst name="defaults">
      <str name="config">data-config.xml</str>
     </lst>
    </requestHandler>
    ```

3. And now the `data-config.xml` file:

    ```
    <dataConfig>
     <dataSource type="FileDataSource" encoding="UTF-8" />
     <document>
      <entity name="page" processor="XPathEntityProcessor"
    stream="true" forEach="/mediawiki/page/" url="/solrcookbook/data/
    enwiki-20120802-pages-articles.xml"transformer="RegexTransformer">
        <field column="id" xpath="/mediawiki/page/id" />
        <field column="name" xpath="/mediawiki/page/title" />
        <field column="revision_id" xpath="/mediawiki/page/revision/id"
    />
        <field column="contents" xpath="/mediawiki/page/revision/text"
    />
        <field column="$skipDoc" regex="^#REDIRECT .*"
    replaceWith="true" sourceColName="contents"/>
    ```

```
        </entity>
      </document>
    </dataConfig>
```

4. Now let's start indexing by sending the following query to Solr:

```
http://localhost:8983/solr/dataimport?command=full-import
```

After the import is done, we will have the data indexed.

How it works...

The Wikipedia data I used in this example is available under the Wikipedia downloads page at `http://download.wikimedia.org/enwiki/`. I've chosen the `pages-articles.xml.bz2` file (actually it was named `enwiki-20120802-pages-articles.xml.bz2`) which is about 6 GB. We only want to index some of the data from the file: page identifier, name, revision, and page contents. I also wanted to skip articles that are only linking to other articles in Wikipedia.

The field definition part of the `schema.xml` file is fairly simple and contains only four fields and there is nothing unusual within it, so I'll skip commenting on it.

The `solrconfig.xml` file contains the handler definition with the information about the Data Import Handler configuration filename.

Next we have the `data-config.xml` file where the actual configuration is written. We have a new data source type here named `FileDataSource`. This data source will read the data from a local directory. You can use `HttpDataSource` if you want to read data from an outer location. The XML tag defining the data source also specifies the file encoding (the `encoding` attribute) and in our example it's `UTF-8`. Next we have an entity definition, which has a name under which it will be visible, a processor which will process our data. The `processor` attribute is only mandatory when not using a database source. This value must be set to `XPathEntityProcessor` in our case. The `stream` attribute, which is set to `true`, informs Data Import Handler to stream the data from the file which is a must in our case when the data is large. Following that we have a `forEach` attribute which specifies an **XPath** expression – this path will be iterated over. There is a location of the data file defined in the `url` attribute and a transformer defined in the `transformer` attribute. **A transformer** is a mechanism that will transform every row of data and process it before sending it to Solr.

Under the entity definition we have field mapping definitions. We have columns which are the same as the index field names thus I skipped the `name` field. There is one additional attribute named `xpath` in the mapping definitions. It specifies the XPath expression that defines where the data is located in the XML file. If you are not familiar with XPath please refer to the `http://www.w3schools.com/xpath/default.asp` tutorial.

We also have a special column named `$skipDoc`. It tells Solr which documents to skip (if the value of the column is `true` then Solr will skip the document). The column is defined by a regular expression (attribute `regex`), a column to which the regular expression applies (attribute `sourceColName`), and the value that will replace all the occurrences of the given regular expression (`replaceWith` attribute). If the regular expression matches (in this case, if the data in the column specified by the `sourceColName` attribute starts with `#REDIRECT`), then the `$skipDoc` column will be set to `true` and thus the document will be skipped.

The actual indexing time was more than four hours on my machine, so if you try to index the sample Wikipedia data please take that into consideration.

How to modify data while importing with Data Import Handler

After we indexed the users and made the indexing incremental (the _How to properly configure Data Import Handler_ and _How to import data using Data Import Handler and delta query_ recipes), we were asked if we could modify the data a bit. Actually it would be perfect if we could split name and surname into two fields in the index while those two reside in a single column in the database. And of course, updating the database is not an option (trust me – it almost never is). Can we do that? Of course we can, we just need to add some more configuration details in Data Import Handler and use a transformer. This task will show you how to do that.

Getting ready

Please refer to the _How to properly configure Data Import Handler_ recipe in this chapter to get to know the basics about the Data Import Handler configuration. Also, to be able to run examples in this chapter, you need to run Solr in the servlet container run on Java 6 or later. I assume that Solr is set up according to the description given in the mentioned recipe.

How to do it...

Let's assume that we have a database table. To select users from our table we use the following SQL query:

```
SELECT user_id, user_name, description FROM users
```

The response may look like this:

```
| user_id | user_name      | description |
| 1       | John Kowalski  | superuser   |
| 2       | Amanda Looks   | user        |
```

Our task is to split the name from the surname and place it in two fields: `name` and `surname`.

1. First of all change the index structure, so our field definition part of `schema.xml` should look like the following code:

```
<field name="id" type="string" indexed="true" stored="true"
required="true"/>
<field name="firstname" type="string" indexed="true"
stored="true"/>
<field name="surname" type="string" indexed="true" stored="true"/>
<field name="description" type="text" indexed="true"
stored="true"/>
```

2. Now we have to add a `db-data-config.xml` file:

```
<dataConfig>
 <dataSource driver="org.postgresql.Driver"
url="jdbc:postgresql://localhost:5432/users" user="users"
password="secret" />
 <script><![CDATA[
   function splitName(row) {
    var nameTable = row.get('user_name').split(' ');
    row.put('firstname', nameTable[0]);
    row.put('surname', nameTable[1]);
    row.remove('name');
    return row;
   }
 ]]></script>
 <document>
  <entity name="user" transformer="script:splitName" query="SELECT
  user_id, user_name, description from users">
   <field column="user_id" name="id" />
   <field column="firstname" />
   <field column="surname" />
   <field column="description" />
  </entity>
 </document>
</dataConfig>
```

3. And now you can follow the normal indexing procedure which was discussed in the *How to properly configure Data Import Handler* recipe in this chapter.

How it works...

The first two listings are the sample SQL query and the result given by a database. Next we have a field definition part of the `schema.xml` file which defines four fields. Look at the example database rows once again. See the difference? We have four fields in our index while our database rows have only three columns. We must split the contents of the `user_name` column into two index fields: `firstname` and `surname`. To do that, we will use JavaScript language and the script transformer functionality of Data Import Handler.

The `solrconfig.xml` file is the same as the one discussed in the *How to properly configure Data Import Handler* recipe in this chapter, so I'll skip that as well.

Next we have the updated contents of the `db-data-config.xml` file which we use to define the behavior of Data Import Handler. The first and the biggest difference is the `script` tag that will be holding our scripts that parse the data. The scripts should be held in the CDATA section. I defined a simple function called `splitName` that takes one parameter, database row (remember that the functions that operate on entity data should always take one parameter). The first thing in the function is getting the contents of the `user_name` column, split it with the space character, and assign it into a JavaScript table. Then we create two additional columns in the processed row – `firstname` and `surname`. The contents of those rows come from the JavaScript table we created. Then we remove the `user_name` column because we don't want it to be indexed. The last operation is the returning of the processed row.

To enable script processing you must add one additional attribute to the entity definition – the `transformer` attribute with the contents such as `script:functionName`. In our example, it looks like this: `transformer:"script:splitName"`. It tells Data Import Handler to use the defined function name for every row returned by the query.

And that's how it works. The rest is the usual indexing process described in the *How to properly configure Data Import Handler* task in this chapter.

There's more...

If you want to use a different language other than JavaScript, then you have to specify it in the `language` attribute of the `<script>` tag. Just remember that the scripting language that you want to use must be supported by Java 6. The example definition would look as follows:

```
<script language="ECMAScript">...</script>
```

Updating a single field of your document

Imagine that you have a system where you store a document your users upload. In addition to that, your users can add other users to have access to the files they uploaded. As you probably know, before Solr 4.0, when you wanted to update a single field in a document you had to re-index the whole document. Solr 4.0 allows you to update a single field if you fulfill some basic requirements. So let's see how we can do that in Solr 4.0.

How to do it...

For the purpose of the recipe, let's assume we have the following index structure (put the following entries to your `schema.xml` file's `fields` section):

```
<field name="id" type="string" indexed="true" stored="true"
required="true" />
<field name="file" type="text_general" indexed="true" stored="true"/>
<field name="user" type="string" indexed="true" stored="true"
multiValued="true" />
```

In addition to that, we need the `_version_` field:

```
<field name="_version_" type="long" indexed="true" stored="true"/>
```

And that's all when it comes to the `schema.xml` file. In addition to that, let's assume we have the following data indexed:

```
<add>
 <doc>
  <field name="id">1</field>
  <field name="file">Sample file</field>
  <field name="user">gro</field>
  <field name="user">negativ</field>
 </doc>
</add>
```

So, we have a sample file and two user names specifying which users of our system can access that file. But what if we would like to add another user called `jack`. Is that possible? Yes, with Solr 4.0 it is. To add the value to a field which has multiple values, we should send the following command:

```
curl 'localhost:8983/solr/update?commit=true' -H 'Content-type:application/json' -d '[{"id":"1","user":{"add":"jack"}}]'
```

Let's see if it worked by sending the following query:

```
http://localhost:8983/solr/select?q=*:*&indent=true
```

The response sent by Solr was as follows:

```xml
<?xml version="1.0" encoding="UTF-8"?>
<response>
 <lst name="responseHeader">
  <int name="status">0</int>
  <int name="QTime">0</int>
  <lst name="params">
   <str name="indent">true</str>
   <str name="q">*:*</str>
  </lst>
 </lst>
 <result name="response" numFound="1" start="0">
  <doc>
   <str name="id">1</str>
   <str name="file">Sample file</str>
   <arr name="user">
    <str>gro</str>
    <str>negativ</str>
    <str>jack</str>
   </arr>
   <long name="_version_">1411121765349851136</long></doc>
 </result>
</response>
```

As you can see it worked without any problems. Imagine that now one of the users changed the name of the document, and we would also like to update the `file` field of that document to match that change. In order to do so, we should send the following command:

```
curl 'localhost:8983/solr/update?commit=true' -H 'Content-type:application/json' -d '[{"id":"1","file":{"set":"New file name"}}]'
```

And again, we send the same query as before to see if the command succeeded:

```xml
<?xml version="1.0" encoding="UTF-8"?>
<response>
 <lst name="responseHeader">
  <int name="status">0</int>
  <int name="QTime">1</int>
  <lst name="params">
   <str name="indent">true</str>
   <str name="q">*:*</str>
  </lst>
 </lst>
 <result name="response" numFound="1" start="0">
  <doc>
```

```
        <str name="id">1</str>
        <str name="file">New file name</str>
        <arr name="user">
         <str>gro</str>
         <str>negativ</str>
         <str>jack</str>
        </arr>
       <long name="_version_">1411121902871642112</long></doc>
      </result>
     </response>
```

It worked again. So now let's see how Solr does that.

How it works...

As you can see the index structure is pretty simple; we have a document identifier, its name, and users that can access that file. As you can see all the fields in the index are marked as stored (`stored="true"`). This is required for the partial update functionality to work. This is because, under the hood, Solr takes all the values from the fields and updates the one we mentioned to be updated. So it is just a typical document indexing, but instead of you having to provide all the information, it's Solr's responsibility to get it from the index.

Another thing that is required for the partial update functionality to work is the `_version_` field. You don't have to set it during indexing, it is used internally by Solr. The example data we are indexing is also very simple. It is a single document with two users defined.

```
[{"id":"1","user":{"add":"jack"}}]
```

The interesting stuff comes with the update command. As you can see, that command is run against a standard update handler you run indexing against. The `commit=true` parameter tells Solr to perform the commit operation right after update. The `-H 'Content-type:application/json'` part is responsible for setting the correct HTTP headers for the update request. Next we have the request contents itself. It is sent as a JSON object. We specified that we are interested in the document with the identifier "1" (`"id":"1"`). We want to change the `user` field and we want to add the `jack` value to that field (the `add` command). So as you can see, the `add` command is used when we want to add a new value to a field which can hold multiple values.

The second command shown as an example shows how to change the value of a single-valued field. It is very similar to what we had before, but instead of using the `add` command, we use the `set` command. And again, as you can see, it worked perfectly.

Handling multiple currencies

Imagine a situation where you run an e-commerce site and you sell your products all over the world. One day you say that you would like to calculate the currencies by yourself and have all the goodies that Solr gives you on all the currencies you support. You could of course add multiple fields, one for each currency. On the other hand, you can use the new functionality introduced in Solr 3.6 and create a field that will use the provided currency exchange rates.

How to do it...

This recipe will show you how to configure and use multiple currencies using a single field in the index:

1. Let's start with creating a sample index structure, by modifying the `fields` section in your `schema.xml` file so it looks like the following code:

```
<field name="id" type="string" indexed="true" stored="true"
required="true" />
<field name="name" type="text_general" indexed="true"
stored="true" />
<field name="price" type="currencyField" indexed="true"
stored="true" />
```

2. In addition to that, we need to provide the definition for the type the `price` field is based on (add the following entry to the `types` section in your `schema.xml` file):

```
<fieldType class="solr.CurrencyField" name="currencyField"
defaultCurrency="USD" currencyConfig="currencyExchange.xml" />
```

3. Another file that we need to create is the `currencyExchange.xml` file, which should be placed in the `conf` directory of your collection and have the following contents:

```
<currencyConfig version="1.0">
  <rates>
   <rate from="USD" to="EUR" rate="0.743676" comment="European
   Euro" />
   <rate from="USD" to="HKD" rate="7.801922" comment="HONG KONG
   Dollar" />
   <rate from="USD" to="GBP" rate="0.647910" comment="UNITED
   KINGDOM Pound" />
  </rates>
</currencyConfig>
```

4. Now we can index some example data. For this recipe, I decided to index the following documents:

```
<add>
  <doc>
    <field name="id">1</field>
    <field name="name">Test document one</field>
    <field name="price">10.10,USD</field>
  </doc>
  <doc>
    <field name="id">2</field>
    <field name="name">Test document two</field>
    <field name="price">12.01,USD</field>
  </doc>
</add>
```

5. Let's now check if that works. Our second document costs `12.01` USD and we have defined the exchange rate for European Euro as `0.743676`. This gives us about 7.50 EUR for the first document and about 8.90 EUR for the second one. Let's check that by sending the following query to Solr:

```
http://localhost:8983/solr/select?q=name:document&fq=price:[8.00,E
UR TO 9.00,EUR]
```

6. The result returned by Solr is as follows:

```
<?xml version="1.0" encoding="UTF-8"?>
 <response>
  <lst name="responseHeader">
   <int name="status">0</int>
   <int name="QTime">1</int>
   <lst name="params">
    <str name="fq">price:[8.00,EUR TO 9.00,EUR]</str>
    <str name="q">name:document</str>
   </lst>
  </lst>
  <result name="response" numFound="1" start="0">
   <doc>
    <str name="id">2</str>
    <str name="name">Test document two</str>
    <str name="price">12.01,USD</str></doc>
  </result>
 </response>
```

As you can see, we got the document we wanted.

How it works...

The idea behind the functionality is simple – we create a field based on a certain type and we provide a file with a currency exchange rate, and that's all. After that we can query our Solr instance with the use of all the currencies we defined exchange rates for. But now, let's discuss all the previous configuration changes in detail.

The index structure is very simple; it contains three fields of which one is responsible for holding the price of the document and is based on the `currencyField` type. This type is based on `solr.CurrencyField`. Its `defaultCurrency` attribute specifies the default currency for all the fields using this type. This is important, because Solr will return prices in the defined default currency, no matter what currency is used during the query. The `currencyConfig` attribute specifies the name of the file with the exchange rate definition.

Our `currencyExchange.xml` file provides exchange rate for three currencies:

- EUR
- HKD
- GBP

The file should be structured similar to the example one previously shown. This means that each exchange rate should have the `from` attribute telling Solr from which currency the exchange will be done, the `to` attribute specifying to which currency the exchange will be done, and the `rate` attribute specifying the actual exchange rate. In addition to that, it can also have the `comment` attribute if we want to include some short comment.

During indexing, we need to specify the currency we want the data to be indexed with. In the previous example, we indexed data with USD. This is done by specifying the price, a colon character, and the currency code after it. So `10.10,USD` will mean ten dollars and ten cents in USD.

The last thing is the query. As you can see, you can query Solr with different currencies from the one used during indexing. This is possible because of the provided exchange rates file. As you can see, when we use a range query for a price field, we specify the value, the colon character, and the currency code after it. Please remember that if you provide a currency code unknown to Solr, it will throw an exception saying that the currency is not known.

There's more...

You can also have the exchange rates being updated automatically by specifying the currency provider.

Setting up your own currency provider

Specifying the currency exchange rate file is great, but we need to update that file because the exchange rates change constantly. Luckily for us, Solr committers thought about it and gave us the option to provide an exchange rate provider instead of a plain file. The provider is a class responsible for providing the exchange rate data. The default exchange rate provider available in Solr uses exchange rates from `http://openexchangerates.org`, which are updated hourly. In order to use it, we need to modify our `currencyField` field type definition and introduce three new properties (and remove the `currencyConfig` one):

- ▶ `providerClass`: This class implements the exchange rates provider, which in our case will be the default one available in Solr – `solr.OpenExchangeRatesOrgProvider`

- ▶ `refreshInterval`: This determines how often to refresh the rates (specified in minutes)

- ▶ `ratesFileLocation`: This determines the location of the file with rates in open exchange format

So the final configuration should look like the following snippet:

```
<fieldType name="currencyField" class="solr.CurrencyField"
providerClass="solr.OpenExchangeRatesOrgProvider"
refreshInterval="120" ratesFileLocation="http://192.168.10.10/latest.
json"/>
```

You can download the sample exchange file from the `http://openexchangerates.org` site after creating an account there.

Detecting the document's language

Imagine a situation where you have users from different countries and you would like to give them a choice to only see content you index that is written in their native language. Sounds quite interesting, right? Let us see how we can identify the language of the documents during indexing and store that information along with the documents in the index for later use.

How to do it...

For the language identification we will use one of the Solr **contrib** modules, but let's start from the beginning.

1. For the purpose of the recipe, I assume that we will be using the following index structure (add the following to the `fields` section of your `schema.xml` file):

   ```
   <field name="id" type="string" indexed="true" stored="true"
   required="true" multiValued="false" />
   ```

```
<field name="name" type="text_general" indexed="true"
stored="true"/>
<field name="description" type="text_general" indexed="true"
stored="true" />
<field name="langId" type="string" indexed="true" stored="true" />
```

We will use the `langId` field to store the information about the identified language.

2. The next thing we need to do is create a `langid` directory somewhere on your filesystem (I'll assume that the directory is created in the same directory that Solr is installed) and copy the following libraries to that directory:

   ❑ `apache-solr-langid-4.0.0.jar` (from the `dist` directory of Apache Solr distribution)

   ❑ `jsonic-1.2.7.jar` (from the `contrib/langid/lib` directory of Apache Solr distribution)

   ❑ `langdetect-1.1.jar` (from the `contrib/langid/lib` directory of Apache Solr distribution)

3. Next we need to add some information to the `solrconfig.xml` file. First we need to inform Solr that we want it to load the additional libraries. We do that by adding the following entry to the `config` section of that file:

   ```
   <lib dir="../../langid/" regex=".*\.jar" />
   ```

4. In addition to that we configure a new update processor by adding the following to the `config` section of the `solrconfig.xml` file:

   ```
   <updateRequestProcessorChain name="langid">
    <processor class="org.apache.solr.update.processor.
   LangDetectLanguageIdentifierUpdateProcessorFactory">
      <str name="langid.fl">name,description</str>
      <str name="langid.langField">langId</str>
      <str name="langid.fallback">en</str>
    </processor>
    <processor class="solr.LogUpdateProcessorFactory" />
    <processor class="solr.RunUpdateProcessorFactory" />
   </updateRequestProcessorChain>
   ```

5. Now, we need some data to be indexed. I decided to use the following test data (stored in a `data.xml` file):

   ```
   <add>
    <doc>
     <field name="id">1</field>
     <field name="name">First</field>
     <field name="description">>Water is a chemical substance with
   the chemical formula H2O. A water molecule contains one oxygen
   and two hydrogen atoms connected by   covalent bonds. Water is a
   ```

```
liquid at ambient conditions, but it often co-exists on Earth with
its solid state, ice, and gaseous state (water vapor or steam).
Water also
exists in a liquid crystal state near hydrophilic surfaces. [1]
[2] Under nomenclature used to name chemical compounds, Dihydrogen
monoxide is the scientific name for water, though it is almost
never used.</field>
 </doc>
 <doc>
  <field name="id">2</field>
  <field name="name">Zweite</field>
  <field name="description">Wasser (H2O) ist eine chemische
Verbindung aus den Elementen Sauerstoff (O) und Wasserstoff
(H). Wasser ist die einzige chemische Verbindung auf der Erde,
die in der Natur in allen drei Aggregatzuständen vorkommt.
Die Bezeichnung Wasser wird dabei besonders für den flüssigen
Aggregatzustand verwendet. Im festen (gefrorenen) Zustand spricht
man von Eis, im gasförmigen Zustand von Wasserdampf.</field>
 </doc>
</add>
```

6. And now the indexing. To index the above test file I used the following commands:

```
curl 'http://localhost:8983/solr/update?update.chain=langid'
--data-binary @data.xml -H 'Content-type:application/xml'
```

```
curl 'http://localhost:8983/solr/update?update.chain=langid'
--data-binary '<commit/>' -H 'Content-type:application/xml'
```

7. After sending the previous two commands, we can finally test if that worked. We will just ask Solr to return all the documents by sending the q=*:* query. The following results will be returned:

```
<?xml version="1.0" encoding="UTF-8"?>
<response>
 <lst name="responseHeader">
  <int name="status">0</int>
  <int name="QTime">6</int>
  <lst name="params">
   <str name="q">*:*</str>
  </lst>
 </lst>
 <result name="response" numFound="2" start="0">
  <doc>
   <str name="id">1</str>
   <str name="name">First</str>
   <str name="description">&gt;Water is a chemical substance with
the
```

```
chemical formula H2O. A water molecule contains one oxygen and two
hydrogen atoms connected by covalent bonds. Water is a liquid at
ambient conditions, but it often co-exists on Earth with its solid
state, ice, and gaseous state (water vapor or steam). Water also
exists in a liquid crystal state near hydrophilic surfaces.[1]
[2] Under nomenclature used to name chemical compounds, Dihydrogen
monoxide is the scientific name for water, though it is almost
never used.</str>
    <str name="langId">en</str></doc>
    <doc>
     <str name="id">2</str>
     <str name="name">Zweite</str>
     <str name="description">Wasser (H2O) ist eine chemische
Verbindung
aus den Elementen Sauerstoff (O) und Wasserstoff (H). Wasser ist
die einzige chemische Verbindung auf der Erde, die in der Natur
in allen drei Aggregatzuständen vorkommt. Die Bezeichnung Wasser
wird dabei besonders für den flüssigen Aggregatzustand verwendet.
Im festen (gefrorenen) Zustand spricht man von Eis, im gasförmigen
Zustand von Wasserdampf.</str>
    <str name="langId">de</str></doc>
   </result>
  </response>
```

As you can see, the `langId` field was filled with the correct language.

How it works...

The index structure we used is quite simple; it contains four fields and we are most interested in the `langId` field which won't be supplied with the data, but instead of that we want Solr to fill it.

The mentioned libraries are needed in order for the language identification to work. The `lib` entry in the `solrconfig.xml` file tells Solr to look for all the JAR files from the `../../langid` directory. Remember to change that to reflect your setup.

Now the update request processor chain definition comes. We need that definition to include `org.apache.solr.update.processor.LangDetectLanguageIdentifierUpdateProcessorFactory` in order to detect the document language. The `langid.fl` property tells the defined processor which fields should be used to detect the language. `langid.langField` specifies to which field the detected language should be written. The last property, `langid.fallback`, tells the language detection library what language should be set if it fails to detect a language. The `solr.LogUpdateProcessorFactory` and `solr.RunUpdateProcessorFactory` processors are there to log the updates and actually run them.

As for data indexing, in order to use the defined update request processor chain, we need to tell Solr that we want it to be used. In order to do that, when sending data to Solr we specify the additional parameter called `update.chain` with the name of the update chain we want to use, which in our case is `langid`. The `--data-binary` switch tells the `curl` command to send that data in a binary format and the `-H` switch tells `curl` which content type should be used. In the end we send the `commit` command to write the data to the Lucene index.

There's more...

If you don't want to use the previously mentioned processor to detect the document language, you can use the one that uses the Apache Tika library:

Language identification based on Apache Tika

If `LangDetectLanguageIdentifierUpdateProcessorFactory` is not good enough for you, you can try using language identification based on the Apache Tika library. In order to do that you need to provide all the libraries from the `contrib/extraction` directory in the Apache Solr distribution package instead of the ones from `contrib/langid/lib`, and instead of using the `org.apache.solr.update.processor.LangDetectLanguageIdentifierUpdateProcessorFactory` processor use `org.apache.solr.update.processor.TikaLanguageIdentifierUpdateProcessorFactory`. So the final configuration should look like the following code:

```
<updateRequestProcessorChain name="langid">
 <processor class="org.apache.solr.update.processor.
 TikaLanguageIdentifierUpdateProcessorFactory">
  <str name="langid.fl">name,description</str>
  <str name="langid.langField">langId</str>
  <str name="langid.fallback">en</str>
 </processor>
 <processor class="solr.LogUpdateProcessorFactory" />
 <processor class="solr.RunUpdateProcessorFactory" />
</updateRequestProcessorChain>
```

However, remember to still specify the `update.chain` parameter during indexing or add the defined processor to your update handler configuration.

Optimizing your primary key field indexing

Most of the data stored in Solr has some kind of primary key. Primary keys are different from most of the fields in your data as each document has a unique value stored; because they are primary in most cases they are unique. Because of that, a search on this primary field is not always as fast as you would expect when you compare it to databases. So, is there anything we can do to make it faster? With Solr 4.0 we can, and this recipe will show you how to improve the execution time of queries run against unique fields in Solr.

How to do it...

Let's assume we have the following field defined as a unique key for our Solr collection. So, in your `schema.xml` file, you would have the following:

> ▶ In your `fields` section you would have the following:
>
> ```
> <field name="id" type="string" indexed="true" stored="true"
> required="true" />
> ```

> ▶ After your fields section the following entry could be found:
>
> ```
> <uniqueKey>id</uniqueKey>
> ```

The following steps will help you optimize the indexing of your primary key field:

1. Now, we would like to use the Lucene flexible indexing and use `PulsingCodec` to handle our `id` field. In order to do that we introduce the following field type (just place it in the `types` section of your `schema.xml` file):

   ```
   <fieldType name="string_pulsing" class="solr.StrField"
   postingsFormat="Pulsing40"/>
   ```

2. In addition to that, we need to change the `id` field definition to use the new type. So, we should change the `type` attribute from `string` to `string_pulsing`:

   ```
   <field name="id" type="string_pulsing" indexed="true"
   stored="true" required="true" />
   ```

3. In addition to that we need to put the following entry in the `solrconfig.xml` file:

   ```
   <codecFactory class="solr.SchemaCodecFactory"/>
   ```

And that's all. Now you can start indexing your data.

How it works...

The changes we made use the new feature introduced in Apache Lucene 4.0 and in Solr – the so-called **flexible indexing**. It allows us to modify the way data is written into an inverted index and thus configure it to our own needs. In the previous example, we used `PulsingCodec` (`postingsFormat="Pulsing40"`) in order to store the unique values in a special way. The idea behind that codec is that the data for low frequency terms is written in a special way to save a single I/O seek operation when retrieving a document or documents for those terms from the index. That's why in some cases, when you do a noticeable amount of search to your unique field (or any high cardinality field indexed with `PulsingCodec`), you can see a drastic performance increase for that fields.

The last change, the one we made to the `solrconfig.xml` file, is required; without it Solr wouldn't let us use specified codes and would throw an exception during startup. It just specifies which codec factory should be used to create codec instances.

Please keep in mind that the previously mentioned method is very case dependent and you may not see a great performance increase with the change.

3
Analyzing Your
Text Data

In this chapter, we will cover:

- ▶ Storing additional information using payloads
- ▶ Eliminating XML and HTML tags from text
- ▶ Copying the contents of one field to another
- ▶ Changing words to other words
- ▶ Splitting text by CamelCase
- ▶ Splitting text by white space only
- ▶ Making plural words singular without stemming
- ▶ Lowercasing the whole string
- ▶ Storing geographical points in the index
- ▶ Stemming your data
- ▶ Preparing text to perform an efficient trailing wildcard search
- ▶ Splitting text by numbers and non-white space characters
- ▶ Using Hunspell as a stemmer
- ▶ Using your own stemming dictionary
- ▶ Protecting words from being stemmed

Introduction

The process of data indexing can be divided into parts. One of the parts, actually one of the last parts of that process, is **data analysis**. It's one of the crucial parts of data preparation. It defines how your data will be written into an index. It defines its structure and so on. In Solr, data behavior is defined by **types**. A type's behavior can be defined in the context of the indexing process or the context of the query process, or both. Furthermore, a type definition is composed of a **tokenizer** (or multiple ones–one for querying and one for indexing) and filters (both token filters and character filters).

A tokenizer specifies how your data will be pre-processed after it is sent to the appropriate field. **Analyzer** operates on the whole data that is sent to the field. Types can only have one tokenizer. The result of the tokenizer's work is a stream of objects called **tokens**. Next in the analysis chain are the filters. They operate on the tokens in the token stream. They can do anything with the tokens – change them, remove them, or make them lowercase, for example. Types can have multiple filters.

One additional type of filter is character filters. They do not operate on tokens from the token stream. They operate on the data that is sent to the field, and they are invoked before the data is sent to the analyzer.

This chapter will focus on data analysis and how to handle common day-to-day analysis questions and problems.

Storing additional information using payloads

Imagine you have a powerful preprocessing tool that can extract information about all the words in the text. Your boss would like you to use it with Solr or at least store the information it returns in Solr. So what can you do? We can use something called **payload** to store that data. This recipe will show you how to do it.

How to do it...

I assume that we already have an application that takes care of recognizing the part of speech in our text data. What we need to add is the data to the Solr index. To do that we will use a payload – a metadata that can be stored with each occurrence of a term.

1. First of all, you need to modify the index structure. To do this, we will add the new field type to the `schema.xml` file (the following entries should be added to the `types` section):

```
<fieldtype name="partofspeech" class="solr.TextField">
 <analyzer>
  <tokenizer class="solr.WhitespaceTokenizerFactory"/>
  <filter class="solr.DelimitedPayloadTokenFilterFactory"
encoder="integer" delimiter="|"/>
 </analyzer>
</fieldtype>
```

2. Now we'll add the field definition part to the `schema.xml` file (the following entries should be added to the `fields` section):

```
<field name="id" type="string" indexed="true" stored="true"
required="true" />
<field name="text" type="text" indexed="true" stored="true" />
<field name="speech" type="partofspeech" indexed="true"
stored="true" multivalued="true" />
```

3. Now let's look at what the example data looks like (I named it `ch3_payload.xml`):

```
<add>
 <doc>
  <field name="id">1</field>
  <field name="text">ugly human</field>
  <field name="speech">ugly|3 human|6</field>
 </doc>
 <doc>
  <field name="id">2</field>
  <field name="text">big book example</field>
  <field name="speech">big|3 book|6 example|1</field>
 </doc>
</add>
```

4. The next step is to index our data. To do that, we run the following command from the `exampledocs` directory (put the `ch3_payload.xml` file there):

```
java -jar post.jar ch3_payload.xml
```

5. To check if the payloads were written to the index, we will use the analysis capabilities or the Solr administration panel. We will test the `test|7` term with the associated payload. The following is what it looks like:

How it works...

What information can the payload hold? It may hold information that is compatible with the encoder type you define for the `solr.DelimitedPayloadTokenFilterFactory` filter. In our case, we don't need to write our own encoder – we will use the supplied one to store integers. We will use it to store the boost of the term. For example, nouns will be given a token boost value of 6, while the adjectives will be given a boost value of 3.

So first, we have the type definition. We defined a new type in the `schema.xml` file named `partofspeech` based on the Solr text field (attribute `class="solr.TextField"`). Our tokenizer splits the given text on whitespace characters. Then we have a new filter which handles our payloads. The filter defines an encoder which in our case is an integer (attribute `encoder="integer"`). Furthermore it defines a delimiter which separates the term from the payload. In our case the separator is the pipe character (`|`).

Finally we have the field definitions. In our example we only define three fields:

- ▶ Identifier
- ▶ Text
- ▶ Recognized speech part with payload

Now let's take a look at the example data. We have two simple fields – id and text. The one that we are interested in is the speech field. Look at how it is defined. It contains pairs which are made of a term, a delimiter, and a boost value. For example, book|6. In the example, I decided to boost nouns with a boost value of 6 and adjectives with the boost value of 3. I also decided that words that cannot be identified by my application, which is used to identify parts of speech, will be given a boost of 1. Pairs are separated with a space character, which in our case will be used to split those pairs – that is the task of the tokenizer which we defined earlier.

To index the documents we use simple post tools provided with the example deployment of Solr. To use it, invoke the command shown in the example. The post tools will send the data to the default update handler found under the address http://localhost:8983/solr/update. The following parameter is the file that is going to be sent to Solr. You can also post a list of files, not only a single one.

As you can see on the provided screenshot, payload is being properly encoded and written to the index – you can see [0 0 0 7] in the payload section of the solr.DelimitedPayloadTokenFilterFactory filter.

Eliminating XML and HTML tags from text

There are many real-life situations when you have to clean your data. Let's assume that you want to index web pages that your client sends you. You don't know anything about the structure of that page; one thing you know is that you must provide a search mechanism that will enable searching through the content of the pages. Of course you could index the whole page, splitting it by whitespaces, but then you would probably hear the clients complain about the HTML tags being searchable and so on. So before we enable searching the contents of the page, we need to clean the data. In this example we need to remove the HTML tags. This recipe will show you how to do it with Solr.

How to do it...

1. Let's start with assuming that our data looks like this (the ch3_html.xml file):

```
<add>
 <doc>
   <field name="id">1</field>
   <field name="html"><html><head><title>My page</title></
head><body><p>This is a <b>my</b><i>sample</i> page</body></
html></field>
```

```
    </doc>
  </add>
```

2. Now let's take care of the `schema.xml` file. First add the type definition to the `schema.xml` file:

```
<fieldType name="html_strip" class="solr.TextField">
  <analyzer>
    <charFilter class="solr.HTMLStripCharFilterFactory"/>
    <tokenizer class="solr.WhitespaceTokenizerFactory"/>
    <filter class="solr.LowerCaseFilterFactory"/>
  </analyzer>
</fieldType>
```

3. The next step is to add the following to the field definition part of the `schema.xml` file:

```
<field name="id" type="string" indexed="true" stored="true"
required="true" />
<field name="html" type="html_strip" indexed="true" stored="false"
/>
```

4. We can now index our data and have the HTML tags removed, right? Let's check that, by going to the analysis section of the Solr administration pages and passing the `<html><head><title>My page</title></head><body><p>This is a <b>my</b><i>sample</i> page</body></html>` text to analysis there:

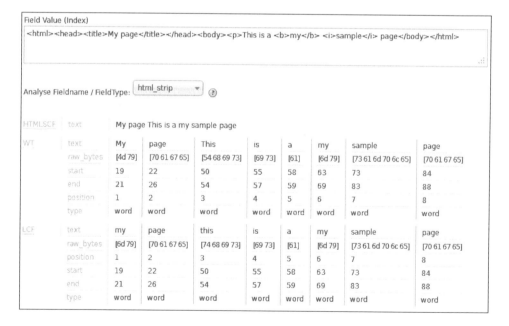

How it works...

First of all we have the data example. In the example we see one file with two fields, the identifier and some HTML data nested in the CDATA section. You must remember to surround HTML data in CDATA tags if they are full pages and start from HTML tags like our example. Otherwise Solr will have problems with parsing the data. But if you only have some tags present in the data, you shouldn't worry.

Next we have the `html_strip` type definition. It is based on `solr.TextField` to enable full text searching. Following that we have a character filter which handles the HTML and the XML tag stripping. The character filters are invoked before the data is sent to the tokenizer. This way they operate on un-tokenized data. In our case the character filter strips the HTML and XML tags, attributes, and so on and then sends the data to the tokenizer which splits the data by whitespace characters. The one and only filter defined in our type makes the tokens lowercase to simplify the search.

If you want to check how your data was indexed, remember not to be mistaken when you choose to store the field contents (attribute `stored="true"`). The stored value is the original one sent to Solr, so you won't be able to see the filters in action. If you wish to check the actual data structures, take a look at the Luke utility (a utility that lets you see the index structure and field values, and operate on the index). Luke can be found at the following address: `http://code.google.com/p/luke`. Instead of using Luke, I decided to use the analysis capabilities of the Solr administration pages and see how the `html` field behaves when we pass the example value provided in the example data file.

Copying the contents of one field to another

Imagine that you have many big XML files that hold information about the books that are stored on library shelves. There is not much data, just a unique identifier, the name of the book and the author. One day your boss comes to you and says: "Hey, we want to facet and sort on the basis of book author". You can change your XML and add two fields, but why do that, when you can use Solr to do that for you? Well, Solr won't modify your data, but can copy the data from one field to another. This recipe will show you how to do that.

How to do it...

In order to achieve what we want, we need the contents of the `author` field to be present in the fields named `author`, `author_facet`, and `author_sort`.

1. Let's assume that our data looks like the following code:

```
<add>
 <doc>
  <field name="id">1</field>
  <field name="name">Solr Cookbook</field>
```

```
     <field name="author">John Kowalsky</field>
    </doc>
    <doc>
     <field name="id">2</field>
     <field name="name">Some other book</field>
     <field name="author">Jane Kowalsky</field>
    </doc>
   </add>
```

2. Now let's add the following fields' definition to the `fields` section of your `schema.xml` file:

```
<field name="id" type="string" indexed="true" stored="true"
required="true"/>
<field name="author" type="text" indexed="true" stored="true"
multiValued="true"/>
<field name="name" type="text" indexed="true" stored="true"/>
<field name="author_facet" type="string" indexed="true"
stored="false"/>
<field name="author_sort" type="alphaOnlySort" indexed="true"
stored="false"/>
```

3. In order to make Solr copy data from the `author` field to the `author_facet` and `author_sort` field we need to define the copy fields in the `schema.xml` file (place the following entries right after the `field` section):

```
<copyField source="author" dest="author_facet"/>
<copyField source="author" dest="author_sort"/>
```

4. Now we can index our example data file by running the following command from the `exampledocs` directory (put the `data.xml` file there):

```
java -jar post.jar data.xml
```

How it works...

As you can see in the example, we only have three fields defined in our sample data XML file. There are two fields which we are not particularly interested in – id and name. The field that interests us the most is the author field. As I have previously mentioned, we want to place the contents of that field into three fields:

▶ author (the actual field that will be holding the data)

▶ author_sort

▶ author_facet

To do that we use copy fields. Those instructions are defined in the `schema.xml` file, right after the field definitions; that is, after the `</fields>` tag. To define a copy field, we need to specify a source field (attribute `source`) and a destination field (attribute `dest`).

After the definitions, like those in the example, Solr will copy the contents of the source fields to the destination fields during the indexing process. There is one thing that you have to be aware of – the content is copied before the analysis process takes place. That means that the data is copied as it is stored in the source.

There's more...

Solr also allows us to do more with copy fields than a simple copying from one field to another.

Copying contents of dynamic fields to one field

You can also copy multiple fields' content to one field. To do that you should define a copy field like so:

```
<copyField source="*_author" dest="authors"/>
```

The definition, like the one previously mentioned, would copy all of the fields that end with `_author` to one field named `authors`. Remember that if you copy multiple fields to one field, the destination field should be defined as multi-valued.

Limiting the number of characters copied

There may be situations where you only need to copy a defined number of characters from one field to another. To do that we add the `maxChars` attribute to the copy field definition. It can look like the following line of code:

```
<copyField source="author" dest="author_facet" maxChars="200"/>
```

The preceding definition tells Solr to copy up to 200 characters from the `author` field to the `author_facet` field. This attribute can be very useful when copying the content of multiple fields to one field.

Changing words to other words

Let's assume we have an e-commerce client and we are providing a search system based on Solr. Our index has hundreds of thousands of documents which mainly consist of books. And everything works fine! Then one day, someone from the marketing department comes into your office and says that he wants to be able to find books that contain the word "machine" when he types "electronics" into the search box. The first thing that comes to mind is, "Hey, I'll do it in the source and index that". But that is not an option this time, because there can be many documents in the database that have those words. We don't want to change the whole database. That's when synonyms come into play and this recipe will show you how to use them.

How to do it...

To make the example as simple as possible, I assumed that we only have two fields in our index.

1. Let's start by defining our index structure by adding the following field definition section to the `schema.xml` file (just add it to your `schema.xml` file in the `field` section):

```
<field name="id" type="string" indexed="true" stored="true"
required="true" />
<field name="description" type="text_syn" indexed="true"
stored="true" />
```

2. Now let's add the `text_syn` type definition to the `schema.xml` file as shown in the following code snippet:

```
<fieldType name="text_syn" class="solr.TextField">
 <analyzer type="query">
  <tokenizer class="solr.WhitespaceTokenizerFactory"/>
  <filter class="solr.LowerCaseFilterFactory"/>
 </analyzer>
 <analyzer type="index">
  <tokenizer class="solr.WhitespaceTokenizerFactory"/>
  <filter class="solr.SynonymFilterFactory" synonyms="synonyms.
txt" ignoreCase="true" expand="false" />
  <filter class="solr.LowerCaseFilterFactory"/>
 </analyzer>
</fieldType>
```

3. As you have noticed there is a file mentioned – `synonyms.txt`. Let's take a look at its contents:

```
machine => electronics
```

The `synonyms.txt` file should be placed in the same directory as other configuration files, which is usually the `conf` directory.

4. Finally we can look at the analysis page of the Solr administration panel to see if the synonyms are properly recognized and applied:

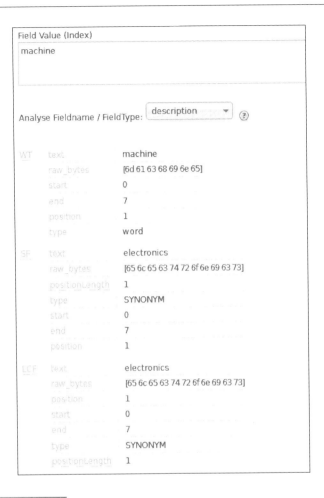

How it works...

First we have our field definition. There are two fields, an identifier and a description. The second one should be of interest r to us ight now. It's based on the new type `text_syn` which is shown in the second listing.

Now about the new type, `text_syn` – it's based on the `solr.TextField` class. Its definition is divided; it behaves in one way while indexing and in a different way while querying. So the first thing we see is the query time analyzer definition. It consists of the tokenizer that splits the data on the basis of whitespace characters, and then the lowercase filter converts all the tokens to lowercase. The interesting part is the index time behavior. It starts with the same tokenizer, but then the synonyms filter comes into play. Its definition starts like all the other filters – with a factory definition. Next we have a `synonyms` attribute which defines which file contains the synonyms definition. Following that we have the `ignoreCase` attribute which tells Solr to ignore the case of the tokens and the contents of the synonyms file.

The last attribute named `expand` is set to false. This means that Solr won't be expanding the synonyms – all equivalent synonyms will be reduced to the first synonym in the line. If the attribute is set to true, all synonyms will be expanded to all equivalent forms.

The example `synonyms.txt` file tells Solr that when the word "machine" appears in the field based on the `text_syn` type it should be replaced by "electronics". But not vice versa. Each synonym rule should be placed in a separate line in the `synonyms.txt` file. Also remember that the file should be written in the UTF-8 file encoding. This is crucial and you should always remember it because Solr will expect the file to be encoded in UTF-8.

As you can see in the provided screenshot from the Solr administration pages, the defined synonym was properly applied during the indexing phase.

There's more...

There is one more thing associated to using synonyms in Solr.

Equivalent synonyms setup

Let's get back to our example for a second. What if the person from the marketing department says that he/she wants not only to be able to find books that have the word "machine" to be found when entering the word "electronics", but also all the books that have the word "electronics", to be found when entering the word "machine". The answer is simple. First, we would set the `expand` attribute (of the filter) to `true`. Then we would change our `synonyms.txt` file to something like this:

```
machine, electronics
```

As I said earlier Solr would expand synonyms to equivalent forms.

Splitting text by CamelCase

Let's suppose that you run an e-commerce site with an electronic assortment. The marketing department can be a source of many great ideas. Imagine that your colleague from this department comes to you and says that they would like your search application to be able to find documents containing the word "PowerShot" by entering the words "power" and "shot" into the search box. So can we do that? Of course, and this recipe will show you how.

How to do it...

1. Let's start by creating the following index structure (add this to your `schema.xml` file to the field definition section):

```
<field name="id" type="string" indexed="true" stored="true"
required="true" />
```

```
<field name="description" type="text_split" indexed="true"
stored="true" />
```

2. To split text in the `description` field, we should add the following type definition to the `schema.xml` file:

```
<fieldType name="text_split" class="solr.TextField">
 <analyzer>
  <tokenizer class="solr.WhitespaceTokenizerFactory"/>
  <filter class="solr.WordDelimiterFilterFactory"
generateWordParts="1" splitOnCaseChange="1"/>
  <filter class="solr.LowerCaseFilterFactory" />
 </analyzer>
</fieldType>
```

3. Now let's index the following XML file:

```
<add>
 <doc>
  <field name="id">1</field>
  <field name="description">TextTest</field>
 </doc>
</add>
```

4. Finally, let's run the following query in the web browser:

```
http://localhost:8983/solr/select?q=description:test
```

You should get the indexed document as the response:

```
<?xml version="1.0" encoding="UTF-8"?>
 <response>
  <lst name="responseHeader">
   <int name="status">0</int>
   <int name="QTime">1</int>
   <lst name="params">
    <str name="q">description:test</str>
   </lst>
  </lst>
  <result name="response" numFound="1" start="0">
   <doc>
    <str name="id">1</str>
    <str name="description">TextTest</str></doc>
  </result>
 </response>
```

How it works...

Let's see how things work. First of all we have the field definition part of the `schema.xml` file. This is pretty straightforward. We have two fields defined–one that is responsible for holding information about the identifier (the `id` field) and the second one that is responsible for the product description (the `description` field).

Next we see the interesting part. We name our type `text_split` and have it based on a text type, `solr.TextField`. We also told Solr that we want our text to be tokenized by whitespaces by adding the whitespace tokenizer (the `tokenizer` tag). To do what we want to do–split by case change–we need more than this. Actually we need a filter named `WordDelimiterFilter` which is created by the `solr.WordDelimiterFilterFactory` class and a `filter` tag. We also need to define the appropriate behavior of the filter, so we add two attributes – `generateWordParts` and `splitOnCaseChange`. The values of those two parameters are set to 1 which means that they are turned on. The first attribute tells Solr to generate word parts, which means that the filter will split the data on non-letter characters. We also add the second attribute which tells Solr to split the tokens by case change.

What will that configuration do with our sample data? As you can see we have one document sent to Solr. The data in the `description` field will be split into two words: `text` and `test`. Please remember that we won't see the analyzed text in the Solr response, we only see the stored fields and the original content of those, not the analyzed one.

Splitting text by whitespace only

One of the most common problems that you probably came across is having to split text with whitespaces in order to segregate words from each other, to be able to process it further. This recipe will show you how to do it.

How to do it...

1. Let's start with the assumption that we have the following index structure (add this to your `schema.xml` file in the field definition section):

```
<field name="id" type="string" indexed="true" stored="true"
required="true" />
<field name="description_string" type="string" indexed="true"
stored="true" />
<field name="description_split" type="text_split" indexed="true"
stored="true" />
```

2. To split the text in the `description` field, we should add the following type definition:

```
<fieldType name="text_split" class="solr.TextField">
 <analyzer>
```

```
    <tokenizer class="solr.WhitespaceTokenizerFactory"/>
   </analyzer>
  </fieldType>
```

3. To test our type, I've indexed the following XML file:

```
<add>
 <doc>
  <field name="id">1</field>
  <field name="description_string">test text</field>
  <field name="description_text">test text</field>
 </doc>
</add>
```

4. Finally, let's run the following query in the web browser:

```
http://localhost:8983/solr/select?q=description_split:text
```

   In the response to the preceding query, we got the indexed document:

```
<?xml version="1.0" encoding="UTF-8"?>
 <response>
  <lst name="responseHeader">
   <int name="status">0</int>
   <int name="QTime">1</int>
   <lst name="params">
    <str name="q">description_split:text</str>
   </lst>
  </lst>
  <result name="response" numFound="1" start="0">
   <doc>
    <str name="id">1</str>
    <str name="description_string">test text</str>
    <str name="description_split">test text</str></doc>
  </result>
 </response>
```

5. On the other hand, we won't get the indexed document in the response after running the following query:

```
http://localhost:8983/solr/select?q=description_string:text
```

   The response to the preceding query:

```
<?xml version="1.0" encoding="UTF-8"?>
 <response>
  <lst name="responseHeader">
   <int name="status">0</int>
   <int name="QTime">0</int>
   <lst name="params">
```

```
        <str name="q">description_string:text</str>
      </lst>
    </lst>
    <result name="response" numFound="0" start="0">
    </result>
  </response>
```

How it works...

Let's see how things work. First of all we have the field definition part of the `schema.xml` file. This is pretty straightforward. We have three fields defined – one for the identifier of the document (the `id` field), and one named `description_string` which is based on a string field and thus not analyzed. The third one is the `description_split` field which is based on our `text_split` type and will be tokenized on the basis of whitespace characters.

Next we see the interesting part. We named our type `text_split` and had it based on a text type – `solr.TextField`. We told Solr that we want our text to be tokenized by whitespaces by adding a whitespace tokenizer (the `tokenizer` tag). Because there are no filters defined, the text will only be tokenized by whitespace characters and nothing more.

That's why our sample data in the field `description_text` will be split into two words, `test` and `text`. On the other hand, the text in the `description_string` field won't be split. That's why the first example query will result in one document in the response, while the second example won't find the example document. Please remember that we won't see the analyzed text in the Solr response, we only see stored fields and we see the original content of those, not the analyzed one.

Making plural words singular without stemming

Nowadays it's nice to have **stemming algorithms** (algorithms that will reduce words to their stems or root form) in your application, which will allow you to find the words such as `cat` and `cats` by typing `cat`. But let's imagine you have a search engine that searches through the contents of books in the library. One of the requirements is changing the plural forms of the words from plural to singular – nothing less, nothing more. Can Solr do that? Yes, the newest version can and this recipe will show you how to do that.

How to do it...

1. First of all let's start with a simple two field index (add this to your `schema.xml` file to the field definition section):

```
<field name="id" type="string" indexed="true" stored="true"
required="true"/>
<field name="description" type="text_light_stem" indexed="true"
stored="true" />
```

2. Now let's define the `text_light_stem` type which should look like this (add this to your `schema.xml` file):

```
<fieldType name="text_light_stem" class="solr.TextField">
 <analyzer>
  <tokenizer class="solr.WhitespaceTokenizerFactory"/>
  <filter class="solr.EnglishMinimalStemFilterFactory" />
  <filter class="solr.LowerCaseFilterFactory"/>
 </analyzer>
</fieldType>
```

3. Now let's check the analysis tool of the Solr administration pages. You should see that words such as `ways` and, `keys` are changed to their singular forms. Let's check the for that words using the analysis page of the Solr administration pages:

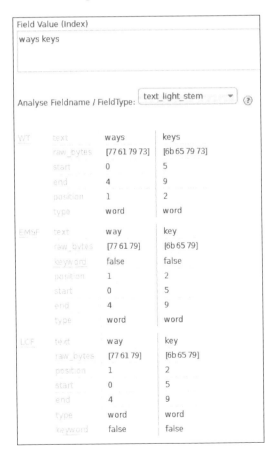

How it works...

First of all we need to define the fields in the `schema.xml` file. To do that we add the contents from the first example into that file. It tells Solr that our index will consist of two fields – the `id` field which will be responsible for holding information about the unique identifier of the document, and the `description` file which will be responsible for holding the document description.

The `description` field is actually where the magic is being done. We defined a new field type for that field and we called it `text_light_stem`. The field definition consists of a tokenizer and two filters. If you want to know how this tokenizer behaves please refer to the *Splitting text by whitespace only* recipe in this chapter. The first filter is a new one. This is the light stemming filter that we will use to perform minimal stemming. The class that enables Solr to use that filter is `solr.EnglishMinimalStemFilterFactory`. This filter takes care of the process of light stemming. You can see that using the analysis tools of the Solr administration panel. The second filter defined is the lowercase filter – you can see how it works by referring to the *How to lowercase the whole string* recipe in this chapter.

After adding this to your `schema.xml` file you should be able to use the light stemming algorithm.

There's more...

Light stemming supports a number of different languages. To use the light stemmers for your respective language, add the following filters to your type:

Language	Filter
Russian	`solr.RussianLightStemFilterFactory`
Portuguese	`solr.PortugueseLightStemFilterFactory`
French	`solr.FrenchLightStemFilterFactory`
German	`solr.GermanLightStemFilterFactory`
Italian	`solr.ItalianLightStemFilterFactory`
Spanish	`solr.SpanishLightStemFilterFactory`
Hungarian	`solr.HungarianLightStemFilterFactory`
Swedish	`solr.SwedishLightStemFilterFactory`
Finish	`solr.FinnishLightStemFilterFactory`
Indonesian	`solr.IndonesianStemFilterFactory` (with `stemDerivational="false"` attribute)
Norwegian	`solr.NorwegianLightStemFilterFactory`

In the case of `solr.IndonesianStemFilterFactory`, you need to add the `stemDerivational="false"` attribute in order to have it working as a light stemmer.

Lowercasing the whole string

Imagine you have a system where you only want to have perfect matches for names of the documents. No matter what the cause of such a decision is, you would want such a functionality. However there is one thing you would like to have – you would like your search to be case independent, so it doesn't matter if the document or query is lower cased or uppercased. Can we do something with that in Solr? Of course Solr can do that, and this recipe will describe how to do it.

How to do it...

1. We start by defining the following index structure (add this to your `schema.xml` file in the field definition section):

```
<field name="id " type="string" indexed="true" stored="true"
required="true" />
<field name="name" type="string_lowercase" indexed="true"
stored="true" />
<field name="description" type="text" indexed="true" stored="true"
/>
```

2. To make our strings lowercase, we should add the following type definition to the `schema.xml` file:

```
<fieldType name="string_lowercase" class="solr.TextField">
 <analyzer>
   <tokenizer class="solr.KeywordTokenizerFactory"/>
   <filter class="solr.LowerCaseFilterFactory"/>
 </analyzer>
</fieldType>
```

3. In order to test if everything is working as it should we need to index the following XML file:

```
<add>
 <doc>
   <field name="id">1</field>
   <field name="name">Solr Cookbook</field>
   <field name="description">Simple description</field>
 </doc>
</add>
```

4. Then we will run the following query in the web browser:

```
http://localhost:8983/solr/select?q=name:"solr cookbook"
```

You should get the indexed document in response. You should also be able to get the indexed document in response to the following query:

```
http://localhost:8983/solr/select?q=name:"solr Cookbook"
```

How it works...

Let's see how things work. First of all we have the field definition part of the schema.xml file. This is pretty straightforward. We have three fields defined. First, the field named id which is responsible for holding our unique identifier. The second one is the name field which is actually our lowercased string field. The third field will hold the description of our documents and is based on the standard text type defined in the example Solr deployment.

Now let's get back to our name field. It's based on the string_lowercase type. The string_lowercase type consists of an analyzer which is defined as a tokenizer and one filter. The solr.KeywordTokenizerFactory filter tells Solr that the data in that field should not be tokenized in any way. It just should be passed as a single token to the token stream. Next we have our filter, which changes all the characters to their lowercased equivalents. And that's how this field analysis is performed.

The example queries show how the field behaves. It doesn't matter if you type lowercase or uppercase characters, the document will be found anyway. What matters is that you must type the whole string as it is because we used the keyword tokenizer which, as I already said, is not tokenizing but just passing the whole data through the token stream as a single token.

Storing geographical points in the index

Imagine that up till now your application stores information about companies – not much information, just unique identification and the company name. But now, your client wants to store the location of the companies. In addition to that, your users would like to sort by distance and filter by distance from a given point. Is this doable with Solr? Of course it is and this recipe will show you how to do it.

How to do it...

1. For the purpose of this recipe, let's create a sample index structure. To do this, describe the companies that we store in the index with three fields which are defined as follows (add this to your schema.xml file to the field definition section):

```
<field name="id" type="string" indexed="true" stored="true"
required="true" />
<field name="name" type="text" indexed="true" stored="true" />
<field name="location" type="location" indexed="true"
stored="true" />
```

2. Next we will also add one dynamic field (add this to your `schema.xml` file in the field definition section):

```
<dynamicField name="*_coordinate" type="tdouble" indexed="true"
stored="false" />
```

3. The next step is to define the `location` type which should look like the following code:

```
<fieldType name="location" class="solr.LatLonType"
subFieldSuffix="_coordinate"/>
```

4. In addition to that, we will need the `tdouble` field type, which should look like the following code:

```
<fieldType name="tdouble" class="solr.TrieDoubleField"
precisionStep="4" positionIncrementGap="0"/>
```

5. The next step is to create the example data looking like the following code (I named the data file `task9.xml`):

```
<add>
 <doc>
  <field name="id">1</field>
  <field name="name">Solr.pl company</field>
  <field name="location">54.02,23.10</field>
 </doc>
</add>
```

6. And now let's index our data. To do that, we run the following command from the `exampledocs` directory (put the `task9.xml` file there):

```
java -jar post.jar task9.xml
```

7. After indexing we should be able to use the query, such as the following one, to get our data:

```
http://localhost:8983/solr/select?q=*:*&fq={!geofilt
sfield=location}&pt=54.00,23.00&d=10
```

The response should look like this:

```
<?xml version="1.0" encoding="UTF-8"?>
 <response>
  <lst name="responseHeader">
   <int name="status">0</int>
   <int name="QTime">0</int>
   <lst name="params">
    <str name="pt">54.00,23.00</str>
```

```
      <str name="d">10</str>
      <str name="fq">{!geofiltsfield=location}</str>
      <str name="q">*:*</str>
     </lst>
    </lst>
    <result name="response" numFound="1" start="0">
     <doc>
      <str name="id">1</str>
      <str name="name">Solr.pl company</str>
      <str name="location">54.02,23.10</str>
     </doc>
    </result>
   </response>
```

How it works...

First of all we have three fields and one dynamic field defined in our `schema.xml` file. The first field is the one responsible for holding the unique identifier. The second one holds the name of the company. The third one named `location` is responsible for holding geographical points and is based on the location `type`. The dynamic field – `*_coordinate` will be used internally by our `location` type. It uses the `tdouble` field which was taken from the `schema.xml` file distributed with Solr.

Next we have our `location` type definition. It's based on the `solr.LatLonType` class which is specially designed for spatial search and is defined by a single attribute – `subFieldSuffix`. That attribute specifies which fields (in our case it's the dynamic `*_coordinate` field) will be used internally for holding the actual values of latitude and longitude.

So how does this type of field actually work? When defining a two-dimensional field, like we did, there are actually three fields created in the index. The first field is named like the field we added in the `schema.xml` file, so in our case it is `location`. This field will be responsible for holding the stored value of the field. And one more thing – this field will only be created when we set the field attribute `store` to `true`.

The next two fields are based on the defined dynamic field. Their names will be `location _0_coordinate` and `location_1_coordinate` in our case. First we have the field name, the `_` character, then the index of the value, and finally the suffix defined by the `subFieldSuffix` attribute of the type.

We can now look at the way the data is indexed. Please take a look at the example data file. You can see that the values in each pair are separated by the comma character, and that's how you can add the data to the index:

```
http://localhost:8983/solr/select?q=*:*&fq={!geofilt sfield=location}
&pt=54.00,23.00&d=10
```

Querying is a bit different. We send a query to retrieve all the documents from the index (q=*:*). In addition to that, we want to filter the results by distance (the `geofilt` filter) with the use of the `location` field (sfield=location). fq={!geofiltsfield=location} uses the Solr local params syntax to send a distance filter. It can look strange comparing it to a standard query, but it works. In addition to that, we've specified the point we will calculate the distance from (the `pt` parameter) as 54.00,23.00. This is a pair of latitude and longitude values separated by a comma character. The last parameter is d, which specifies the maximum distance that documents can be, from the given point, to be considered as a match. We specified it as 10 kilometers (d=10). As you can see, even though our document had its point defined as 54.02,23.10 we found it with our query because of the distance we specified.

Stemming your data

One of the most common requirements I meet is **stemming** – the process of reducing the word to their root form (or stems). Let's imagine the book e-commerce store, where you store the books' names and descriptions. We want to be able to find words such as shown or showed when you type the word show and vice versa. To achieve that we can use stemming algorithms. This recipe will show you how to add stemming to your data analysis.

How to do it...

1. We need to start with the index structure. Let's assume that our index consists of three fields (add this to your schema.xml file to the field definition section):

    ```
    <field name="id" type="string" indexed="true" stored="true"
    required="true" />
    <field name="name" type="text" indexed="true" stored="true" />
    <field name="description" type="text_stem" indexed="true"
    stored="true" />
    ```

2. Now let's define our text_stem type which should look like the following code:

    ```
    <fieldType name="text_stem" class="solr.TextField">
      <analyzer>
        <tokenizer class="solr.WhitespaceTokenizerFactory"/>
        <filter class="solr.SnowballPorterFilterFactory" />
      </analyzer>
    </fieldType>
    ```

3. Now we can index our data – to do that we need to create an example data file, for example, the following code:

    ```
    <add>
     <doc>
      <field name="id">1</field>
      <field name="name">Solr cookbook</field>
    ```

```
  <field name="description">This is a book that I'll show</field>
 </doc>
 <doc>
  <field name="id">2</field>
  <field name="name">Solr cookbook 2</field>
  <field name="description">This is a book I showed</field>
 </doc>
</add>
```

4. After indexing, we can test how our data was analyzed. To do that, let's run the following query:

```
http://localhost:8983/solr/select?q=description:show
```

The result we get from Solr is as follows:

```
<?xml version="1.0" encoding="UTF-8"?>
 <response>
  <lst name="responseHeader">
   <int name="status">0</int>
   <int name="QTime">1</int>
   <lst name="params">
    <str name="q">description:show</str>
   </lst>
  </lst>
  <result name="response" numFound="2" start="0">
   <doc>
    <str name="id">1</str>
    <str name="name">Solr cookbook</str>
    <arr name="description">
     <str>This is a book that I'll show</str>
    </arr>
   </doc>
   <doc>
    <str name="id">2</str>
    <str name="name">Solr cookbook 2</str>
    <arr name="description">
     <str>This is a book I showed</str>
    </arr>
   </doc>
  </result>
 </response>
```

That's right, Solr found two documents matching the query which means that our fields and types are working as intended.

How it works...

Our index consists of three fields; one holding the unique identifier of the document, the second one holding the name of the document, and the third one holding the document description. The last field is the field that will be stemmed.

The stemmed field is based on a Solr text field and has an analyzer that is used at query and indexing time. It is tokenized on the basis of the whitespace characters, and then the stemming filter is used. What does the filter do? It tries to bring the words to its root form, which means that words such as shows, showing, and show will all be changed to show – or at least they should be changed to that form.

Please note that in order to properly use stemming algorithms they should be used at query and indexing time. This is a must because of the stemming results.

As you can see, our test data consists of two documents. Take a look at the description. One of the documents contains the word showed and the other has the word show in their description fields. After indexing and running the sample query, Solr would return two documents in the results which means that the stemming did its job.

There's more...

There are too many languages that have stemming support integrated into Solr to mention them all. If you are using a language other than English, please refer to the http://wiki. apache.org/solr/LanguageAnalysis page of the Solr Wiki to find the appropriate filter.

Preparing text to perform an efficient trailing wildcard search

Many users coming from traditional RDBMS systems are used to wildcard searches. The most common of them are the ones using * characters which means zero or more characters. You have probably seen searches like the one as follows:

```
AND name LIKE 'ABC12%'
```

So how to do that with Solr and not kill our Solr server? This task will show you how to prepare your data and make efficient searches.

How to do it...

1. The first step is to create a proper index structure. Let's assume we have the following one (add this to your `schema.xml` file to the field definition section):

```
<field name="id" type="string" indexed="true" stored="true"
required="true" />
<field name="name" type="string_wildcard" indexed="true"
stored="true" />
```

2. Now, let's define our `string_wildcard` type (add this to the `schema.xml` file):

```
<fieldType name="string_wildcard" class="solr.TextField">
  <analyzer type="index">
    <tokenizer class="solr.WhitespaceTokenizerFactory"/>
    <filter class="solr.EdgeNGramFilterFactory" minGramSize="1"
    maxGramSize="25" side="front"/>
  </analyzer>
  <analyzer type="query">
    <tokenizer class="solr.WhitespaceTokenizerFactory"/>
  </analyzer>
</fieldType>
```

3. The third step is to create the example data which looks like the following code:

```
<add>
  <doc>
    <field name="id">1</field>
    <field name="name">XYZ1234ABC12POI</field>
  </doc>
</add>
```

4. Now send the following query to Solr:

```
http://localhost:8983/solr/select?q=name:XYZ1
```

The Solr response for the previous query is as follows:

```
<?xml version="1.0" encoding="UTF-8"?>
 <response>
  <lst name="responseHeader">
   <int name="status">0</int>
   <int name="QTime">1</int>
   <lst name="params">
    <str name="q">name:XYZ1</str>
   </lst>
  </lst>
  <result name="response" numFound="1" start="0">
   <doc>
```

```
    <str name="id">1</str>
    <str name="name">XYZ1234ABC12POI</str>
  </doc>
 </result>
</response>
```

As you can see, the document has been found, so our setup is working as intended.

How it works...

First of all let's look at our index structure defined in the `schema.xml` file. We have two fields – one holding the unique identifier of the document (the `id` field) and the second one holding the name of the document (the `name` field) which is actually the field we are interested in.

The `name` field is based on the new type we defined – `string_wildcard`. This type is responsible for enabling trailing wildcards, the ones that will enable the `LIKE 'WORD%'` SQL queries. As you can see the field type is divided into two analyzers, one for the data analysis during indexing and the other for query processing. The querying analyzer is straight; it just tokenizes the data on the basis of whitespace characters. Nothing more, nothing less.

Now the indexing time analysis (of course we are talking about the `name` field). Similar to the query time, during indexing the data is tokenized on the basis of whitespace characters, but there is also an additional filter defined. The `solr.EdgeNGramFilterFactory` class is responsible for generating the filter called **n-grams**. In our setup, we tell Solr that the minimum length of an n-gram is 1 (the `minGramSize` attribute) and the maximum length is 25 (the `maxGramSize` attribute). We also defined that the analysis should be started from the beginning of the text (the `side` attribute set to `front`). So what would Solr do with our example data? It will create the following tokens from the example text: X, XY, XYZ, XYZ1, XYZ12, and so on. It will create tokens by adding the next character from the string to the previous token, up to the maximum length of the n-gram filter that is given in the filter configuration.

So by typing the example query, we can be sure that the example document will be found because of the n-gram filter defined in the configuration of the field. We also didn't define the n-gram filter in the querying stage of analysis because we didn't want our query to be analyzed in such a way that it could lead to false positive hits.

This functionality, as described, can also be used successfully to provide autocomplete features to your application (if you are not familiar with the autocomplete feature please take a look at `http://en.wikipedia.org/wiki/Autocomplete`).

Please remember that using n-grams will make your index a bit larger. Because of that you should avoid having n-grams on all the fields in the index. You should carefully decide which fields should use n-grams and which should not.

There's more...

If you would like your field to be able to simulate `SQL LIKE '%ABC'` queries, you should change the `side` attribute of the `solr.EdgeNGramFilterFactory` class to the `back` value. The configuration should look like the following code snippet:

```
<filter class="solr.EdgeNGramFilterFactory" minGramSize="1"
maxGramSize="25" side="back"/>
```

It would change the end from which Solr starts to analyze the data. In our case it would start from the end, and thus would produce n-grams as follows: `I`, `OI`, `POI`,`2POI`, `12POI`, and so on.

See also

▸ If you want to propose another solution for that kind of search, please refer to the recipe *Splitting text by numbers and non-whitespace characters* in this chapter

Splitting text by numbers and non-whitespace characters

Analyzing the text data is not only about stemming, removing diacritics (if you are not familiar with the word, please take a look at `http://en.wikipedia.org/wiki/Diacritic`), and choosing the right format for the data. Let's assume that our client wants to be able to search by words and numbers that construct product identifiers. For example, he would like to be able to find the product identifier `ABC1234XYZ` by using `ABC`, `1234`, or `XYZ`.

How to do it...

1. Let's start with the index that consists of three fields (add this to your `schema.xml` file to the field definition section):

```
<field name="id" type="string" indexed="true" stored="true"
required="true" />
<field name="name" type="text" indexed="true" stored="true"/>
<field name="description" type="text_split" indexed="true"
stored="true" />
```

2. The second step is to define our `text_split` type which should look like the following code (add this to your `schema.xml` file):

```
<fieldType name="text_split" class="solr.TextField">
  <analyzer>
```

```
    <tokenizer class="solr.WhitespaceTokenizerFactory"/>
    <filter class="solr.WordDelimiterFilterFactory"
generateWordParts="1" generateNumberParts="1" splitOnNumerics="1"
/>
  <filter class="solr.LowerCaseFilterFactory"/>
  </analyzer>
</fieldType>
```

3. Now you can index your data. To do that let's create an example data file:

```
<add>
  <doc>
    <field name="id">1</field>
    <field name="name">Test document</field>
    <field name="description">ABC1234DEF BL-123_456
    adding-documents</field>
  </doc>
</add>
```

4. After indexing we can test how our data was analyzed. To do that let's run the following query:

```
http://localhost:8983/solr/select?q=description:1234
```

Solr found our document which means that our field is working as intended. The response from Solr will be as follows:

```
<?xml version="1.0" encoding="UTF-8"?>
 <response>
  <lst name="responseHeader">
   <int name="status">0</int>
   <int name="QTime">1</int>
   <lst name="params">
    <str name="q">description:1234</str>
   </lst>
  </lst>
  <result name="response" numFound="1" start="0">
   <doc>
    <str name="id">1</str>
    <str name="name">Test document</str>
    <str name="description">ABC1234DEF BL-123_456 adding-
documents</str></doc>
  </result>
 </response>
```

How it works...

We have our index defined as three fields in the `schema.xml` file. We have a unique identifier (an `id` field) indexed as a `string` value. We have a document name (the `name` field) indexed as `text` (type which is provided with the example deployment of Solr), and a document description (a `description` field) which is based on the `text_split` field which we defined ourselves.

Our type is defined to make the same text analysis, both on query time and on index time. It consists of the whitespace tokenizer and two filters. The first filter is where the magic is done. The `solr.WordDelimiterFilterFactory` behavior, in our case, is defined by the following parameters:

- `generateWordParts`: If this parameter is set to `1`, it tells the filter to generate parts of the word that are connected by non-alphanumeric characters such as the dash character. For example, token `ABC-EFG` would be split into `ABC` and `EFG`.

- `generateNumberParts`: If this parameter is set to `1`, it tells the filter to generate words from numbers connected by non-numeric characters, such as the dash character. For example, token `123-456` would be split into `123` and `456`.

- `splitOnNumerics`: If this parameter is set to `1`, it tells the filter to split letters and numbers from each other. This means that token `ABC123` would be split in to `ABC` and `123`.

The second filter is responsible for changing the words that lowercased the equivalents and is discussed in the recipe *How to lowercase the whole string* in this chapter.

Therefore, after sending our test data to Solr we can run the example query to see if we defined our filter properly. In addition, you probably know the result; yes, the result will contain one document – the one that we send to Solr. That is because the word `ABC1234DEF` is split into `ABC`, `1234`, and `DEF` tokens, and thus can be found by the example query.

There's more...

In case you would like to preserve the original token that is passed to `solr.WordDelimiterFilterFactory`, add the following attribute to the filter definition:

```
preserveOriginal="1"
```

See also

- If you would like to know more about `solr.WordDelimiterFilterFactory`, please refer to the recipe *Splitting text by CamelCase* in this chapter

Using Hunspell as a stemmer

Solr supports numerous stemmers for various languages. You can use various stemmers for English, and there are ones available for French, German, and most of the European languages. But sometimes they provide stemming results that are not of great quality. Alternatively, maybe you are wondering if there is a stemmer out there that supports your language, which is not included in Solr. No matter what the reason, if you are looking for a different stemmer you should look at the Hunspell filter if it suits your needs, and this recipe will show you how to use it in Solr.

Getting ready

Before starting, please check the `http://wiki.openoffice.org/wiki/Dictionaries` page to see if Hunspell supports your language.

How to do it...

1. We should start by creating an index structure (just add the following entries to the `fields` section of your `schema.xml` file) which looks like the following code:

   ```
   <field name="id" type="string" indexed="true" stored="true"
   required="true" multiValued="false" />
   <field name="name" type="text_english" indexed="true"
   stored="true"/>
   <field name="description" type="text_english" indexed="true"
   stored="true" />
   ```

2. Now we should define the `text_english` type as follows (if you don't have it in your `schema.xml` file, please add it to the `types` section of the file):

   ```
   <fieldType name="text_english" class="solr.TextField"
   positionIncrementGap="100">
     <analyzer>
       <tokenizer class="solr.StandardTokenizerFactory"/>
       <filter class="solr.LowerCaseFilterFactory"/>
       <filter class="solr.PorterStemFilterFactory"/>
     </analyzer>
   </fieldType>
   ```

3. Let's assume that we are not satisfied with the quality of `solr.PorterStemFilterFactory` and we would like to have that improved by using Hunspell. In order to do that, we need to change the `solr.PorterStemFilterFactory` definition to the following one:

   ```
   <filter class="solr.HunspellStemFilterFactory" dictionary="en_
   GB.dic" affix="en_GB.aff" ignoreCase="true" />
   ```

So the final `text_english` type configuration would look like the following code:

```
<fieldType name="text_english" class="solr.TextField"
positionIncrementGap="100">
  <analyzer>
    <tokenizer class="solr.StandardTokenizerFactory"/>
    <filter class="solr.LowerCaseFilterFactory"/>
    <filter class="solr.HunspellStemFilterFactory" dictionary=
    "en_GB.dic" affix="en_GB.aff" ignoreCase="true" />
  </analyzer>
</fieldType>
```

4. The last thing we need to do is place the `en_GB.dic` and `en_GB.aff` files in the Solr `conf` directory (the one where you have all your configuration files stored). Those files can be found at the `http://wiki.openoffice.org/wiki/Dictionaries` page. They are the dictionaries for English used in Great Britain. And that's all; nothing more needs to be done.

How it works...

Our index structure is very simple – it contains three fields of which two (`name` and `description`) are used for full text searching, and we want those fields to use the `text_english` field type and thus use `solr.HunspellStemFilterFactory` for stemming.

The configuration of the `solr.HunspellStemFilterFactory` filter factory is not difficult. Of course, there are a few attributes of the `filter` tag that need to be specified:

- ▶ `class`: This specifies the class implementing the filter factory we want to use, which in our case is `solr.HunspellStemFilterFactory`.
- ▶ `dictionary`: This specifies the name of the `.dic` file of the dictionary we want to use.
- ▶ `affix`: This specifies the name of the `.aff` file of the dictionary we want to use.
- ▶ `ignoreCase`: This is used to ignore cases when matching words against the dictionary. In our case, we want to ignore cases.

The last thing we need to do is provide Solr with the dictionary files so that the Hunspell filter can do its work. Although this is simple, this part is crucial. The dictionaries define how well Hunspell will work. Before using a new dictionary, you should always properly conduct A/B testing and see if things did not get worse in your case.

One last thing about the dictionaries. If you would like to use other languages with Hunspell, the only thing you will need to do is provide the new dictionary file and change the name of the dictionaries, so change the `dictionary` and `affix` attributes of the `solr.HunspellStemFilterFactory` definition.

Using your own stemming dictionary

Sometimes, stemmers provided with Lucene and Solr don't do what you would like them to do. That's because most of them are based on an algorithmic approach and even the best algorithms can come to a place where you won't like the results of their work and you would like to make some modifications. Of course, modifications to the algorithm code can be challenging and we don't usually do that. The good thing is that Solr supports a method of overriding the stemmer work and this recipe will show you how to use it.

Getting ready

Before we continue please remember that the method described in this recipe may not work with custom stemmers that are not provided with Solr.
How to do it... Let's say that we want some of the words to be stemmed in a way we want. For example,
we want the word dogs to be stemmed as doggie (of course that's only an example).

1. What we have to do first is write the words dogs and doggie in a file (let's call it override.txt). Words should be separated from each other by a tab character and each line of the file should contain a single stemming overwrite. For example, our override.txt file could look like this:

    ```
    dogs doggie
    ```

2. Now we should put the override.txt file in the same directory as the schema.xml file (usually its conf). Please remember to have that file written in UTF-8 encoding. If you have characters from the classic ASCII character set, they won't be recognized properly if you don't use UTF-8.

3. Next we need to add the solr.StemmerOverrideFilterFactory filter to our text types. I assume we only use text_english with the following definition (put the following definition to your types section of the schema.xml file):

    ```
    <fieldType name="text_english" class="solr.TextField"
    positionIncrementGap="100">
      <analyzer>
        <tokenizer class="solr.StandardTokenizerFactory"/>
        <filter class="solr.LowerCaseFilterFactory"/>
        <filter class="solr.PorterStemFilterFactory"/>
      </analyzer>
    </fieldType>
    ```

In order for our list of protected words to work, we need to put `solr.StemmerOverrideFilterFactory` before the stemming, which is `solr.PorterStemFilterFactory` in our case. The final type definition for `text_english` would look like the following code:

```
<fieldType name="text_english" class="solr.TextField"
positionIncrementGap="100">
  <analyzer>
    <tokenizer class="solr.StandardTokenizerFactory"/>
    <filter class="solr.LowerCaseFilterFactory"/>
    <filter class="solr.StemmerOverrideFilterFactory"
    dictionary="dict.txt" />
    <filter class="solr.PorterStemFilterFactory"/>
  </analyzer>
</fieldType>
```

This is what the analysis page of the Solr administration pages shows:

4. That's all. Now, the fields that are based on the `text_english` type will not be stemmed.

How it works...

The work of the `solr.StemmerOverrideFilterFactory` class is simple – it changes the words we want it to change and then marks them as protected so that the stemmer won't do any further processing of those words. In order for this functionality to work properly, you should remember to put `solr.StemmerOverrideFilterFactory` before any stemmers in your analysis chain.

The actual configuration of `solr.StemmerOverrideFilterFactory` is pretty simple and similar to other filters. It requires two attributes; the usual `class` attribute, which informs Solr which filter factory should be used in order to create the filter, and the `dictionary` attribute, which specifies the name of the file containing the dictionary that we want to use for our custom stemming.

Looking at the analysis page of the Solr administration pages, we can see that our `dogs` word was protected from being stemmed with the default stemmer and changed to what we wanted, that is, `doggie`.

Protecting words from being stemmed

Sometimes, the stemming filters available in Solr do more than you would like them to do. For example, they can stem brand names or the second name of a person. Sometimes, you would like to protect some of the words that have a special meaning in your system or you know that some words would cause trouble to a stemmer or stemmers. This recipe will show you how to do it.

Getting started

Before we continue, please remember that the method described in this recipe may not work with custom stemmers that are not provided with Solr.

How to do it...

In order to have the defined words protected we need a list of them. Let's say that we don't want the words `cats` and `dogs` to be stemmed.

1. To achieve that, we should start by writing the words we want to be protected from stemming into a file. Let's create the file called `dontstem.txt` with the following contents:

   ```
   cats
   dogs
   ```

2. Now let's put the created file in the same directory as the `schema.xml` file (usually it's the `conf` directory). Please remember to have that file written in UTF-8 encoding. If you have characters from the classic ASCII character set they won't be recognized properly if you don't use UTF-8.

3. Now, we need to add the `solr.KeywordMarkerFilterFactory` filter to our text types. I assume we only use the `text_english` type with the following definition:

```
<fieldType name="text_english" class="solr.TextField"
positionIncrementGap="100">
  <analyzer>
    <tokenizer class="solr.StandardTokenizerFactory"/>
    <filter class="solr.LowerCaseFilterFactory"/>
    <filter class="solr.PorterStemFilterFactory"/>
  </analyzer>
</fieldType>
```

In order for our list of protected words to work, we need to put `solr.KeywordMarkerFilterFactory` before the stemming, which is `solr.PorterStemFilterFactory` in our case. So the final type definition for the `text_english` type would look like the following code:

```
<fieldType name="text_english" class="solr.TextField"
positionIncrementGap="100">
  <analyzer>
    <tokenizer class="solr.StandardTokenizerFactory"/>
    <filter class="solr.LowerCaseFilterFactory"/>
    <filter class="solr.KeywordMarkerFilterFactory"
    protected="dontstem.txt" />
    <filter class="solr.PorterStemFilterFactory"/>
  </analyzer>
</fieldType>
```

This is what the analysis page of the Solr administration pages shows:

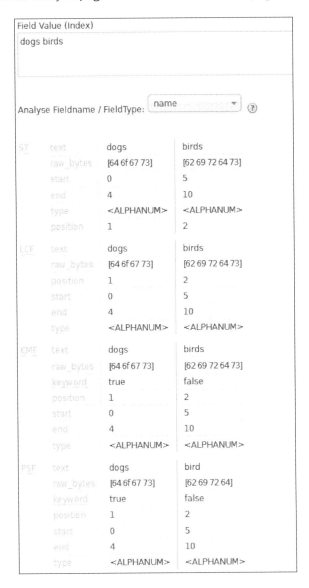

4. That's all. Now, the fields that are based on the `text_english` type won't
    be stemmed.

How it works...

The whole idea is pretty simple. With the use of `solr.KeywordMarkerFilterFactory`, we mark the protected words and that information is used by the stemmers available in Solr and Lucene. In order for this functionality to work properly, you should remember to put the `solr.KeywordMarkerFilterFactory` filter before any stemmers in your analysis chain.

The actual configuration of `solr.KeywordMarkerFilterFactory` is pretty simple and similar to other filters. It requires two attributes; the usual `class` attribute, which informs Solr which filter factory should be used in order to create the filter, and the attribute `protected` which specifies the name of the file containing words that we want to protect from stemming.

Looking at the analysis page of the Solr administration pages, we can see that our `dogs` word was protected from being stemmed, compared to the `birds` word which was changed to `bird`.

4
Querying Solr

In this chapter, we will cover:

- ▶ Asking for a particular field value
- ▶ Sorting results by a field value
- ▶ How to search for a phrase, not a single word
- ▶ Boosting phrases over words
- ▶ Positioning some documents over others in a query
- ▶ Positioning documents with words closer to each other first
- ▶ Sorting results by a distance from a point
- ▶ Getting documents with only a partial match
- ▶ Affecting scoring with functions
- ▶ Nesting queries
- ▶ Modifying returned documents
- ▶ Using parent-child relationships
- ▶ Ignoring typos in terms of the performance
- ▶ Detecting and omitting duplicate documents
- ▶ Using field aliases
- ▶ Returning a value of a function in the results

Introduction

Making a simple query is not a hard task, but making a complex one, with faceting, local params, parameters dereferencing, and phrase queries can be a challenging task. On the top of all that, you must remember to write your query with performance factors in mind. That's why something that is simple at first sight can turn into something more challenging such as writing a good, complex query. This chapter will try to guide you through some of the tasks you may encounter during your everyday work with Solr.

Asking for a particular field value

There are many cases where you will want to ask for a particular field value. For example, when searching for the author of a book in the Internet library or an e-commerce shop. Of course Solr can do that, and this recipe will show you how to do it.

How to do it...

1. Let's start with the following index structure (just add the following to your `schema.xml` file to the field definition section):

    ```
    <field name="id" type="string" indexed="true" stored="true"
    required="true" />
    <field name="title" type="text" indexed="true" stored="true" />
    <field name="author" type="string" indexed="true" stored="true"/>
    ```

2. To ask for a value in the author field, send the following query to Solr:

    ```
    http://localhost:8983/solr/select?q=author:rafal
    ```

That's all. The documents you'll get from Solr will be the ones with the requested value in the `author` field. Remember that the query shown in the example uses the standard query parser, not DisMax.

How it works...

We defined three fields in the index, but this was only for the purpose of the example. As you can see in the previous query, to ask for a particular field value, you need to send a `q` parameter syntax such as `FIELD_NAME:VALUE`, and that's all there is to it. Of course you can add the logical operator to the query to make it more complex. Remember that if you omit the field name from the query your values will be checked again in the default search field that is defined in the `schema.xml` file.

There's more...

When asking for a particular field value, there are a few things that are useful to know:

Querying for a particular value using the DisMax query parser

Sometimes you may need to ask for a particular field value when using the DisMax query parser. Unfortunately the DisMax query parser doesn't support full Lucene query syntax and thus you can't send a query like that, but there is a solution to it. You can use the extended DisMax query parser which is an evolved DisMax query parser. It has the same list of functionalities as DisMax and it also supports full Lucene query syntax. The following is the query shown in this task, but by using `edismax`, it would look like the following:

```
http://localhost:8983/solr/select?q=author:rafal&defType=edismax
```

Querying for multiple values in the same field

You may sometimes need to ask for multiple values in a single field. For example, let's suppose that you want to find the `solr` and `cookbook` values in the `title` field. To do that you should run the following query (notice the brackets surrounding the values):

```
http://localhost:8983/solr/select?q=author:(solr cookbook)
```

Sorting results by a field value

Imagine an e-commerce site where you can't choose the sorting order of the results, you can only browse the search results page-by-page and nothing more. That's terrible, right? That's why with Solr you can specify the sort fields and order in which your search results should be sorted. This recipe will show you how to do it.

How to do it...

Let's assume that you want to sort your data by an additional field, for example, the field that contains the name of the author of the book.

1. First we add the following to your `schema.xml` file's `field` section:

```
<field name="id" type="string" indexed="true" stored="true"
required="true" />
<field name="title" type="text" indexed="true" stored="true" />
<field name="author" type="string" indexed="true" stored="true"/>
```

2. Now, let's create a simple data file which will look like the following code:

```
<add>
 <doc>
```

```
 <field name="id">1</field>
 <field name="title">Solr cookbook</field>
 <field name="author">Rafal Kuc</field>
</doc>
<doc>
 <field name="id">2</field>
 <field name="title">Solr results</field>
 <field name="author">John Doe</field>
</doc>
<doc>
 <field name="id">3</field>
 <field name="title">Solr perfect search</field>
 <field name="author">John Doe</field>
</doc>
</add>
```

3. As I wrote earlier, we want to sort the result list by author name in ascending order. Additionally, we want the books that have the same author to be sorted by relevance in the descending order. To do that we must send the following query to Solr:

```
http://localhost:8983/solr/select?q=solr&sort=author+asc,
score+desc
```

The results returned by Solr are as follows:

```
<?xml version="1.0" encoding="UTF-8"?>
 <response>
  <lst name="responseHeader">
   <int name="status">0</int>
   <int name="QTime">1</int>
   <lst name="params">
    <str name="q">solr</str>
    <str name="sort">author asc,score desc</str>
   </lst>
  </lst>
  <result name="response" numFound="3" start="0">
   <doc>
    <str name="id">2</str>
    <str name="title">Solr results</str>
    <str name="author">John Doe</str>
   </doc>
   <doc>
    <str name="id">3</str>
```

```
    <str name="title">Solr perfect search</str>
    <str name="author">John Doe</str>
   </doc>
   <doc>
    <str name="id">1</str>
    <str name="title">Solr cookbook</str>
    <str name="author">Rafal Kuc</str>
   </doc>
  </result>
 </response>
```

As you can see, our data is sorted exactly how we wanted it to be.

How it works...

As you can see I defined three fields in our index. The most interesting to us is the `author` field, based on which we will perform the sorting operation. Notice one thing – the type on which the field is based is the `string` type. In order to sort the values of the field from the index, you need to prepare your data well, that is, use the appropriate number types (the ones based on the `Trie` types), and to sort the text field using the `string` field type (or text type using the `KeywordTokenizer` type and a lowercase filter).

The following what you see is the data which is very simple – it only adds three documents to the index.

I've added one additional parameter to the query that was sent to Solr – the `sort` parameter. This parameter defines the sort field with the order. Each field must be followed by the order in which the data should be sorted; `asc` which tells Solr to sort the data in the ascending order, and `desc` which tells Solr to sort in the descending order. Pairs of field and order should be delimited with the comma character as shown in the example.

The result list that Solr returned tells us that we did a perfect job on defining the sort order.

How to search for a phrase, not a single word

Imagine that you have an application that searches within millions of documents that are generated by a law company. One of the requirements is to search the titles of the documents as a phrase, but with stemming and lowercasing. So a string-based field is not an option. In that case, is it possible to achieve this using Solr? Yes, and this recipe will show you how to do that.

How to do it...

1. First let's define the following type (add this part to your `schema.xml` file):

```
<fieldType name="text" class="solr.TextField"
positionIncrementGap="100">
 <analyzer>
  <tokenizer class="solr.WhitespaceTokenizerFactory"/>
  <filter class="solr.LowerCaseFilterFactory"/>
  <filter class="solr.SnowballPorterFilterFactory"
language="English"/>
 </analyzer>
</fieldType>
```

2. Now let's add the following fields to our `schema.xml` file:

```
<field name="id" type="string" indexed="true" stored="true"
required="true" />
<field name="title" type="text" indexed="true" stored="true" />
```

3. The third step is to create an example data which looks like the following code:

```
<add>
 <doc>
  <field name="id">1</field>
  <field name="title">2012 report</field>
 </doc>
 <doc>
  <field name="id">2</field>
  <field name="title">2009 report</field>
 </doc>
 <doc>
  <field name="id">3</field>
  <field name="title">2012 draft report</field>
 </doc>
</add>
```

4. Now let's try to find the documents that have the phrase `2012 report` in them. To do that, make the following query to Solr:

```
http://localhost:8983/solr/select?q=title:"2012 report"
```

The result should be as follows:

```
<?xml version="1.0" encoding="UTF-8"?>
 <response>
  <lst name="responseHeader">
   <int name="status">0</int>
```

```
      <int name="QTime">1</int>
      <lst name="params">
       <str name="q">title:"2012 report"</str>
      </lst>
     </lst>
     <result name="response" numFound="1" start="0">
      <doc>
       <str name="id">1</str>
       <str name="title">2012 report</str>
      </doc>
     </result>
    </response>
```

The debug query (the `debugQuery=on` parameter) shows us the Lucene query that was created:

```
    <str name="parsedquery">PhraseQuery(title:"2012 report")</str>
```

As you can see we only got one document which is perfectly good. Now let's see how that happened.

How it works...

As I said in the *Introduction* section, our requirement was to search for phrases over fields that are stemmed and lowercased. If you want to know more about stemming please refer to the *Stemming your data* recipe in *Chapter 3, Analyzing Your Text Data*. Lowercasing is described in the *Lowercasing the whole string* recipe in *Chapter 3*.

We only need two fields because we will only search the title, and return the title and unique identifier of the field; thus the configuration is as shown in the example.

The example data is quite simple so I'll skip commenting on it.

The query is something that we should be more interested in. The query is made to the standard Solr query parser, thus we can specify the field name and the value we are looking for. The query differs from the standard word searching query by the use of the " character at the start and end of the query. It tells Solr to use the phrase query instead of the term query. Using the phrase query means that Solr will search for the whole phrase not a single word. That's why only the document with identifier 1 was found, because the third document did not match the phrase.

The debug query only ensured that the phrase query was made instead of the usual term query, and Solr showed us that we created the right query.

When using queries there is one thing that is very useful to know.

Defining the distance between words in a phrase

You may sometimes need to find documents that match a phrase, but are separated by some other words. Let's assume that you would like to find the first and third document in our example. This means that you want documents that could have an additional word between the word 2010 and report. To do that, we add a so-called **phrase slop** to the phrase. In our case the distance (slop) between words can be the maximum of one word, so we add the ~1 part after the phrase definition:

```
http://localhost:8983/solr/select?q=title:"2012 report"~1
```

Boosting phrases over words

Imagine you are a search expert at a leading e-commerce shop in your region. One day disaster strikes and your marketing department says that the search results are not good enough. They would like you to favor documents that have the exact phrase typed by the user over the documents that have matches for separate words. Can you do it? Of course you can, and this recipe will show you how to achieve it.

Getting ready

Before you start reading this task I suggest you read the *How to search for a phrase not a single word* recipe in this chapter. It will allow you to understand the recipe better.

How to do it...

I assume that we will be using the DisMax query parser, not the standard one. We will also use the same schema.xml file that was used in the *How to search for a phrase not a single word* recipe in this chapter.

1. Let's start with our sample data file which looks like the following code:

```
<add>
 <doc>
  <field name="id">1</field>
  <field name="title">Annual 2012 report last draft</field>
 </doc>
 <doc>
  <field name="id">2</field>
  <field name="title">2011 report</field>
```

```
   </doc>
   <doc>
    <field name="id">3</field>
    <field name="title">2012 draft report</field>
   </doc>
  </add>
```

2. As I already mentioned, we would like to boost those documents that have phrase
    matches over others matching the query. To do that, run the following query to your
    Solr instance:

```
http://localhost:8983/solr/select?defType=dismax&pf=title^100&q=20
12+report&qf=title&q.op=AND
```

You should get the following response:

```
<?xml version="1.0" encoding="UTF-8"?>
 <response>
  <lst name="responseHeader">
   <int name="status">0</int>
   <int name="QTime">1</int>
   <lst name="params">
    <str name="pf">title^100</str>
    <str name="q">2012 report</str>
    <str name="qf">title</str>
    <str name="q.op">AND</str>
    <str name="defType">dismax</str>
   </lst>
  </lst>
  <result name="response" numFound="2" start="0">
   <doc>
    <str name="id">1</str>
    <str name="title">Annual 2012 report last draft</str>
   </doc>
   <doc>
    <str name="id">3</str>
    <str name="title">2012 draft report</str>
   </doc>
  </result>
 </response>
```

3. To visualize the results better, I decided to include the results returned by Solr for the
    same query but without adding the `pf` parameter, and received the following results:

```
<?xml version="1.0" encoding="UTF-8"?>
 <response>
```

```
<lst name="responseHeader">
 <int name="status">0</int>
 <int name="QTime">0</int>
 <lst name="params">
  <str name="qf">title</str>
  <str name=" defType">dismax</str>
  <str name="q.op">AND</str>
  <str name="q">2012 report</str>
 </lst>
</lst>
<result name="response" numFound="2" start="0">
 <doc>
  <str name="id">3</str>
  <str name="title">2012 draft report</str>
 </doc>
 <doc>
  <str name="id">1</str>
  <str name="title">Annual 2012 report last draft</str>
 </doc>
</result>
</response>
```

As you can see we fulfilled our requirement.

How it works...

Some of the parameters that are present in the example query may be new to you. The first parameter is `defType` that tells Solr which query parser we will be using. In this example we will be using the DisMax query parser (if you are not familiar with the DisMax query parser please have a look at the following address `http://wiki.apache.org/solr/DisMax`). One of the features of this query parser is the ability to tell what field should be used to search for phrases, and we do that by adding the `pf` parameter. The `pf` parameter takes a list of fields with the boost that corresponds to them, for example, `pf=title^100` which means that the phrase found in the title field will be boosted with a value of `100`. The `q` parameter is the standard query parameter that you are familiar with. This time we passed the words we are searching for and the logical operator `AND`. This means that we are looking for documents which contain the words `2012` and `report`. You should remember that you can't pass queries such as `fieldname:value` to the `q` parameter and use the DisMax query parser. The fields you are searching against should be specified using the `qf` parameter. In our case we told Solr that we will be searching against the `title` field. We also included the `q.op=AND` parameter because we want `AND` to be our logical operator for the query.

The results show us that we found two documents. The one that matches the exact query is returned first and that is what we intended to achieve.

There's more...

You can of course boost phrases with standard query parsers, but that's not as elegant as the DisMax query parser method. To achieve similar results, you should run the following query to your Solr instance:

```
http://localhost:8983/solr/select?q=title:(2012+AND+report)+OR+title:
"2012+report"^100
```

The above query tells Solr to search for the words `2010` and `report` in a `title` field, and search for a `2012 report` phrase and, if found, to boost that phrase with the value of 100.

Positioning some documents over others on a query

Imagine a situation when your client tells you that he/she wants to promote some of his/her products by placing them at the top of the search result list. Additionally, the client would like the product list to be flexible, that is, he/she would like to be able to define the list for some queries and not for others. Many thoughts come into your mind such as boosting, index time boosting, or maybe some special field to achieve that. But don't bother, Solr can help you with a component that is known as `solr.QueryElevationComponent`.

How to do it...

The following recipe will help you to place document over others based on your priorities:

1. First of all let's modify the `solrconfig.xml` document. We need to add the component definition. To do that add the following section to your `solrconfig.xml` file:

   ```
   <searchComponent name="elevator" class="solr.
   QueryElevationComponent" >
     <str name="queryFieldType">string</str>
     <str name="config-file">elevate.xml</str>
   </searchComponent>
   ```

2. Now let's add the proper request handler that will include the elevation component. We will name it `/promotion`. Add this to your `solrconfig.xml` file:

   ```
   <requestHandler name="/promotion" class="solr.SearchHandler">
     <lst name="defaults">
   ```

```
<str name="echoParams">explicit</str>
<int name="rows">10</int>
<str name="df">name</str>
</lst>
<arr name="last-components">
<str>elevator</str>
</arr>
</requestHandler>
```

3. You may notice that the query elevation component contained information about a mysterious `elevate.xml` file. Let's assume that we want the documents with identifiers 3 and 1 to be in the first two places in the results list for the `solr` query. For now you need to create that file in the configuration directory of your Solr instance and paste the following content:

```
<?xml version="1.0" encoding="UTF-8" ?>
<elevate>
<query text="solr">
<doc id="3" />
<doc id="1" />
</query>
</elevate>
```

4. Now it's time for the `schema.xml` file. Our field definition part of the file should contain the following code:

```
<field name="id" type="string" indexed="true" stored="true"
required="true" />
<field name="name" type="text" indexed="true" stored="true" />
```

5. Now let's index the following data file:

```
<add>
<doc>
<field name="id">1</field>
<field name="name">Solr cookbook</field>
</doc>
<doc>
<field name="id">2</field>
<field name="name">Solr master pieces</field>
</doc>
<doc>
<field name="id">3</field>
<field name="name">Solr annual report</field>
</doc>
</add>
```

6. Now we can run Solr and test our configuration. To do that let's run the following query:

```
http://localhost:8983/solr/promotion?q=solr
```

The previous query should return the following result:

```xml
<?xml version="1.0" encoding="UTF-8"?>
 <response>
  <lst name="responseHeader">
   <int name="status">0</int>
   <int name="QTime">2</int>
   <lst name="params">
    <str name="q">solr</str>
   </lst>
  </lst>
  <result name="response" numFound="3" start="0">
   <doc>
    <str name="id">3</str>
    <str name="name">Solr annual report</str>
   </doc>
   <doc>
    <str name="id">1</str>
    <str name="name">Solr cookbook</str>
   </doc>
   <doc>
    <str name="id">2</str>
    <str name="name">Solr master pieces</str>
   </doc>
  </result>
 </response>
```

The query without using the elevation component returned the following result:

```xml
<?xml version="1.0" encoding="UTF-8"?>
 <response>
  <lst name="responseHeader">
   <int name="status">0</int>
   <int name="QTime">1</int>
   <lst name="params">
    <str name="q">solr</str>
   </lst>
  </lst>
  <result name="response" numFound="3" start="0">
   <doc>
    <str name="id">1</str>
    <str name="name">Solr cookbook</str>
   </doc>
```

```
<doc>
 <str name="id">2</str>
 <str name="name">Solr master pieces</str>
</doc>
<doc>
 <str name="id">3</str>
 <str name="name">Solr annual report</str>
</doc>
</result>
</response>
```

As you can see the component worked. Now let's see how it works.

How it works...

The first part of the configuration defines a new search component with a name under which the component will be visible to other components and the search handler (the `name` attribute). In our case the component name is `elevator` and it's based on the `solr.QueryElevationComponent` class (the `class` attribute). The following that we have are two additional attributes that define the elevation component's behavior:

- `queryFieldType`: This attribute tells Solr what type of field should be used to parse the query text that is given to the component (for example, if you want the component to ignore the letter case, you should set this parameter to the `field` type that lowercases its contents)

- `config-file`: This specifies the configuration file which will be used by the component

The next part of the `solrconfig.xml` configuration procedure is the search handler definition. It simply tells Solr to create a new search handler with the name of `/promotion` (to be the value of the `name` attribute) and using the `solr.SearchHandler` class (the `class` attribute). In addition to that, the handler definition also tells Solr to include the component named `elevator` in this search handler. This means that this search handler will use our defined component. For your information, you can use more than one search component in a single search handler. We've also included some standard parameters to the handler, such as `df`, which specifies the default search field.

What we see next is the actual configuration of the `elevator` component. You can see that there is a query defined (the `query` XML tag) with an attribute `text="solr"`. This defines the behavior of the component when a user passes `solr` to the `q` parameter. Under this tag you can see a list of the documents' unique identifiers that will be placed at the top of the results list for the defined query. Each document is defined by a `doc` tag and an `id` attribute (which have to be defined on the basis of `solr.StrField`) which holds the unique identifier. You can have multiple `query` tags in a single configuration file which means that the elevation component can be used for a variety of queries.

The index configuration and example datafile are fairly simple. The index contains two fields that are responsible for holding information about the document. In the example datafile, we can see three documents present. As the explanation is not crucial, I'll skip discussing it further.

The query you see in the example returns all the documents. The query is made to our new handler with just a simple one word `q` parameter (the default search field is set to `name` in the `schema.xml` file). Recall the `elevate.xml` file and the documents we defined for the query we just passed to Solr. We told Solr that we want the document with `id=3` in the first place of the results list and we want the document with `id=1` in the second place of the results list. As you can see, the documents were positioned exactly as we wanted them so it seems that the component did its job.

There's more...

There is one more thing I would like to say about the query elevation functionality in Solr.

Excluding documents with QueryElevationComponent

The elevate component can not only place documents on top of the results list, but it can also exclude documents from the results list. To do that you should add the `exclude="true"` attribute to the document definition in your `elevate.xml` file. This is what the example file would look like:

```xml
<?xml version="1.0" encoding="UTF-8" ?>
<elevate>
 <query text="solr">
  <doc id="3" />
  <doc id="1" exclude="true" />
  <doc id="2" exclude="true" />
 </query>
</elevate>
```

See also

If you would like to know how to mark the documents that were positioned by the `solr.QueryElevationComponent` class, please read the *Modifying returned documents* recipe in this chapter.

Positioning documents with words closer to each other first

Imagine an e-commerce book shop where the users have only one way to find books, that is, by searching. Most of the users requested that the OR operator should be the default logical operator, so that we can have many results for most of the popular queries. Once every few days an angry user calls the call center and says that by typing "solr cookbook" the first few pages are not relevant to the query he/she typed in, so in other words this is not what he/she searched for. So that's the problem, now what can be done? The answer is to boost documents with query words closer to each other. This recipe will show you how to do it.

How to do it...

For the purpose of this task I will be using the DisMax query parser.

1. Let's start with the following index structure (just add the following to your schema.xml file to the field definition section):

   ```
   <field name="id" type="string" indexed="true" stored="true"
   required="true" />
   <field name="title" type="text" indexed="true" stored="true" />
   <field name="author" type="string" indexed="true" stored="true"/>
   ```

2. Now, let's index the following data:

   ```
   <add>
    <doc>
     <field name="id">1</field>
     <field name="title">Solr perfect search cookbook</field>
    </doc>
    <doc>
     <field name="id">2</field>
     <field name="title">Solr example cookbook</field>
    </doc>
    <doc>
     <field name="id">3</field>
     <field name="title">Solr cookbook</field>
    </doc>
   </add>
   ```

3. In addition to that we need to define a new request handler in the solrconfig.xml file, which looks like the following code:

   ```
   <requestHandler name="/closer" class="solr.
   StandardRequestHandler">
   ```

```
<lst name="defaults">
  <str name="q">_query_:"{!dismax qf=$qfQuery mm=1 pf=$pfQuery
bq=$boostQuery v=$mainQuery}"</str>
  <str name="qfQuery">title</str>
  <str name="pfQuery">title^1000</str>
  <str name="boostQuery">_query_:"{!dismax qf=$boostQueryQf
mm=100% v=$mainQuery}"^100</str>
  <str name="boostQueryQf">title</str>
  <str name="df">title</str>
 </lst>
</requestHandler>
```

4. As I wrote earlier, we want to get the documents with the words typed by the user close to each other first in the result list. Let's assume our user typed in the dreaded `solr cookbook` query. To handle the query we use the new `/closer` request handler we defined earlier and we send the query using the `mainQuery` parameter, not the `q` one (I'll describe why this is so later). So the whole query looks as follows:

```
http://localhost:8983/solr/closer?mainQuery=solr+cookbook&fl=score,
id,title
```

The result list returned by Solr is the following:

```
<?xml version="1.0" encoding="UTF-8"?>
 <response>
  <lst name="responseHeader">
   <int name="status">0</int>
   <int name="QTime">3</int>
  </lst>
  <result name="response" numFound="3" start="0"
maxScore="0.93303263">
   <doc>
    <str name="id">3</str>
    <str name="title">Solr cookbook</str>
    <float name="score">0.93303263</float>
   </doc>
   <doc>
    <str name="id">1</str>
    <str name="title">Solr perfect search cookbook</str>
    <float name="score">0.035882458</float>
   </doc>
   <doc>
    <str name="id">2</str>
    <str name="title">Solr example cookbook</str>
    <float name="score">0.035882458</float>
```

```
        </doc>
      </result>
    </response>
```

We received the documents in the way we wanted. Now let's look at how that happened.

How it works...

First of all we have the index structure. For the purpose of the example, I assumed that our book description will consist of three fields and we will be searching with the use of the `title` field which is based on the standard text field defined in the standard `schema.xml` file provided with the Solr distribution.

As you can see in the provided data file example there are three books. The first book has two other words between the words `solr` and `cookbook`. The second book has one word between the given words, and the third book has the words next to each other. In a perfect situation, we would like to have the third book from the example file as the first one in the result list, the second book from the file in the second place, and the first book from the example data file as the last in the results list.

Now let's take a look at our new request handler. We defined it to be available under a name `/closer` (the `name` attribute of the `requestHandler` tag). We also said that it should be based on the `solr.StandardRequestHandler` class (in the `class` attribute). Next, in the `defaults` list we have a number of parameters defining the query behavior we want to achieve. First of all we have the `q` parameter. This contains the query constructed with the use of local params. The `_query_:"..."` part of the `q` parameter is a way of specifying the new query. We tell Solr that we want to use DisMax query parser (the `!dismax` part) and we want to pass the value of the `qfQuery` parameter as the `qf` DisMax parser parameter. We also want the "minimum should match" parameter to be equal one (`mm=1`), we want a phrase query to be used (the one which is defined in the `pfQuery` (`pf=$pfQuery`) parameter) and we want the boost query to be used – the one that is defined in the `boostQuery` parameter (`bq=$boostQuery`). Finally we specify that we will pass the actual user query not with the `q` parameter, but instead with the `mainQuery` parameter (`v=$mainQuery`).

Next we have `boostQuery` – another query constructed using local parameters. As you can see we use the DisMax query parser (the `!dismax` query part), and we specify the `qf` and `mm` DisMax query parser parameters. The value of the `qf` parameter will be taken from the `boostQueryQf` parameter and the value of the `mm` parameter is set to `100%`, so we want the boost query to return only the documents that have all the words specified by the user. The `v` attribute is responsible for passing the actual query, which in our case will be stored in the `mainQuery` (`v=$mainQuery` part) parameter. We also said that we want our boost query to be boosted by 100 (the `^100` part of the query). The `boostQueryQf` parameter is used by the boost query to specify which fields should be used for search, in the query used for boosting. Finally, the `df` parameter specifies the default search field.

Now let's discuss what the query is actually doing. The first query tells Solr to return all the documents with at least one of the words that the user entered (this is defined by setting the mm parameter to 1). But we also say that we want to boost phrases; that's why we use a phrase query on the title field. In addition to that we specified that we want to use our boost query, which will increase the boost of all the documents that have all the words entered by the user (mm=100%). Combining all those factors we will end up with results that have the top documents occupied by those documents that have all the words entered by the user present in the title field and where all those words are close to each other.

The query is simple. We specify that we want to get a calculated score in the results for each document, we want the id field, and the title field. We also pass the mainQuery parameter because we have the v attribute of both the q and boostQuery parameters set to the $mainQuery parameter. This means that Solr will take the mainQuery parameter value and pass it to the v parameter of those queries. Because we prepared our request handler configuration and pasted it into solrconfig.xml, now at query time we only need to pass a single parameter that passes the words specified by our users.

The last thing is the results list. As you can see the documents are sorted in the way we wanted them to be. You should take a look at one thing – the score field. This field shows how relevant the document is to the query we sent to Solr.

Sorting results by a distance from a point

Suppose we have a search application that is storing information about the companies. Every company is described by a name and two floating point numbers that represent the geographical location of the company. One day your boss comes to your room and says that he/she wants the search results to be sorted by distance from the user's location. This recipe will show you how to do it.

Getting ready

Before continuing please read the *Storing geographical points in the index* recipe from *Chapter 3, Analyzing Your Text Data*.

How to do it...

1. Let's begin with the following index (add the following to your schema.xml file to the fields section):

```
<field name="id" type="string" indexed="true" stored="true"
required="true" />
<field name="name" type="text" indexed="true" stored="true"/>
```

```
<field name="location" type="location" indexed="true"
stored="true" />
<dynamicField name="*_coordinate" type="tdouble" indexed="true"
stored="false" />
```

2. We also have the following type defined in the `schema.xml` file:

    ```
    <fieldType name="location" class="solr.LatLonType"
    subFieldSuffix="_coordinate"/>
    ```

    I assumed that the user location will be provided from the application that is making a query.

3. Now let's index our example data file, which looks like the following code:

    ```
    <add>
     <doc>
      <field name="id">1</field>
      <field name="name">Company 1</field>
      <field name="location">56.4,40.2</field>
     </doc>
     <doc>
      <field name="id">2</field>
      <field name="name">Company 2</field>
      <field name="location">50.1,48.9</field>
     </doc>
     <doc>
      <field name="id">3</field>
      <field name="name">Company 3</field>
      <field name="location">23.18,39.1</field>
     </doc>
    </add>
    ```

4. So our user is standing at the North Pole and is using our search application. Now let's assume that we want to get the companies sorted in such a way that the ones that are nearer the user are at the top of the results list. The query to find such companies could look like the following query:

    ```
    http://localhost:8983/solr/select?q=company&sort=geodist(location,
    0.0,0.0)+asc
    ```

    The result of that query would look as follows:

    ```
    <?xml version="1.0" encoding="UTF-8"?>
     <response>
      <lst name="responseHeader">
       <int name="status">0</int>
    ```

```
<int name="QTime">1</int>
<lst name="params">
 <str name="q">company</str>
 <str name="sort">geodist(location,0.0,0.0) asc</str>
</lst>
</lst>
<result name="response" numFound="3" start="0">
 <doc>
  <str name="id">3</str>
  <str name="name">Company 3</str>
  <str name="location">23.18,39.1</str>
 </doc>
 <doc>
  <str name="id">1</str>
  <str name="name">Company 1</str>
  <str name="location">56.4,40.2</str>
 </doc>
 <doc>
  <str name="id">2</str>
  <str name="name">Company 2</str>
  <str name="location">50.1,48.9</str>
 </doc>
 </result>
</response>
```

If you would like to calculate the distance by hand, you would see that the results are sorted as they should be.

How it works...

As you can see in the index structure and in the data, every company is described by the following three fields:

- ▶ id: This specifies the unique identifier
- ▶ name: This specifies the company name
- ▶ location: This specifies the latitude and longitude of the company location

I'll skip commenting on how the actual location of the company is stored. If you want to read more about it, please refer to the *Storing geographical points in the index* recipe from *Chapter 3, Analyzing Your Text Data*.

We wanted to get the companies that match the given query and are sorted in the ascending order from the North Pole. To do that we run a standard query with a non-standard sort. The sort parameter consists of a function name, `geodist`, which calculates the distance between points. In our example the function takes three parameters:

► The first parameter specifies the field in the index that should be used to calculate the distance

► The second parameter is the latitude value of the point from which the distance will be calculated

► The third parameter is the longitude value of the point from which the distance will be calculated

After the function there is the order of the sort which in our case is `asc` (ascending order).

See also

If you would like to learn how to return the calculated distance that we used for sorting please refer to the *Returning the value of a function in results* recipe in this chapter.

Getting documents with only a partial match

Imagine a situation where you have an e-commerce library and you want to make a search algorithm that tries to bring the best search results to your customers. But you noticed that many of your customers tend to make queries with too many words, which result in an empty results list. So you decided to make a query that will require the maximum of two of the words that the user entered to be matched. This recipe will show you how to do it.

Getting ready

This method can only be used with the DisMax query parser. The standard query parser doesn't support the `mm` parameter.

How to do it...

1. Let's begin with creating our index that has the following structure (add this to your `schema.xml` file to the field definition section):

```
<field name="id" type="string" indexed="true" stored="true"
required="true" />
<field name="title" type="text" indexed="true" stored="true" />
```

As you can see our books are described by two fields.

2. Now let's look at the example data:

```
<add>
 <doc>
  <field name="id">1</field>
  <field name="title">Solrcook book revised</field>
 </doc>
 <doc>
  <field name="id">2</field>
  <field name="title">Some book that was revised</field>
 </doc>
 <doc>
  <field name="id">3</field>
  <field name="title">Another revised book</field>
 </doc>
</add>
```

3. The third step is to made a query that will satisfy the requirements. Such a query could look like the following:

```
http://localhost:8983/solr/select?q=book+revised+another+
different+word+that+doesnt+count&defType=dismax&mm=2&q.op=AND
```

The preceding query will return the following results:

```
<?xml version="1.0" encoding="UTF-8"?>
 <response>
  <lst name="responseHeader">
   <int name="status">0</int>
   <int name="QTime">1</int>
   <lst name="params">
    <str name="q.op">AND</str>
    <str name="mm">2</str>
    <str name="q">book revised another different word that doesnt
count</str>
    <str name="defType">dismax</str>
   </lst>
  </lst>
  <result name="response" numFound="3" start="0">
   <doc>
    <str name="id">3</str>
    <str name="title">Another revised book</str>
   </doc>
   <doc>
    <str name="id">2</str>
```

```
     <str name="title">Some book that was revised</str>
    </doc>
    <doc>
     <str name="id">1</str>
     <str name="title">Solrcook book revised</str>
    </doc>
   </result>
  </response>
```

As you can see, even though the query was made up of too many words, the result list contains all the documents from the example file. Now let's see how that happened.

How it works...

The index structure and the data are fairly simple. Every book is described by two fields: a unique identifier and a title.

The query is the thing that we are interested in. We have passed about eight words to Solr (the q parameter), we defined that we want to use the DisMax query parser (the `defType` parameter), and we sent the mysterious mm parameter set to the value of 2. Yes, you are right, the mm parameter, also called `minimum should match`, tells the DisMax query parser how many of the words passed into the query must be matched with the document, to ascertain that the document is a match. In our case we told the DisMax query parser that there should be two or more words matched to identify the document as a match. We've also included `q.op=AND`, so that the default logical operator for the query would be set to `AND`.

You should also note one thing – the document that has three words matched is at the top of the list. The relevance algorithm is still there, which means that the documents with more words that matched the query will be higher in the result list than those that have fewer words that matched the query. The documentation about the mm parameter can be found at `http://wiki.apache.org/solr/DisMaxQParserPlugin`.

Affecting scoring with functions

There are many situations where you would want to have an influence on how the score of the documents is calculated. For example, you would perhaps like to boost the documents on the basis of the purchases of it. Like in an e-commerce boost store, you would like to show relevant results, but you would like to influence them by adding yet another factor to their score. Is it possible? Yes, and this recipe will show you how to do it.

How to do it...

1. Let's start with the following index structure (just add the following to the field section in your `schema.xml` file):

```
<field name="id" type="string" indexed="true" stored="true"
required="true" />
<field name="title" type="text" indexed="true" stored="true" />
<field name="sold" type="int" indexed="true" stored="true" />
```

2. The example data looks like the following code:

```
<add>
 <doc>
  <field name="id">1</field>
  <field name="title">Solrcook book revised</field>
  <field name="sold">5</field>
 </doc>
 <doc>
  <field name="id">2</field>
  <field name="title">Some book revised</field>
  <field name="sold">200</field>
 </doc>
 <doc>
  <field name="id">3</field>
  <field name="title">Another revised book</field>
  <field name="sold">60</field>
 </doc>
</add>
```

3. So we want to boost our documents on the basis of a `sold` field while retaining the relevance sorting. Our user typed `revised` into the search box, so the query would look like the following:

```
http://localhost:8983/solr/select?defType=dismax&qf=title&q=revise
d&fl=*,score
```

And the results would be as follows:

```
<?xml version="1.0" encoding="UTF-8"?>
 <response>
  <lst name="responseHeader">
   <int name="status">0</int>
   <int name="QTime">1</int>
   <lst name="params">
    <str name="qf">title</str>
```

```
    <str name="fl">*,score</str>
    <str name="q">revised</str>
    <str name="defType">dismax</str>
   </lst>
  </lst>
  <result name="response" numFound="3" start="0"
maxScore="0.35615897">
   <doc>
    <str name="id">1</str>
    <str name="title">Solrcook book revised</str>
    <int name="sold">5</int>
    <float name="score">0.35615897</float>
   </doc>
   <doc>
    <str name="id">2</str>
    <str name="title">Some book revised</str>
    <int name="sold">200</int>
    <float name="score">0.35615897</float>
   </doc>
   <doc>
    <str name="id">3</str>
    <str name="title">Another revised book</str>
    <int name="sold">60</int>
    <float name="score">0.35615897</float>
   </doc>
  </result>
 </response>
```

4. Now let's add the sold factor by adding the following to the query:

    ```
    bf=product(sold)
    ```

    So our modified query would look like this:

    ```
    http://localhost:8983/solr/select?defType=dismax&qf=title&q=revise
    d&fl=*,score&bf=product(sold)
    ```

    And the results for the preceding query are as follows:

    ```
    <?xml version="1.0" encoding="UTF-8"?>
     <response>
      <lst name="responseHeader">
       <int name="status">0</int>
       <int name="QTime">36</int>
       <lst name="params">
        <str name="fl">*,score</str>
    ```

```
        <str name="q">revised</str>
        <str name="qf">title</str>
        <str name="bf">product(sold)</str>
        <str name="defType">dismax</str>
      </lst>
    </lst>
    <result name="response" numFound="3" start="0"
  maxScore="163.1048">
      <doc>
       <str name="id">2</str>
       <str name="title">Some book revised</str>
       <int name="sold">200</int>
       <float name="score">163.1048</float>
      </doc>
      <doc>
       <str name="id">3</str>
       <str name="title">Another revised book</str>
       <int name="sold">60</int>
       <float name="score">49.07608</float>
      </doc>
      <doc>
       <str name="id">1</str>
       <str name="title">Solrcook book revised</str>
       <int name="sold">5</int>
       <float name="score">4.279089</float>
      </doc>
    </result>
  </response>
```

As you can see, adding the parameter changed the whole results list. Now let's see why that happened.

How it works...

The schema.xml file is simple. It contains the following three fields:

- id: This field is responsible for holding the unique identifier of the book
- title: This specifies the book title
- sold: This specifies the number of pieces that have been sold during the last month

In the data we have three books. Each of the books has the same number of words in the title. That's why when typing the first query all documents got the same score. As you can see, the first book is the one with the fewest pieces sold and that's not what we want to achieve.

For the same reason we added the `bf` parameter. It tells Solr what function to use to affect the scoring computation (in this case the result of the function will be added to the score of the document). In our case it is the `product` function that returns the product of the values we provide as its arguments; in our case the one and only argument of the function will be the value of the book's `sold` field.

The result list of the modified query clearly shows how the scoring was affected by the function. In the first place of the results list we have the book that was most popular during the last week. The next book is the one which was less popular than the first book, but more popular than the last book. The last book in the results is the least popular book.

See also

If you would like to know more about the functions available in Solr, please go to the Solr wiki page at the following address: `http://wiki.apache.org/solr/FunctionQuery`.

Nesting queries

Imagine a situation where you need a query nested inside another query. Let's imagine that you want to run a query using the standard request handler but you need to embed a query that is parsed by the DisMax query parser inside it. This is possible with Solr 4.0 and this recipe will show you how to do it.

How to do it...

1. Let's start with a simple index that has the following structure (just add the following to the field section in your `schema.xml` file):

    ```
    <field name="id" type="string" indexed="true" stored="true"
    required="true" />
    <field name="title" type="text" indexed="true" stored="true" />
    ```

2. Now let's look at the example data:

    ```
    <add>
    <doc>
     <field name="id">1</field>
     <field name="title">Revised solrcook book</field>
    </doc>
    <doc>
     <field name="id">2</field>
     <field name="title">Some book revised</field>
    </doc>
    <doc>
    ```

```
    <field name="id">3</field>
    <field name="title">Another revised little book</field>
  </doc>
</add>
```

3. Imagine you are using the standard query parser to support the Lucene query syntax, but you would like to boost phrases using the DisMax query parser. At first it seems that it is impossible, but let's assume that we want to find books that have the words book and revised in their title field, and we want to boost the book revised phrase by 10. Let's send a query like so:

```
http://localhost:8983/solr/select?q=book+revised+_query_:"{!dismax
qf=title pf=title^10 v=$qq}"&qq=book+revised&q.op=AND
```

The results of the preceding query should look like the following:

```
<?xml version="1.0" encoding="UTF-8"?>
  <response>
   <lst name="responseHeader">
    <int name="status">0</int>
    <int name="QTime">3</int>
    <lst name="params">
     <str name="q.op">AND</str>
     <str name="qq">book revised</str>
     <str name="q">book revised _query_:"{!dismax qf=title
pf=title^10 v=$qq}"</str>
    </lst>
   </lst>
   <result name="response" numFound="3" start="0">
    <doc>
     <str name="id">2</str>
     <str name="title">Some book revised</str>
    </doc>
    <doc>
     <str name="id">1</str>
     <str name="title">Revised solrcook book</str>
    </doc>
    <doc>
     <str name="id">3</str>
     <str name="title">Another revised little book</str>
    </doc>
   </result>
  </response>
```

As you can see, the results list was sorted exactly the way we wanted. Now let's see how it works.

How it works...

As you can see our index is very simple. It consists of two fields – one holding the unique identifier (the id field) and another one holding the title of the book (the title field).

Let's look at the query. The q parameter is built from two parts. The first one, book+revised, is just a usual query composed from two terms. The second part of the query starts with a strange looking expression, that is, _query_. This expression tells Solr that another query should be made that will affect the results list. Notice that the expression is surrounded with " characters. Then we will see the expression tells Solr to use the DisMax query parser (the !dismax part) and the parameters that will be passed to the parser (qf and pf). The v parameter is used to pass the value of the q parameter. The value passed to the DisMax query parser in our case will be book+revised. This is called **parameter dereferencing**. By using the $qq expression, we tell Solr to use the value of the qq parameter. Of course, we could pass the value to the v parameter, but I wanted to show you how to use the dereferencing mechanism. The qq parameter is set to book+revised and it is used by Solr as a parameter for the query that was passed to the DisMax query parser. The last parameter, q.op=AND tells Solr which logical operator should be used as the default one.

The results show that we achieved exactly what we wanted.

Modifying returned documents

Let's say we are using the elevate component that Solr provides to promote some books when necessary. But as you may already know, the standard Solr response doesn't include the information about document being elevated or not. What we would like to achieve is to get that information somehow from Solr. Actually we would like it to be as simple as running a Solr query and getting the results back. This recipe will show you how to use document transformers with the elevation component.

How to do it...

1. First of all, let's assume we have the following index structure defined in the fields section of our schema.xml file:

   ```
   <field name="id" type="string" indexed="true" stored="true"
   required="true" multiValued="false" />
   <field name="name" type="text" indexed="true" stored="true"/>
   ```

2. We also need to have the elevation component defined along with the search component (place the following entries in your solrconfig.xml file):

   ```
   <requestHandler name="/select" class="solr.SearchHandler">
    <lst name="defaults">
   ```

```
  <str name="echoParams">explicit</str>
  <int name="rows">10</int>
  <str name="df">name</str>
 </lst>
 <arr name="last-components">
  <str>elevator</str>
 </arr>
</requestHandler>

<searchComponent name="elevator" class="solr.
QueryElevationComponent">
 <str name="queryFieldType">string</str>
 <str name="config-file">elevate.xml</str>
</searchComponent>
```

3. The contents of the `elevate.xml` file located in the `conf` directory look like the
    following code:

```
<elevate>
  <query text="book">
    <doc id="3" />
  </query>
</elevate>
```

4. Our example data that we indexed looks like the following code:

```
<add>
 <doc>
  <field name="id">1</field>
  <field name="name">Book 1</field>
 </doc>
 <doc>
  <field name="id">2</field>
  <field name="name">Book 2</field>
 </doc>
 <doc>
  <field name="id">3</field>
  <field name="name">Promoted document</field>
 </doc>
</add>
```

5. Now let's query Solr with the following query:

```
http://localhost:8983/solr/select?q=book&df=name&fl=*,[elevated]
```

And the response we get from Solr is as follows:

```xml
<?xml version="1.0" encoding="UTF-8"?>
<response>
 <lst name="responseHeader">
  <int name="status">0</int>
  <int name="QTime">2</int>
  <lst name="params">
   <str name="q">book</str>
   <str name="df">name</str>
   <str name="fl">*,[elevated]</str>
  </lst>
 </lst>
 <result name="response" numFound="3" start="0">
  <doc>
   <str name="id">3</str>
   <str name="name">Promoted document</str>
   <bool name="[elevated]">true</bool>
  </doc>
  <doc>
   <str name="id">1</str>
   <str name="name">Book 1</str>
   <bool name="[elevated]">false</bool>
  </doc>
  <doc>
   <str name="id">2</str>
   <str name="name">Book 2</str>
   <bool name="[elevated]">false</bool>
  </doc>
 </result>
</response>
```

As you can see each document does not only have its name and identifier, but also the information about whether it was elevated or not.

How it works...

Our index structure consists of two fields, the id field which is our unique key and the name field used for holding the name of the document. Please remember that in order to use the elevation component you have to have a unique key defined in your schema.xml file, and this field has to be based on the string type.

The /select request handler configuration is quite standard, although we've added the last-components sections that define what component should be used during a query. We defined that we want to use the component named elevator.

The next thing we did is the `elevator` search component definition. It is based on the `solr.QueryElevationComponent` class (the `class` attribute) and we set its name to `elevator` (the attribute `name`). In addition to that, we specified two attributes needed by the query elevation component:

▶ `queryFieldType`: This specifies the name of the type that will be used to analyze the incoming text. We specified the `string` type because we want only exact matches to include elevated documents.

▶ `config-file`: This specifies the name of the configuration file that stores the elevation definitions.

The `elevate.xml` file we use for storing the query elevation component is simple. The root tag is named `elevate` and can have multiple `query` tags inside it. Each `query` tag is responsible for elevating documents for a query defined with the `text` attribute. Inside the `query` tag we can have multiple `doc` tags with an `id` attribute, which should have a value of the identifier of the document to which we want add to results or modify positions. In our case, we want the document with an identifier value of `3` to be placed in the first position when users enter the `book` query.

The query we sent was simple; we asked for documents that have `book` in the default field (the `df` parameter) which is `name` in our case. In addition to that, we want all stored fields to be returned (the `*` part of the `fl` parameter) and we also want to activate one of the document transformers, which is responsible for marking the documents that were elevated by the query elevation component, by adding the `[elevated]` part of the `fl` parameter. This transformer adds the `<bool name="[elevated]">true</bool>` field if the document was elevated, and `<bool name="[elevated]">false</bool>` if the document wasn't elevated.

Using parent-child relationships

When using Solr you are probably used to having a flat structure of documents without any relationships. However, there are situations where decomposing relationships is a cost we can't take. Because of that Solr 4.0 comes with a join functionality that allows us to use some basic relationships. For example, imagine that our index consists of books and workbooks and we would like to use that relationship. This recipe will show you how to do it.

How to do it...

1. First of all, let's assume that we have the following index structure (just place the following in the `fields` section of your `schema.xml` file):

```
<field name="id" type="string" indexed="true" stored="true"
required="true" multiValued="false" />
<field name="name" type="text" indexed="true" stored="true"
multiValued="false"/>
```

```
<field name="type" type="string" indexed="true" stored="true"/>
<field name="book" type="string" indexed="true" stored="true"/>
```

2. Now let's look at our test data that we are going to index:

```
<add>
 <doc>
  <field name="id">1</field>
  <field name="name">Book 1</field>
  <field name="type">book</field>
 </doc>
 <doc>
  <field name="id">2</field>
  <field name="name">Book 2</field>
  <field name="type">book</field>
 </doc>
 <doc>
  <field name="id">3</field>
  <field name="name">Workbook A</field>
  <field name="type">workbook</field>
  <field name="book">1</field>
 </doc>
 <doc>
  <field name="id">4</field>
  <field name="name">Workbook B</field>
  <field name="type">workbook</field>
  <field name="book">2</field>
 </doc>
</add>
```

3. Now, let's assume we want to get all the books from Solr that have workbooks for them. Also we want to narrow the books we got to only those that have the character 2 in their names. In order to do that, we run the following query:

```
http://localhost:8983/solr/select/?q={!join from=book to=id}
type:workbook&fq=name:2
```

The Solr response for the preceding query is as follows:

```
<?xml version="1.0" encoding="UTF-8"?>
 <response>
  <lst name="responseHeader">
   <int name="status">0</int>
   <int name="QTime">2</int>
```

```
    <lst name="params">
     <str name="fq">name:2</str>
     <str name="q">{!join from=book to=id}type:workbook</str>
    </lst>
   </lst>
   <result name="response" numFound="1" start="0">
    <doc>
     <str name="id">2</str>
     <str name="name">Book 2</str>
     <str name="type">book</str>
    </doc>
   </result>
  </response>
```

As you can see, the returned document was exactly the one we expected.

How it works...

Although the example index structure is simple I would like to comment on it. The id field is responsible for holding the unique identifier of the document, the name field is the document name, and the type field holds the document's types. The book field is optional and specifies the identifier of the parent document. So you can see that in our example data, we have two parent documents (those with an id field value of 1 and 2) and two child documents (those with an id field value of 3 and 4).

Let's pause for a bit now before looking at the query, and look at our example data. If we only query for workbooks, we would get documents with identifier values of 3 and 4. The parent for the document with the id field equal to 3 is 1, and the parent for the document with the id field equal to 4 is 2. If we filter 1 and 2 with the filter fq=name:2, we should only get the document with the id field value equal to 2 as the result. So looking at the query result it works as intended, but how does the query actually work?

I'll begin the description from the join part, that is, q={!join from=book to=id} type:workbook. As you can see we used local params to choose the different type of query parser – the join query parser (the !join part of the query). We specified that child documents should use the book field (the from parameter) and join it with the id field (the to parameter). The type:workbook part specifies the query we run, that is, we want only those documents that have the workbook value in the type field. The fq parameter, which narrows the result set to only those documents that have the value 2 in the name field, is applied after the join is executed, so we only apply it to the parent documents.

Ignoring typos in terms of performance

Sometimes there are situations where you would like to have some kind of functionality that would allow you to give your user the search results even though he/she made a typo or even multiple typos. In Solr, there are multiple ways to undo that: using a spellchecker component to try and correct the user's mistake, using the fuzzy query, or for example, using the ngram approach. This recipe will concentrate on the third approach and show you how to use ngrams to handle user typos.

How to do it...

For the purpose of the recipe, let's assume that our index is built up of four fields: `identifier`, `name`, `description`, and the `description_ngram` field which will be processed with the ngram filter.

1. So let's start with the fields definition of our index which should look like the following code (place this in your `schema.xml` file in the `fields` section):

```
<field name="id" type="string" indexed="true" stored="true"
required="true" multiValued="false" />
<field name="name" type="text" indexed="true" stored="true"/>
<field name="description" type="text" indexed="true" stored="true"
/>
<field name="description_ngram" type="text_ngram" indexed="true"
stored="false" />
```

2. As we want to use the ngram approach, we will include the following filter in our `text_ngram` field type definition:

```
<filter class="solr.NGramFilterFactory" minGramSize="2"
maxGramSize="2" />
```

The filter will be responsible for dividing the indexed data and queries into two bi-grams. To better illustrate what I mean, take a look at the following screenshot, which shows how the filter worked for the word "multiple":

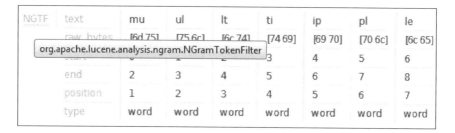

NGTF	text	mu	ul	lt	ti	ip	pl	le
	raw bytes	[6d 75]	[75 6c]	[6c 74]	[74 69]	[69 70]	[70 6c]	[6c 65]
					3	4	5	6
	end	2	3	4	5	6	7	8
	position	1	2	3	4	5	6	7
	type	word	word	word	word	word	word	word

So the whole `text_ngram` type definition will look like the following code:

```
<fieldType name="text_ngram" class="solr.TextField"
positionIncrementGap="100">
 <analyzer>
  <tokenizer class="solr.StandardTokenizerFactory"/>
  <filter class="solr.LowerCaseFilterFactory"/>
  <filter class="solr.NGramFilterFactory" minGramSize="2"
maxGramSize="2" />
 </analyzer>
</fieldType>
```

3. We also need to add the copy field definition to our `schema.xml` file, to automatically copy the value of the `description` field to the `description_ngram` field. The copy field definition looks as follows:

```
<copyField source="description" dest="description_ngram" />
```

4. Now we can index our data. For the purpose of the recipe I used the following data sample:

```
<add>
  <doc>
    <field name="id">1</field>
    <field name="name">Solr Cookbook 4.0</field>
    <field name="description">Solr Cookbook 4.0 contains multiple
    recipes helping you with your every day work with Solr :)</field>
  </doc>
</add>
```

5. After indexing it, I decided to test if my query can handle a single typo in each of the words provided to the query, so I've sent the following query to Solr, where the words I was really interested in were "contains" and "multiple":

```
q=description:(kontains+multyple) description_
ngram:(kontains+multyple)&q.op=OR
```

The result of the query was as follows:

```
<?xml version="1.0" encoding="UTF-8"?>
 <response>
  <lst name="responseHeader">
   <int name="status">0</int>
   <int name="QTime">1</int>
   <lst name="params">
    <str name="indent">true</str>
    <str name="q">description:(kontains multyple) description_
ngram:(kontains multyple)</str>
```

```
      <str name="q.op">OR</str>
     </lst>
    </lst>
    <result name="response" numFound="1" start="0">
     <doc>
      <str name="id">1</str>
      <str name="name">Solr Cookbook 4.0</str>
      <str name="description">Solr Cookbook 4.0 contains multiple
      recipes helping you with your every day work with Solr :)</
      str></doc>
    </result>
   </response>
```

As you can see the document we were interested in was found. So let's see how that worked.

How it works...

As you can see from the index structure, we have two fields, namely `name` and `description`, which we defined to use the `text_ngram` field because we want these fields to support the returning of the search results even when the user enters a typo of some sort. To allow this we use the `solr.NGramFilterFactory` filter with two attributes defined, namely, the `minGramSize` which sets the minimum size of the produced ngram, and the `maxGramSize` which sets the maximum size of the produced ngram. With both of these attributes set to `2`, we configured the `solr.NGramFilterFactory` filter to produce tokens called 2-grams, that are built of two characters. The third attribute of the `filter` tag is the `class` attribute that specifies
the filter factory class we want to use.

Let's concentrate on the provided screenshot (refer to step 2 in the *How to do it...* section) to discuss how the `solr.NGramFilterFactory` filter works in our case. As I wrote earlier, we want the ngram filter to produce grams built up of two characters. You can see how the filter we've chosen works. From the word `multiple` it created the following bi-grams (n-grams built from 2 characters):

```
mu ul lt ti ip pl le
```

So, the idea of the algorithm is quite simple – divide the word, so that we take the first character and the character after it, and we make a bi-gram from it. Then we take the next character and the character after it and create the second bi-gram and so on until we can't make any more bi-grams.

Now if you look at the query there are two words we are looking for and both of them contain a typo. The `kontains` word should be `contain` without a typo and the `multyple` should be `multiple` without a typo. Our query also specifies that the logical query operator we want to use is the `OR` operator. We use it because we want to match all documents with even a single match to any bi-gram. If we turn the `kontains` and `multyple` tokens into bi-grams, we would get the following (I'll use the pipe (|) character to separate the words from each other):

```
ko on nt ta ai in ns | mu ul lt ty yp pl le
```

If we turn the `contains multiple` tokens into bi-grams we would get the following:

```
co on nt ta ai in ns | mu ul lt ti ip pl le
```

If you compare those bi-grams you would see that only three of those differ between the proper words and the ones with typos. The rest of them are the same. Because of that our query finds the document we indexed. You may wonder why we queried both the `description` and `description_ngram` fields. We did that because we don't know if the client's query is the one with typos or without. If it is without, we want the documents with better matches to be higher up on the results lists, than the ones that are not perfectly matched.

Of course all of that doesn't come without any downsides. One of the major downsides of this approach is the growth of the index size because of the number of tokens produced by the ngram filter. The second downside is the number of results produced with such an approach; there will be many more results than you are used to and that's why we did a query to both the `description` and `description_ngram` fields. We wanted to increase the `score` value of the perfectly matched documents (you can also boost the `description` field higher during a query). You can also try having the same approach work with the `edismax` query parser and the "minimum should match" (`mm`) parameter, but this is beyond the scope of this recipe.

Detecting and omitting duplicate documents

Imagine your data consists of duplicates because they come from different sources. For example, you have books that come from different suppliers, but you are only interested in a single book with the same name. Of course you could use the field collapsing feature during the query, but that affects query performance and we would like to avoid that. This recipe will show you how to use the Solr deduplication functionality.

How to do it...

1. We start with the simple index structure. This should be placed in the `fields` section of your `schema.xml` file:

    ```
    <field name="id" type="string" indexed="true" stored="true"
    required="true" multiValued="false" />
    ```

```
<field name="name" type="text" indexed="true" stored="true"
multiValued="false"/>
<field name="type" type="string" indexed="true" stored="true"
multiValued="false"/>
```

2. For the purpose of the recipe, we assume that we have the following data stored in the `data.xml` file:

```
<add>
 <doc>
  <field name="name">This is a book we are indexing and we think
it will be a dupe because it's almost the same as the second document
we are going to index</field>
  <field name="type">book</field>
 </doc>
 <doc>
  <field name="name">This is the book we are indexing and we think
it will be a dupe because it's almost the same as the second
document we are going to index</field>
  <field name="type">book</field>
 </doc>
</add>
```

As you can see, the file contains two documents and they only differ by a single word; the first document contains is the `is a book` phrase, while the second contains the `is the book` phrase. In my opinion the second document is a dupe of the first one.

3. In order to have those two documents detected and overwritten, we need to create a new update request processor chain called `dedupe` and configure `org.apache. solr.update.processor.SignatureUpdateProcessorFactory` as the first update processor. So the appropriate section of our `solrconfig.xml` file should look like the following code:

```
<updateRequestProcessorChain name="dedupe">
 <processor class="org.apache.solr.update.processor.
SignatureUpdateProcessorFactory">
  <bool name="enabled">true</bool>
  <bool name="overwriteDupes">true</bool>
  <str name="signatureField">id</str>
  <str name="fields">name</str>
  <str name="signatureClass">org.apache.solr.update.processor.
TextProfileSignature</str>
 </processor>
 <processor class="solr.LogUpdateProcessorFactory" />
 <processor class="solr.RunUpdateProcessorFactory" />
</updateRequestProcessorChain>
```

4. Now let's index our data by running the following command:

```
curl 'http://localhost:8983/solr/update?update.
chain=dedupe&commit=true' --data-binary @data.xml -H 'Content-
type:application/xml'
```

5. If everything went well, we should only see the second document as the first one should be overwritten. So we should check that by running the following query:

```
http://localhost:8983/solr/select?q=*:*
```

The response to it was the following:

```
<?xml version="1.0" encoding="UTF-8"?>
 <response>
  <lst name="responseHeader">
   <int name="status">0</int>
   <int name="QTime">1</int>
   <lst name="params">
    <str name="q">*:*</str>
   </lst>
  </lst>
  <result name="response" numFound="1" start="0">
   <doc>
    <str name="name">This is the book we are indexing and we think it
    will be a dupe because it's almost the same as the second
    document we are going to index</str>
    <str name="type">book</str>
    <str name="id">a095014df10f76513387af0450768ffb</str>
   </doc>
  </result>
 </response>
```

As you can see we got only a single document, and if you look again at the example data, you would notice that it is the second document we sent, so the first one was overwritten.

How it works...

Our index structure is simple and consists of three fields – the id field which holds the unique identifier, the name field which is a name of the book, and the type field which holds the type of the book.

The example data you see doesn't contain the id field, which isn't a mistake, it was prepared this way on purpose. We want our deduping to use the id field to generate a unique identifier for us and use it to overwrite duplicate documents. Also, you can see that the two sample documents are almost the same, so they should be marked as dupes and we should only see one of them in the index, probably the second one.

Next we define a new update request processor chain in the `solrconfig.xml` file with the name `dedupe` (the `name` property). The first processor we need to add in order to have the deduping functionality is `org.apache.solr.update.processor.SignatureUpdateProcessorFactory`. We do so by setting the `class` attribute of the `processor` tag to the mentioned class. The next few properties configure the `org.apache.solr.update.processor.SignatureUpdateProcessorFactory` behavior. By setting the `enabled` property to `true`, we turn on the deduping mechanism. `overwriteDupes` set to `true` tells Solr that we want the duplicate documents to be overwritten. The `signatureField` field configures the name of the field where the generated signature will be stored, which in our case is the `id` field. This is crucial, because Solr will use that information to identify duplicate documents. The `fields` field contains information of which fields (a list separated by the comma character) should be used to identify the duplication. We decided to use the `name` field. Finally, the `signatureClass` class is the class implementing the signature calculation. We've chosen `org.apache.solr.update.processor.TextProfileSignature` because it works best on longer text and we expect that. You can also choose `org.apache.solr.update.processor.MD5Signature` and `org.apache.solr.update.processor.Lookup3Signature`. The last two processors, `solr.LogUpdateProcessorFactory` and `solr.RunUpdateProcessorFactory`, write information about the update to the log file and run the update.

As you can see in the response for our "match all documents" query, only the second document is present. This is because when the index was empty the first document was indexed. Then, the second document came and it was identified as a dupe and thus it overwrote the first one.

Using field aliases

Imagine your products have multiple prices, and depending on your client's location you search one of the defined fields. So you have a field for price in US dollars, in Euros, and so on. But what you would like to do is return the field you are using for displaying the price of the document as a "price" no matter what field you use. This recipe will show you how to do it.

How to do it...

1. Let's begin with the following index structure (put all the entries in the `fields` section of your `schema.xml` file):

```
<field name="id" type="string" indexed="true" stored="true"
required="true" multiValued="false" />
<field name="name" type="text" indexed="true" stored="true"/>
<field name="price_usd" type="double" indexed="true" stored="true"
/>
<field name="price_eur" type="double" indexed="true" stored="true"
/>
<field name="price_pln" type="double" indexed="true" stored="true"
/>
```

2. We will also use the following test data:

```
<add>
 <doc>
  <field name="id">1</field>
  <field name="name">Solr Cookbook 4.0</field>
  <field name="price_usd">40.00</field>
  <field name="price_pln">120.00</field>
  <field name="price_eur">30.00</field>
 </doc>
</add>
```

3. Let's assume that we have a client from the United States of America and he/she searches for the word `solr` and for products with the price in US dollars ranging from `20` to `50`. The query would look like the following:

```
q=name:solr&fq=price_usd:[20+TO+50]&fl=id,name,price_usd
```

And the results of the preceding query would be as follows:

```
<?xml version="1.0" encoding="UTF-8"?>
 <response>
  <lst name="responseHeader">
   <int name="status">0</int>
   <int name="QTime">1</int>
   <lst name="params">
    <str name="fq">price_usd:[20 TO 50]</str>
    <str name="fl">id,name,price_usd</str>
    <str name="q">name:solr</str>
   </lst>
  </lst>
  <result name="response" numFound="1" start="0">
   <doc>
    <str name="id">1</str>
    <str name="name">Solr Cookbook 4.0</str>
    <double name="price_usd">40.0</double>
   </doc>
  </result>
 </response>
```

4. As you can see, we have our sample document returned but we've got the `price_usd` value returned as well. We would like it to be named `price`. So let's modify our `fl` parameter value, and instead of specifying `id,name,price_usd` we pass `id,name,price:price_usd`. So the whole query would look as follows:

```
q=name:solr&fq=price_usd:[20+TO+50]&fl=id,name,price:price_usd
```

And the returned results would be as follows:

```
<?xml version="1.0" encoding="UTF-8"?>
 <response>
  <lst name="responseHeader">
   <int name="status">0</int>
   <int name="QTime">1</int>
   <lst name="params">
    <str name="fq">price_usd:[20 TO 50]</str>
    <str name="fl">id,name,price:price_usd</str>
    <str name="q">name:solr</str>
   </lst>
  </lst>
  <result name="response" numFound="1" start="0">
   <doc>
    <str name="id">1</str>
    <str name="name">Solr Cookbook 4.0</str>
    <double name="price">40.0</double>
   </doc>
  </result>
 </response>
```

As you can see in the result document we got a field called `price` instead of `price_usd` field. Now, let's see how that works.

How it works...

The index structure is pretty simple, it only contains the field responsible for holding the identifier, name of the document, and three prices in different currencies. All the fields are marked as stored because we want to return them (not all at the same time though) at query time. The sample data is also simple so I decided to skip commenting on that.

The first query is simple. We are searching for the value `solr` in the `name` field and we want only the documents with the value of the `price_usd` field to be between `20` and `50`. We also want to return (the `fl` parameter) the following fields as a document: `id`, `name`, and `price_usd`.

The interesting things come with the second query. As you can see there is a different `fl` parameter that you may be used to. The first part of the `fl` parameter is pretty obvious; we want to return the `id` and `name` fields. The second part is new though; we specified the following value: `price:price_usd`. This means that we want the `price_usd` field to be returned as `price`. That is how field aliasing works; you add the value `ALIAS_NAME:FIELD_NAME` to the `fl` parameter and in the results, instead of `FIELD_NAME`, Solr will return `ALIAS_NAME`.

Returning a value of a function in the results

Imagine you have a service where your users can search for different companies. Your users can enter a simple keyword(s) and then return all the companies matching that keyword(s). But a day comes when you give your users the ability to choose their location, and you would like to show how far they are from each company returned in the results. This recipe will show you how to do it.

Getting ready

Before reading further I advise you to read the *Using field aliases* recipe in the current chapter and the *Storing geographical points in the index* recipe from *Chapter 3, Analyzing Your Text Data.*

How to do it...

1. For the purpose of the recipe, let's assume that we have the following index structure (put the following field's definition into your `schema.xml` file in the `fields` section):

   ```
   <field name="id" type="string" indexed="true" stored="true"
   required="true" multiValued="false" />
   <field name="name" type="text" indexed="true" stored="true"/>
   <field name="loc" type="location" indexed="true" stored="true"/>
   <dynamicField name="*_coordinate"  type="double" indexed="true"
   stored="false" />
   ```

2. Next, we need to define the `location` field type. It should look like the following code (put the following definition in to your `schema.xml` file in the `types` section):

   ```
   <fieldType name="location" class="solr.LatLonType"
   subFieldSuffix="_coordinate"/>
   ```

3. Let's also assume that we have the following data indexed:

   ```
   <add>
    <doc>
     <field name="id">1</field>
     <field name="name">Company 1</field>
     <field name="loc">56.4,40.2</field>
    </doc>
    <doc>
     <field name="id">2</field>
     <field name="name">Company 2</field>
     <field name="loc">50.1,48.9</field>
    </doc>
   ```

```
<doc>
 <field name="id">3</field>
 <field name="name">Company 3</field>
 <field name="loc">23.18,39.1</field>
</doc>
</add>
```

4. Now, in order to get all the documents with the word `company` in the `name` field we would run the following query:

```
q=name:company&fl=*
```

5. We have the information that our client's location is 50.0, 28.0 and we would like to show our client the distance from his/her location to each of the companies we return in the results. In order to do that we add the following part to the `fl` parameter:

```
dist:geodist(loc,50.0,28.0)
```

So the whole query looks like the following:

```
q=name:company&fl=*,dist:geodist(loc,50.0,28.0)
```

And the response from Solr is as follows:

```
<?xml version="1.0" encoding="UTF-8"?>
 <response>
  <lst name="responseHeader">
   <int name="status">0</int>
   <int name="QTime">0</int>
   <lst name="params">
    <str name="q">name:company</str>
    <str name="fl">*,dist:geodist(loc,50.0,28.0)</str>
   </lst>
  </lst>
  <result name="response" numFound="3" start="0">
   <doc>
    <str name="id">1</str>
    <str name="name">Company 1</str>
    <str name="loc">56.4,40.2</str>
    <double name="dist">1077.4200268973314</double>
   </doc>
   <doc>
    <str name="id">2</str>
    <str name="name">Company 2</str>
    <str name="loc">50.1,48.9</str>
    <double name="dist">1487.4260767512278</double>
   </doc>
```

```
<doc>
  <str name="id">3</str>
  <str name="name">Company 3</str>
  <str name="loc">23.18,39.1</str>
  <double name="dist">3134.746384852772</double>
</doc>
</result>
</response>
```

As you can see, in addition to all the stored fields, Solr returned the additional field called `dist`. Let's now see how that worked.

How it works...

The index structure is simple, it contains the identifier (the `id` field), name of the company (the `name` field), and the geographical location of the company (the `loc` field). Description of how geographical points should be stored were described in Chapter 3, *Analyzing Your Text Data*, in the *Storing geographical points in the index* recipe, so please refer to that for the explanation.

The initial query returning all the companies that have the word `company` in their `name` field returns all the stored fields (the `fl=*` part of the query). The interesting part comes with the `dist:geodist(loc,50.0,28.0)` part of the `fl` parameter. As you remember from the *Using field aliases* recipe, we told Solr that we want to have a new field called `dist` returned and we want it to be a value of the `dist` function query which takes three parameters: the field in the index (in our case it is `loc`), the latitude, and the longitude, and returns the distance between the point stored in the `loc` field, and the point described by the latitude and longitude. The value is then returned as the `dist` field of each of the returned documents.

5
Using the Faceting Mechanism

In this chapter we will cover:

- ▶ Getting the number of documents with the same field value
- ▶ Getting the number of documents with the same value range
- ▶ Getting the number of documents matching the query and the sub query
- ▶ Removing filters from faceting results
- ▶ Sorting faceting results in alphabetical order
- ▶ Implementing the autosuggest feature using faceting
- ▶ Getting the number of documents that don't have a value in the field
- ▶ Having two different facet limits for two different fields in the same query
- ▶ Using decision tree faceting
- ▶ Calculating faceting for relevant document groups

Introduction

One of the advantages of Solr is the ability to group results on the basis of some fields' contents. The Solr classification mechanism, called **faceting**, provides the functionalities which can help us in several tasks that we need to do in everyday work, from getting the number of documents with the same values in a field (for example, the companies from the same city) using the ability of date and range faceting, to the autocomplete features based on the faceting mechanism. This chapter will show you how to handle some of the common tasks when using the faceting mechanism.

Getting the number of documents with the same field value

Imagine a situation where besides the search results, you have to return the number of documents with the same field value. For example, imagine that you have an application that allows the user to search for companies in Europe, and your client wants the number of companies in the cities where the companies that were found by the query are located. To do this, you could of course run several queries but Solr provides a mechanism called faceting that can do that for you. This recipe will show you how to do it.

How to do it...

For getting the number of documents with the same field value, follow these steps:

1. To start, let's assume that we have the following index structure (just add this to your `schema.xml` file in the field definition section; we will use the `city` field to do the faceting):

```
<field name="id" type="string" indexed="true" stored="true"
required="true" />
<field name="name" type="text" indexed="true" stored="true" />
<field name="city" type="string" indexed="true" stored="true" />
```

2. The next step is to index the following example data:

```
<add>
<doc>
 <field name="id">1</field>
 <field name="name">Company 1</field>
 <field name="city">New York</field>
</doc>
<doc>
 <field name="id">2</field>
 <field name="name">Company 2</field>
 <field name="city">New Orleans</field>
</doc>
<doc>
 <field name="id">3</field>
 <field name="name">Company 3</field>
 <field name="city">New York</field>
</doc>
</add>
```

3. Let's suppose that our hypothetical user searches for the word `company`. The query that will get us what we want should look like this:

```
http://localhost:8983/solr/select?q=name:company&facet=true&facet.
field=city
```

The result of the query should be like this:

```xml
<?xml version="1.0" encoding="UTF-8"?>
<response>
 <lst name="responseHeader">
  <int name="status">0</int>
  <int name="QTime">1</int>
  <lst name="params">
   <str name="facet">true</str>
   <str name="facet.field">city</str>
   <str name="q">name:company</str>
  </lst>
 </lst>
 <result name="response" numFound="3" start="0">
  <doc>
   <str name="city">New York</str>
   <str name="id">1</str>
   <str name="name">Company 1</str>
  </doc>
  <doc>
   <str name="city">New Orleans</str>
   <str name="id">2</str>
   <str name="name">Company 2</str>
  </doc>
  <doc>
   <str name="city">New York</str>
   <str name="id">3</str>
   <str name="name">Company 3</str>
  </doc>
 </result>
 <lst name="facet_counts">
  <lst name="facet_queries"/>
  <lst name="facet_fields">
   <lst name="city">
           <int name="New York">2</int>
           <int name="New Orleans">1</int>
   </lst>
  </lst>
  <lst name="facet_dates"/>
  <lst name="facet_ranges"/>
 </lst>
</response>
```

As you can see, besides the normal results list, we got faceting results with the numbers that we wanted. Now let's look at how that happened.

How it works...

The index structure and the data are pretty simple and they make the example easier to understand. The company is described by three fields. We are particularly interested in the `city` field. This is the field that we want to use to get the number of companies that have the same value in this field—which basically means that they are in the same city.

To do that, we run a query to Solr and inform the query parser that we want the documents that have the word `company` in the `title` field. Additionally we say that we want to enable the faceting mechanism, by using the `facet=true` parameter. The `facet.field` parameter tells Solr which field to use to calculate faceting numbers. You can specify the `facet.field` parameter multiple times to get faceting numbers for different fields in the same query.

As you can see in the results list, the results of all types of faceting are grouped in the list with the `name="facet_counts"` attribute. The field based faceting is grouped under the list with the `name="facet_fields"` attribute. Every field that you specified using the `facet.field` parameter has its own list which has the attribute `name`, the same as the value of the parameter in the query—in our case it is `city`. Then finally you can see the results that we are interested in: the pairs of values (`name` attribute) and how many documents have the value in the specified field.

There's more...

There are two more things I would like to share about field faceting:

> **How to show facets with counts greater than zero**: The default behavior of Solr is to show all the faceting results irrespective of the counts. If you want to show only the facets with counts greater than zero than you should add the `facet.mincount=1` parameter to the query (you can set this parameter to another value if you are interested in any arbitrary value).

> **Lexicographical sorting of the faceting results**: If you want to sort the faceting results lexicographically, and not by the highest count (which is the default behavior), then you need to add the `facet.sort=index` parameter.

Getting the number of documents with the same value range

Imagine that you have an application where users can search the index to find a car for rent. One of the requirements of the application is to show a navigation panel, where the user can choose the price range for the cars that they are interested in. To do it in an efficient way, we will use range faceting and this recipe will show you how to do it.

How to do it...

For getting the number of documents with the same value range, follow these steps:

1. Let's begin with the following index structure (just add this to your `schema.xml` file in the field definition section; we will use the `price` field to do the faceting):

```
<field name="id" type="string" indexed="true" stored="true"
required="true" />
<field name="name" type="text" indexed="true" stored="true" />
<field name="price" type="float" indexed="true" stored="true" />
```

2. The example data that we will use is like this:

```
<add>
 <doc>
  <field name="id">1</field>
  <field name="name">Super Mazda</field>
  <field name="price">50</field>
 </doc>
 <doc>
  <field name="id">2</field>
  <field name="name">Mercedes Benz</field>
  <field name="price">210</field>
 </doc>
 <doc>
  <field name="id">3</field>
  <field name="name">Bentley</field>
  <field name="price">290</field>
 </doc>
 <doc>
  <field name="id">2</field>
  <field name="name">Super Honda</field>
  <field name="price">99.90</field>
 </doc>
</add>
```

3. Now, as you recall, our requirement was to show the navigation panel with price ranges. To do that, we need to get that data from Solr. We also know that the minimum price for car rent is 1 dollar and the maximum is 400 dollars. To get the price ranges from Solr, we send the following query:

```
http://localhost:8983/solr/select?q=*:*&rows=0&facet=true&facet.
range=price&facet.range.start=0&facet.range.end=400&facet.range.
gap=100
```

The query will produce the following result list:

```
<?xml version="1.0" encoding="UTF-8"?>
<response>
 <lst name="responseHeader">
  <int name="status">0</int>
  <int name="QTime">3</int>
  <lst name="params">
   <str name="facet">true</str>
   <str name="q">*:*</str>
   <str name="facet.range.start">0</str>
   <str name="facet.range">price</str>
   <str name="facet.range.end">400</str>
   <str name="facet.range.gap">100</str>
   <str name="rows">0</str>
  </lst>
 </lst>
 <result name="response" numFound="4" start="0"/>
  <lst name="facet_counts">
   <lst name="facet_queries"/>
   <lst name="facet_fields"/>
   <lst name="facet_dates"/>
   <lst name="facet_ranges">
    <lst name="price">
     <lst name="counts">
      <int name="0.0">2</int>
      <int name="100.0">0</int>
      <int name="200.0">2</int>
      <int name="300.0">0</int>
     </lst>
     <float name="gap">100.0</float>
     <float name="start">0.0</float>
     <float name="end">400.0</float>
    </lst>
   </lst>
  </lst>
</response>
```

So we got exactly what we wanted. Now let's see how it works.

How it works...

As you can see, the index structure is simple. There are three fields, one responsible for the unique identifier, one responsible for the car name, and the last one responsible for the price of rent.

The query is where all the magic is done. As we are not interested in the search results, we ask for all documents in the index (`q=*:*` parameter) and we tell Solr not to return the search results (`rows=0` parameter). Then we tell Solr that we want the faceting mechanism to be enabled for the query (`facet=true` parameter). We will not be using the standard faceting mechanism, that is, the field based faceting. Instead we will use range faceting which is optimized to work with ranges. So, we tell Solr which field will be used for range faceting by adding the parameter `facet.range` with the `price` value. That means that the `price` field will be used for the range faceting calculation. Then we specify the lower boundary from which the range faceting calculation will begin. We do this by adding the `facet.range.start` parameter; in our example we set it to `0`. Next we have the `facet.range.end` parameter which tells Solr when to stop the calculation of the range faceting. The last parameter (`facet.range.gap`) informs Solr about the length of the periods that will be calculated.

Remember that when using the range faceting mechanism you must specify the three parameters:

- `facet.range.start`
- `facet.range.end`
- `facet.range.gap`

Otherwise, the range faceting mechanism won't work.

In the faceting results you can see the periods and the number of documents that were found in each of them. The first period can be found under the `<int name="0.0">` tag. This period consists of prices from 0 to 100 (in mathematical notation it would be `<0; 100>`). It contains two cars. The next period can be found under the `<int name="100.0">` tag and consists of prices from 100 to 200 (in mathematical notation it would be `<100; 200>`), and so on.

Getting the number of documents matching the query and subquery

Imagine a situation where you have an application that has a search feature for cars. One of the requirements is not only to show search results, but also to show the number of cars with the price period chosen by the user. There is also another thing—those queries must be fast because of the number of queries that will be run. Can Solr handle that? The answer is yes. This recipe will show you how to do it.

How to do it...

For getting the number of documents matching the query and subquery, follow these steps:

1. Let's start with creating an index with the following structure (just add this to your `schema.xml` file in the field definition section; we will use the `price` field to do the faceting):

```
<field name="id" type="string" indexed="true" stored="true"
required="true" />
<field name="name" type="text" indexed="true" stored="true" />
<field name="price" type="float" indexed="true" stored="true" />
```

2. Now let's index the following sample data:

```
<add>
<doc>
 <field name="id">1</field>
 <field name="name">Car 1</field>
 <field name="price">70</field>
</doc>
<doc>
 <field name="id">2</field>
 <field name="name">Car 2</field>
 <field name="price">101</field>
</doc>
<doc>
 <field name="id">3</field>
 <field name="name">Car 3</field>
 <field name="price">201</field>
</doc>
<doc>
 <field name="id">4</field>
 <field name="name">Car 4</field>
 <field name="price">99.90</field>
</doc>
</add>
```

Now, recall our requirement cars that match the query (let's suppose that our user typed `car`), and show the counts in the chosen price periods. For the purpose of the recipe let's assume that the user has chosen two periods of prices:

- 10 to 80
- 90 to 300

3. The query to achieve such a requirement should look like this:

```
http://localhost:8983/solr/select?q=name:car&facet=true&facet.
query=price:[10 TO 80]&facet.query=price:[90 TO 300]
```

The result list of the query should look like this:

```
<?xml version="1.0" encoding="UTF-8"?>
<response>
 <lst name="responseHeader">
  <int name="status">0</int>
  <int name="QTime">1</int>
  <lst name="params">
   <str name="facet">true</str>
   <arr name="facet.query">
    <str>price:[10 TO 80]</str>
    <str>price:[90 TO 300]</str>
   </arr>
   <str name="q">name:car</str>
  </lst>
 </lst>
 <result name="response" numFound="4" start="0">
  <doc>
   <str name="id">1</str>
   <str name="name">Car 1</str>
   <float name="price">70.0</float>
  </doc>
  <doc>
   <str name="id">2</str>
   <str name="name">Car 2</str>
   <float name="price">101.0</float>
  </doc>
  <doc>
   <str name="id">3</str>
   <str name="name">Car 3</str>
   <float name="price">201.0</float>
  </doc>
  <doc>
   <str name="id">4</str>
   <str name="name">Car 4</str>
   <float name="price">99.9</float>
  </doc>
 </result>
```

```
<lst name="facet_counts">
 <lst name="facet_queries">
  <int name="price:[10 TO 80]">1</int>
  <int name="price:[90 TO 300]">3</int>
 </lst>
 <lst name="facet_fields"/>
 <lst name="facet_dates"/>
</lst>
</response>
```

How it works...

As you can see, the index structure is simple. There are three fields, one responsible for the unique identifier, one responsible for the car name, and the last one responsible for the price.

Next we have the query. First you can see a standard query where we tell Solr that we want to get all the documents that have the word `car` in the `name` field (the `q=name:car` parameter). Next, we say that we want to use the faceting mechanism by adding the `facet=true` parameter to the query. This time we will use the query faceting type. This means that we can pass the query to the faceting mechanism and as a result we will get the number of documents that match the given query. In our example case, we wanted two periods like this:

 ▸ One from the price of 10 to 80

 ▸ Another from the price of 90 to 300

This is achieved by adding the `facet.query` parameter with the appropriate value. The first period is defined as a standard range query to the `price` field (`price:[10 TO 80]`). The second query is very similar, just with different values. The value passed to the `facet.query` parameter should be a Lucene query written using the default query syntax.

As you can see in the results, the query faceting results are grouped under the `<lst name="facet_queries">` XML tag with the names exactly as in the queries sent to Solr. You can see that Solr correctly calculated the number of cars in each of the periods, which means that this is a perfect solution for us when we can't use the range faceting mechanism.

Removing filters from faceting results

Let's assume for the purpose of this recipe that you have an application that can search for companies within a city and state. But the requirements say that you should show not only the search results but also the number of companies in each city and the number of companies in each state (in the Solr way we say that you want to exclude the filter query from the faceting results). Can Solr do that in an efficient way? Sure it can, and this recipe will show you how to do it.

Getting ready

Before you start reading this recipe, please take a look at the *Getting the number of documents with the same field value* recipe in this chapter.

How to do it...

1. We start with the following index structure (just add this to your `schema.xml` file in the field definition section; we will use the `city` and `state` fields to do the faceting):

```
<field name="id" type="string" indexed="true" stored="true"
required="true" />
<field name="name" type="text" indexed="true" stored="true" />
<field name="city" type="string" indexed="true" stored="true" />
<field name="state" type="string" indexed="true" stored="true" />
```

2. The second step would be to index the following example data:

```
<add>
 <doc>
  <field name="id">1</field>
  <field name="name">Company 1</field>
  <field name="city">New York</field>
  <field name="state">New York</field>
 </doc>
 <doc>
  <field name="id">2</field>
  <field name="name">Company 2</field>
  <field name="city">New Orleans</field>
  <field name="state">Luiziana</field>
 </doc>
 <doc>
  <field name="id">3</field>
  <field name="name">Company 3</field>
  <field name="city">New York</field>
  <field name="state">New York</field>
 </doc>
 <doc>
  <field name="id">4</field>
  <field name="name">Company 4/field>
  <field name="city">New York</field>
  <field name="state">New York</field>
 </doc>
</add>
```

3. Let's suppose that our hypothetical user searched for the word `company`, and told our application that he needs the companies matching the word in the state of `New York`. In that case, the query that will fulfill our requirement should look like this:

```
http://localhost:8983/solr/select?q=name:company&facet=true
&fq={!tag=stateTag}state:"New York"&facet.field={!ex=stateTag}
city&facet.field={!ex=stateTag}state
```

The result for the query will look like this:

```xml
<?xml version="1.0" encoding="UTF-8"?>
<response>
 <lst name="responseHeader">
  <int name="status">0</int>
  <int name="QTime">1</int>
  <lst name="params">
   <str name="facet">true</str>
   <arr name="facet.field">
    <str>{!ex=stateTag}city</str>
    <str>{!ex=stateTag}state</str>
   </arr>
   <str name="fq">{!tag=stateTag}state:"New York"</str>
   <str name="q">name:company</str>
  </lst>
 </lst>
 <result name="response" numFound="3" start="0">
  <doc>
   <str name="id">1</str>
   <str name="name">Company 1</str>
   <str name="city">New York</str>
   <str name="state">New York</str>
  </doc>
  <doc>
   <str name="id">3</str>
   <str name="name">Company 3</str>
   <str name="city">New York</str>
   <str name="state">New York</str>
  </doc>
  <doc>
   <str name="id">4</str>
   <str name="name">Company 4</str>
   <str name="city">New York</str>
   <str name="state">New York</str>
  </doc>
```

```
      </result>
      <lst name="facet_counts">
       <lst name="facet_queries"/>
       <lst name="facet_fields">
        <lst name="city">
         <int name="New York">3</int>
         <int name="New Orleans">1</int>
        </lst>
        <lst name="state">
         <int name="New York">3</int>
         <int name="Luiziana">1</int>
        </lst>
       </lst>
       <lst name="facet_dates"/>
       <lst name="facet_ranges"/>
      </lst>
     </response>
```

Now let's see how it works.

How it works...

The index structure is pretty simple—it contains four fields that describe the company. The search will be performed against the `name` field, while the filtering and the faceting is done with the use of the `state` and `city` fields.

So let's get on with the query. As you can see, we have some typical elements there. First the `q` parameter, which just tells Solr where and what to search for. Then the `facet=true` parameter that enables the faceting mechanism. So far, so good. Following that, you have a strange looking filter query (the `fq` parameter) with the value of `fq={!tag=stateTag}` `state:"New York"`. It tells Solr to only show those results that have `New York` in the `state` field. By adding the `{!tag=stateTag}` part, we basically gave that filter query a name (`stateTag`), which we will use further.

Now, look at the two `facet.field` parameters. Our requirement was to show the number of companies in all states and in all cities. The only thing that was preventing us from getting those numbers was the filter query we added to the query. So let's exclude it from the faceting results. How to do it ? It's simple—just add `{!ex=stateTag}` to the beginning of each of the `facet.field` parameters, like this: `facet.field={!ex=stateTag}city`. It tells Solr to exclude the filter with the passed name.

As you can see in the results list, we got the correct numbers which means that the exclude works as intended.

Sorting faceting results in alphabetical order

Imagine a situation where you have a website, where you present some kind of advertisements, for example, house rental advertisements. One of the requirements is to show a list of cities in which the offer, that matched the query typed by the user, are located. So the first thing you think is to use the faceting mechanism – and that's a good idea. But then, your boss tells you that he is not interested in the counts and you have to sort the results in the alphabetical order. So, is Solr able to do it? Of course it is and this recipe will show you how to do it.

Getting ready

Before you start reading this recipe, please take a look at the *Getting the number of documents with the same field value* recipe in this chapter.

How to do it...

1. For the purpose of the recipe let's assume that we have the following index structure (just add this to your `schema.xml` file to the field definition section; we will use the `city` field to do the faceting):

```
<field name="id" type="string" indexed="true" stored="true"
required="true" />
<field name="name" type="text" indexed="true" stored="true" />
<field name="city" type="string" indexed="true" stored="true" />
```

2. This index structure is responsible for holding information about companies and their location. Now, let's index the example data matching the presented index structure:

```
<add>
<doc>
 <field name="id">1</field>
 <field name="name">House 1</field>
 <field name="city">New York</field>
 </doc>
<doc>
 <field name="id">2</field>
 <field name="name">House 2</field>
 <field name="city">Washington</field>
 </doc>
<doc>
 <field name="id">3</field>
 <field name="name">House 3</field>
```

```
 <field name="city">Washington</field>
</doc>
<doc>
 <field name="id">4</field>
 <field name="name">House 4</field>
 <field name="city">San Francisco</field>
</doc>
</add>
```

3. Let's assume that our hypothetical user typed `house` in the search box. The query to return the search results with the faceting results sorted alphabetically should be like this:

```
http://localhost:8983/solr/select?q=name:house&facet=true&facet.
field=city&facet.sort=index
```

The results returned by Solr for the query should look like this:

```
<?xml version="1.0" encoding="UTF-8"?>
<response>
 <lst name="responseHeader">
  <int name="status">0</int>
  <int name="QTime">1</int>
  <lst name="params">
   <str name="facet">true</str>
   <str name="facet.field">city</str>
   <str name="facet.sort">index</str>
   <str name="q">name:house</str>
  </lst>
 </lst>
 <result name="response" numFound="4" start="0">
  <doc>
   <str name="city">New York</str>
   <str name="id">1</str>
   <str name="name">House 1</str>
  </doc>
  <doc>
   <str name="city">Washington</str>
   <str name="id">2</str>
   <str name="name">House 2</str>
  </doc>
  <doc>
   <str name="city">Washington</str>
   <str name="id">3</str>
   <str name="name">House 3</str>
```

```
    </doc>
    <doc>
     <str name="city">San Francisco</str>
     <str name="id">4</str>
     <str name="name">House 4</str>
    </doc>
   </result>
   <lst name="facet_counts">
    <lst name="facet_queries"/>
    <lst name="facet_fields">
     <lst name="city">
      <int name="New York">1</int>
      <int name="San Francisco">1</int>
      <int name="Washington">2</int>
     </lst>
    </lst>
    <lst name="facet_dates"/>
    <lst name="facet_ranges"/>
   </lst>
  </response>
```

As you can see the faceting results returned by Solr are not sorted by counts but in alphabetical order. Now let's see how it works.

How it works...

The index structure and the example data are only here to help us make a query so I'll skip discussing them.

The query shown in the recipe differs from the standard faceting query by only one parameter—`facet.sort`. It tells Solr how to sort the faceting results. The parameter can be assigned one of two values:

- ▶ `count` – which tells Solr to sort the faceting results placing the highest counts first
- ▶ `index` – which tells Solr to sort the faceting results by index order, which means that the results will be sorted lexicographically

For the purpose of the recipe we chose the second option and as you can see in the returned results, we got what we wanted.

Implementing the autosuggest feature using faceting

There are plenty of web-based applications that help users choose what they want to search for. One of the features that helps users is the autocomplete (or autosuggest) feature, like the one that most of the most used search engines have. Let's assume that we have an e-commerce library and we want to help the user to choose a book title—we want to enable autosuggest on the basis of the title. This recipe will show you how to do that.

Getting ready

Before you start reading this recipe, please take a look at the *Getting the number of documents with the same field value* recipe in this chapter.

How to do it...

1. Let's begin with the assumption of having the following index structure (just add this to your `schema.xml` file in the fields definition section):

    ```
    <field name="id" type="string" indexed="true" stored="true"
    required="true" />
    <field name="title" type="text" indexed="true" stored="true" />
    <field name="title_autocomplete" type="lowercase" indexed="true"
    stored="true">
    ```

2. We also want to add some field copying to do some operations automatically. To do that we need to add the following line after the `fields` section in your `schema.xml` file:

    ```
    <copyField source="title" dest="title_autocomplete" />
    ```

3. The lowercase field type should look like this (just add this to your `schema.xml` file to the type definitions):

    ```
    <fieldType name="lowercase" class="solr.TextField">
     <analyzer>
     <tokenizer class="solr.KeywordTokenizerFactory"/>
     <filter class="solr.LowerCaseFilterFactory" />
     </analyzer>
    </fieldType>
    ```

4. Now, let's index a sample data file which could look like this:

```
<add>
 <doc>
  <field name="id">1</field>
  <field name="title">Lucene or Solr ?</field>
 </doc>
 <doc>
  <field name="id">2</field>
  <field name="title">My Solr and the rest of the world</field>
 </doc>
 <doc>
  <field name="id">3</field>
  <field name="title">Solr recipes</field>
 </doc>
 <doc>
  <field name="id">4</field>
  <field name="title">Solr cookbook</field>
 </doc>
</add>
```

5. Let's assume that our hypothetical user typed the letters so in the search box and we want to give him the first 10 suggestions with the highest counts. We also want to suggest the whole titles, not just single words. To do that, we should send the following query to Solr:

```
http://localhost:8983/solr/select?q=*:*&rows=0&facet=true&facet.
field=title_autocomplete&facet.prefix=so
```

As a result for the query, Solr returned the following output:

```
<?xml version="1.0" encoding="UTF-8"?>
<response>
 <lst name="responseHeader">
  <int name="status">0</int>
  <int name="QTime">16</int>
  <lst name="params">
   <str name="facet">true</str>
   <str name="q">*:*</str>
   <str name="facet.prefix">so</str>
   <str name="facet.field">title_autocomplete</str>
   <str name="rows">0</str>
  </lst>
 </lst>
```

```
<result name="response" numFound="4" start="0"/>
<lst name="facet_counts">
 <lst name="facet_queries"/>
 <lst name="facet_fields">
  <lst name="title_autocomplete">
   <int name="solr cookbook">1</int>
   <int name="solr recipes">1</int>
  </lst>
 </lst>
 <lst name="facet_dates"/>
 <lst name="facet_ranges"/>
</lst>
</response>
```

As you can see, we got what we wanted in the faceting results. Now let's see how it works.

How it works...

You can see that our index structure defined in the `schema.xml` file is pretty simple. Every book is described by two fields, `id` and `title`. The additional field will be used to provide the autosuggest feature.

The copy field section is there to automatically copy the contents of the `title` field to the `title_autocomplete` field.

The `lowercase` field type is a type we will use to provide the autocomplete feature; this is the same for lowercase words typed by the users as well as uppercase words. If we want to show different results for uppercased and lowercased letters then the `string` type will be sufficient.

Now let's take a look at the query. As you can see we are searching the whole index (the parameter `q=*:*`), but we are not interested in any search results (the `rows=0` parameter). We tell Solr that we want to use the faceting mechanism (`facet=true` parameter) and that it will be field-based faceting on the basis of the `title_autocomplete` field (the `facet.field=title_autocomplete` parameter). The last parameter, `facet.prefix`, can be something new. Basically it tells Solr to return only those faceting results that begin with the prefix specified as the value of this parameter, which in our case is the value of `so`. The use of this parameter enables us to show the suggestions that the user is interested in, and we can see in the results that we achieved what we wanted.

There's more...

There is one more thing I would like to say about autosuggestion functionality.

Suggesting words not whole phrases

If you want to suggest words instead of a whole phrase you don't have to change much of the previous configuration. Just change the type of `title_autocomplete` to the type based on `solr.TextField` (for example, the `text_ws` field type). You should remember, though, not to use heavily analyzed text (like stemmed text) to be sure that your word won't be modified too much.

Getting the number of documents that don't have a value in the field

Let's imagine we have an e-commerce library where we put some of our books on a special promotion, for example, we give them away for free. We want to share that knowledge with our customers and say: *Hey! You searched for Solr, we found this, but we also have X books that are free!* To do that, we index the books that are free without the price defined. But how do you make a query to Solr to retrieve the data that we want? This recipe will show you how.

Getting ready

Before you start reading this recipe, please take a look at the *Getting the number of documents matching the query and the subquery* recipe in this chapter.

How to do it...

1. Let's begin with the following index structure (just add this to your `schema.xml` file in the field definition section):

    ```
    <field name="id" type="string" indexed="true" stored="true"
    required="true" />
    <field name="title" type="text" indexed="true" stored="true" />
    <field name="price" type="float" indexed="true" stored="true">
    ```

2. We will also use the following sample data:

    ```
    <add>
     <doc>
      <field name="id">1</field>
      <field name="title">Lucene or Solr ?</field>
      <field name="price">11</field>
     </doc>
     <doc>
      <field name="id">2</field>
      <field name="title">My Solr and the rest of the world</field>
      <field name="price">44</field>
     </doc>
    ```

```
<doc>
 <field name="id">3</field>
 <field name="title">Solr recipes</field>
 <field name="price">15</field>
</doc>
<doc>
 <field name="id">4</field>
 <field name="title">Solr cookbook</field>
</doc>
</add>
```

As you can see, the first three documents have a value in the `price` field, while the last one doesn't. So now, for the purpose of the example, let's assume that our hypothetical user is trying to find books that have `solr` in their `title` field.

3. Besides the search results, we want to show the number of documents that don't have a value in the `price` field. To do that, we send the following query to Solr:

```
http://localhost:8983/solr/select?q=title:solr&facet=true&facet.
query=!price:[* TO *]\
```

The query should result in the following output from Solr:

```
<?xml version="1.0" encoding="UTF-8"?>
<response>
 <lst name="responseHeader">
  <int name="status">0</int>
  <int name="QTime">0</int>
  <lst name="params">
   <str name="facet">true</str>
   <str name="facet.query">!price:[* TO *]</str>
   <str name="q">title:solr</str>
  </lst>
 </lst>
 <result name="response" numFound="4" start="0">
  <doc>
   <str name="id">3</str>
   <float name="price">15.0</float>
   <str name="title">Solr recipes</str>
  </doc>
  <doc>
   <str name="id">4</str>
   <str name="title">Solr cookbook</str>
  </doc>
  <doc>
```

```
        <str name="id">1</str>
        <float name="price">11.0</float>
        <str name="title">Lucene or Solr ?</str>
       </doc>
       <doc>
        <str name="id">2</str>
        <float name="price">44.0</float>
        <str name="title">My Solr and the rest of the world</str>
       </doc>
      </result>
      <lst name="facet_counts">
       <lst name="facet_queries">
        <int name="!price:[* TO *]">1</int>
       </lst>
       <lst name="facet_fields"/>
       <lst name="facet_dates"/>
       <lst name="facet_ranges"/>
      </lst>
     </response>
```

As you can see we got the proper results. Now let's see how it works.

How it works...

You can see that our index structure defined in the `schema.xml` file is pretty simple. Every book is described by three fields, `id`, `title`, and `price`. Their names speak for the type of information they will hold.

The query is in most parts something you should be familiar with. First, we tell Solr that we are searching for documents that have the word `solr` in the `title` field (the `q=title:solr` parameter). Then we say that we want to have the faceting mechanism enabled by adding the `facet=true` parameter. Then we add a facet query parameter that tells Solr to return the number of documents that don't have a value in the `price` field. We do that by adding the `facet.query=!price:[* TO *]` parameter. How does that work? You should be familiar with how the `facet.query` parameter works, so I'll skip that part. The `price:[* TO *]` expression tells Solr to count all the documents that have a value in the `price` field. By adding the `!` character before the fieldname, we tell Solr to negate the condition and in fact we get the number of documents that don't have any value in the specified field.

Having two different facet limits for two different fields in the same query

Imagine a situation where you have a database of cars in your application. Besides the standard search results, you want to show two faceting by field results. The first of those two faceting results, the number of cars in each category, should be shown without any limits, while the second faceting, the one showing the cars by their manufacturer, should be limited to a maximum of 10 results. Can we achieve it in one query? Yes, we can, and this recipe will show you how to do it.

Getting ready

Before you start reading this recipe please take a look at the *Getting the number of documents with the same field value* recipe in this chapter.

How to do it...

1. For the purpose of the recipe, let's assume that we have the following index structure (just add this to your `schema.xml` file in the field definition section; we will use the `category` and `manufacturer` fields to do the faceting):

    ```
    <field name="id" type="string" indexed="true" stored="true"
    required="true" />
     <field name="name" type="text" indexed="true" stored="true" />
     <field name="category" type="string" indexed="true" stored="true"
    />
    <field name="manufacturer" type="string" indexed="true"
    stored="true" />
    ```

2. We will need some sample data. For example we can use a file that has the following content:

    ```
    <add>
     <doc>
      <field name="id">1</field>
      <field name="name">Super Mazda car</field>
      <field name="category">sport</field>
      <field name="manufacturer">mazda</field>
     </doc>
     <doc>
    ```

```
      <field name="id">2</field>
      <field name="name">Mercedes Benz car</field>
      <field name="category">limousine</field>
      <field name="manufacturer">mercedes</field>
    </doc>
    <doc>
      <field name="id">3</field>
      <field name="name">Bentley car</field>
      <field name="category">limousine</field>
      <field name="manufacturer">bentley</field>
    </doc>
    <doc>
      <field name="id">4</field>
      <field name="name">Super Honda car</field>
      <field name="category">sport</field>
      <field name="manufacturer">honda</field>
    </doc>
  </add>
```

3. For the purpose of the example, let's assume that our hypothetical user is trying to search the index for the word `car`. To do that we should send Solr the following query:

```
http://localhost:8983/solr/select?q=name:car&facet=true&facet.
field=category&facet.field=manufacturer&f.category.facet.limit=-
1&f.manufacturer.facet.limit=10
```

The query resulted in the following response from Solr:

```
<?xml version="1.0" encoding="UTF-8"?>
<response>
 <lst name="responseHeader">
  <int name="status">0</int>
  <int name="QTime">1</int>
  <lst name="params">
   <str name="f.category.facet.limit">-1</str>
   <str name="facet">true</str>
   <str name="q">name:car</str>
   <arr name="facet.field">
    <str>category</str>
    <str>manufacturer</str>
   </arr>
   <str name="f.manufacturer.facet.limit">10</str>
  </lst>
 </lst>
 <result name="response" numFound="4" start="0">
  <doc>
```

```
  <str name="id">3</str>
  <str name="name">Bentley car</str>
  <str name="category">limousine</str>
  <str name="manufacturer">bentley</str>
 </doc>
 <doc>
  <str name="id">1</str>
  <str name="name">Super Mazda car</str>
  <str name="category">sport</str>
  <str name="manufacturer">mazda</str>
 </doc>
 <doc>
  <str name="id">2</str>
  <str name="name">Mercedes Benz car</str>
  <str name="category">limousine</str>
  <str name="manufacturer">mercedes</str>
 </doc>
 <doc>
  <str name="id">4</str>
  <str name="name">Super Honda car</str>
  <str name="category">sport</str>
  <str name="manufacturer">honda</str>
 </doc>
 </result>
 <lst name="facet_counts">
  <lst name="facet_queries"/>
  <lst name="facet_fields">
   <lst name="category">
    <int name="limousine">2</int>
    <int name="sport">2</int>
   </lst>
   <lst name="manufacturer">
    <int name="bentley">1</int>
    <int name="honda">1</int>
    <int name="mazda">1</int>
    <int name="mercedes">1</int>
   </lst>
  </lst>
  <lst name="facet_dates"/>
  <lst name="facet_ranges"/>
 </lst>
</response>
```

Now let's see how it works.

How it works...

Our data is very simple. As you can see in the field definition section of the `schema.xml` file and the example data, every document is described by four fields—id, `name`, `category`, and `manufacturer`. I think that their names speak for themselves and I don't need to discuss them.

The first parts of the query are pretty standard. We ask for documents which have the word `car` in their `name` field. Then we tell Solr to enable faceting (the `facet=true` parameter) and we tell it what field will be used to calculate faceting results (the `facet.field=category` and the `facet.field=manufacturer` parameters). Then we specify the limits. By adding the parameter limits in a way shown in the example (`f.FIELD_NAME.facet.limit`) we tell Solr to set the limits for the faceting calculation for the particular field. In our example query, by adding the `f.category.facet.limit=-1` parameter we told Solr that we don't want any limits on the number of faceting results for the `category` field. By adding the `f.manufacturer.facet.limit=10` parameter we told Solr that we want a maximum of `10` faceting results for the manufacturer field.

Following the pattern you can specify per-field values for faceting properties such as sorting and minimum count.

Using decision tree faceting

Imagine that in our store we have products divided into categories. In addition to that, we store information about the stock of the items. Now, we want to show our crew how many of the products in the categories are in stock and how many we are missing. The first thing that comes to mind is using the faceting mechanism and some additional calculation. But why bother, when Solr 4.0 can do that calculation for us with the use of so called **pivot faceting**. This recipe will show you how to use it.

How to do it...

The following steps illustrate the use of pivot faceting:

1. Let's start with the following index structure (just add this to your `schema.xml` file in the field definition section; we will use the `category` and `stock` fields to do the faceting):

   ```
   <field name="id" type="string" indexed="true" stored="true"
   required="true" />
   <field name="name" type="text" indexed="true" stored="true" />
   <field name="category" type="string" indexed="true" stored="true"
   />
   <field name="stock" type="boolean" indexed="true" stored="true" />
   ```

2. Now let's index the following example data:

```
<add>
 <doc>
  <field name="id">1</field>
  <field name="name">Book 1</field>
  <field name="category">books</field>
  <field name="stock">true</field>
 </doc>
 <doc>
  <field name="id">2</field>
  <field name="name">Book 2</field>
  <field name="category">books</field>
  <field name="stock">true</field>
 </doc>
 <doc>
  <field name="id">3</field>
  <field name="name">Workbook 1</field>
  <field name="category">workbooks</field>
  <field name="stock">false</field>
 </doc>
 <doc>
  <field name="id">4</field>
  <field name="name">Workbook 2</field>
  <field name="category">workbooks</field>
  <field name="stock">true</field>
 </doc>
</add>
```

3. Let's assume we are running a query from the administration panel of our shop and we are not interested in the documents at all; we only want to know how many documents are in stock or out of stock for each of the categories. The query implementing that logic should look like this:

```
http://localhost:8983/solr/select?q=*:*&rows=0&facet=true&facet.pivot=category,stock
```

The response to the query is as follows:

```
<?xml version="1.0" encoding="UTF-8"?>
<response>
 <lst name="responseHeader">
  <int name="status">0</int>
  <int name="QTime">76</int>
  <lst name="params">
   <str name="facet">true</str>
```

```
      <str name="indent">true</str>
      <str name="facet.pivot">category,stock</str>
      <str name="q">*:*</str>
      <str name="rows">0</str>
   </lst>
 </lst>
 <result name="response" numFound="4" start="0">
 </result>
 <lst name="facet_counts">
  <lst name="facet_queries"/>
  <lst name="facet_fields"/>
  <lst name="facet_dates"/>
  <lst name="facet_ranges"/>
  <lst name="facet_pivot">
   <arr name="category,stock">
    <lst>
     <str name="field">category</str>
     <str name="value">books</str>
     <int name="count">2</int>
     <arr name="pivot">
      <lst>
       <str name="field">stock</str>
       <bool name="value">true</bool>
       <int name="count">2</int>
      </lst>
     </arr>
    </lst>
    <lst>
     <str name="field">category</str>
     <str name="value">workbooks</str>
     <int name="count">2</int>
     <arr name="pivot">
      <lst>
       <str name="field">stock</str>
       <bool name="value">false</bool>
       <int name="count">1</int>
      </lst>
      <lst>
       <str name="field">stock</str>
       <bool name="value">true</bool>
       <int name="count">1</int>
      </lst>
     </arr>
    </lst>
   </arr>
  </lst>
 </lst>
</response>
```

You will notice that we received what we wanted, now let's see how it works.

How it works...

Our data is very simple. As you can see in the field definition section of the `schema.xml` file and the example data, every document is described by four fields—`id`, `name`, `category`, and `stock`. I think that their names speak for themselves and I don't need to discuss them.

The interesting things start with the query. We specified that we want the query to match all the documents (`q=*:*` parameter), but we don't want to see any documents in the response (`rows=0` parameter). In addition to that, we want to have faceting calculation (`facet=true` parameter) and we want to use the decision tree faceting, also known as pivot faceting. We do that by specifying which fields should be included in the tree faceting. In our case we want the top level of the pivot facet to be calculated on the basis of the `category` field, and the second level (the one nested in the `category` field calculation) should be based on the values available in the `stock` field. Of course, if you would like to have another value of another field nested under the `stock` field you can do that by adding another field to the `facet.pivot` query parameter. Assuming you would like to see faceting on the `price` field nested under the `stock` field, your `facet.pivot` parameter would look like this: `facet.pivot=category,stock,price`.

As you can see in the response, each nested faceting calculation result is written inside the `<arr name="pivot">` XML tag. So let's look at the response structure. The first level of your facet pivot tree is based on the `category` field. You can see two books (`<int name="count">2</int>`) in the `books` category (`<str name="value">books</str>`), and these books have the `stock` field (`<str name="field">stock</str>`) set to `true` (`<bool name="value">true</bool>`). For the `workbooks` category, the situation is a bit different, because you can see two different sections there—one for documents with the `stock` field equal to `false`, and the other with the `stock` field set to `true`. But in the end, the calculation is correct and that's what we wanted!

Calculating faceting for relevant documents in groups

If you have ever used the field collapsing functionality of Solr you may be wondering if there is a possibility of using that functionality and faceting. Of course there is, but the default behavior still works so that you get the faceting calculation on the basis of documents not document groups. In this recipe, we will learn how to query Solr so that it returns facets calculated for the most relevant document in each group in order for your user facet counts to be more or less grouped.

Getting ready

Before reading this recipe please look at the *Using field to group results*, *Using query to group results*, and *Using function query to group results* recipes in *Chapter 8*, *Using Additional Solr Functionalities*. Also, if you are not familiar with faceting functionality, please read the first three recipes in this chapter.

How to do it...

1. As a first step we need to create an index. For the purpose of the recipe let's assume that we have the following index structure (just add this to your `schema.xml` file to the field definition section):

```
<field name="id" type="string" indexed="true" stored="true"
required="true" />
<field name="name" type="text" indexed="true" stored="true" />
<field name="category" type="string" indexed="true" stored="true"
/>
<field name="stock" type="boolean" indexed="true" stored="true" />
```

2. The second step is to index the data. We will use some example data which looks like this:

```
<add>
 <doc>
  <field name="id">1</field>
  <field name="name">Book 1</field>
  <field name="category">books</field>
  <field name="stock">true</field>
 </doc>
 <doc>
  <field name="id">2</field>
  <field name="name">Book 2</field>
  <field name="category">books</field>
  <field name="stock">true</field>
 </doc>
 <doc>
  <field name="id">3</field>
  <field name="name">Workbook 1</field>
  <field name="category">workbooks</field>
  <field name="stock">false</field>
 </doc>
 <doc>
  <field name="id">4</field>
  <field name="name">Workbook 2</field>
  <field name="category">Workbooks</field>
  <field name="stock">true</field>
 </doc>
</add>
```

3. So now it's time for our query. So, let's assume we want our results to be grouped on the values of the `category` field, and we want the faceting to be calculated on the `stock` field. And remember that we are only interested in the most relevant document from each result group when it comes to faceting. So, the query that would tell Solr to do what we want should look like this:

```
http://localhost:8983/solr/select?q=*:*&facet=true&facet.
field=stock&group=true&group.field=category&group.truncate=true
```

The results for the query would look as follows:

```xml
<?xml version="1.0" encoding="UTF-8"?>
<response>
<lst name="responseHeader">
<int name="status">0</int>
<int name="QTime">2</int>
<lst name="params">
<str name="facet">true</str>
<str name="q">*:*</str>
<str name="group.truncate">true</str>
<str name="group.field">category</str>
<str name="group">true</str>
<str name="facet.field">stock</str>
</lst>
</lst>
<lst name="grouped">
<lst name="category">
<int name="matches">4</int>
<arr name="groups">
<lst>
<str name="groupValue">books</str>
<result name="doclist" numFound="2" start="0">
<doc>
<str name="id">1</str>
<str name="name">Book 1</str>
<str name="category">books</str>
<bool name="stock">true</bool></doc>
</result>
</lst>
<lst>
<str name="groupValue">workbooks</str>
        <result name="doclist" numFound="2" start="0">
         <doc>
          <str name="id">3</str>
```

```
                   <str name="name">Workbook 1</str>
                   <str name="category">workbooks</str>
                   <bool name="stock">false</bool>
                 </doc>
               </result>
             </lst>
           </arr>
         </lst>
       </lst>
       <lst name="facet_counts">
        <lst name="facet_queries"/>
        <lst name="facet_fields">
         <lst name="stock">
          <int name="false">1</int>
          <int name="true">1</int>
         </lst>
        </lst>
        <lst name="facet_dates"/>
        <lst name="facet_ranges"/>
       </lst>
     </response>
```

As you can see everything worked as it should. Now let's see how it works.

How it works...

Our data is very simple. As you can see in the field definition section of the `schema.xml` file and the example data, every document is described by four fields—`id`, `name`, `category`, and `stock`. I think that their names speak for themselves and I don't need to discuss them.

As it comes to the query, we fetch all the documents from the index (the `q=*:*` parameter). Next, we say that we want to use faceting and we want it to be calculated on the `stock` field. We want a grouping mechanism to be active and we want to group documents on the basis of the `category` field (all the query parameters responsible for defining the faceting and grouping behavior are described in the appropriate recipes in this book, so please look at those if you are not familiar with those parameters). And finally something new—the `group.truncate` parameter is set to `true`. If set to `true`, like in our case, facet counts will be calculated using only the most relevant document in each of the calculated groups. So in our case, for the group with the `category` field equal to `books`, we have the `true` value in the `stock` field and for the second group we have `false` in the `stock` field. Of course we are looking at the most relevant documents, so the first ones in our case. So, as you can easily see, we've got two facet counts for the `stock` field, both with a count of `1`, which is what we would expect.

There is one thing more—at the time of writing this book, the `group.truncate` parameter was not supported when using distributed search, so please be aware of that.

6
Improving Solr Performance

In this chapter we will cover:

- ▶ Paging your results quickly
- ▶ Configuring the document cache
- ▶ Configuring the query result cache
- ▶ Configuring the filter cache
- ▶ Improving Solr performance right after the start up or commit operation
- ▶ Caching whole result pages
- ▶ Improving faceting performance for low cardinality fields
- ▶ What to do when Solr slows down during indexing
- ▶ Analyzing query performance
- ▶ Avoiding filter caching
- ▶ Controlling the order of execution of filter queries
- ▶ Improving the performance of numerical range queries

Introduction

Performance of the application is one of the most important factors. Of course, there are other factors, such as usability and availability—we could recite many more—but one of the most crucial is **performance**. Even if our application is perfect in terms of usability, the users won't be able to use it if they will have to wait for minutes for the search results.

The standard Solr deployment is fast enough, but sooner or later a time will come when you will have to optimize your deployment. This chapter and its recipes will try to help you with the optimization of Solr deployment.

If your business depends on Solr, you should keep monitoring it even after optimization. There are numerous solutions available in the market, from the generic and open-sourced ones such as **Gangila** (`http://ganglia.sourceforge.net/`) to search-specific ones such as **Scalable Performance Monitoring** (`http://www.sematext.com/spm/index.html`) from **Sematext**.

Paging your results quickly

Imagine a situation where you have a user constantly paging through the search results. For example, one of the clients I was working for was struggling with the performance of his website. His users tend to search for a word and then page through the result pages – the statistical information gathered from the application logs showed that typical users changed the page about four to seven times. Apart from improving the query relevance (which isn't what we will talk about in this recipe), we decided to optimize the paging. How do we do that? This recipe will show you.

How to do it...

So, let's get back to my client deployment. As I mentioned, typical users typed a word into the search box and then used the paging mechanism to go through a maximum of seven pages. My client's application was showing 20 documents on a single page. So, it can be easily calculated that we need about 140 documents in advance, apart from the first 20 documents returned by the query.

1. So what we did was actually pretty simple. First of all, we modified the `queryResultWindowSize` property in the `solrconfig.xml` file and changed it to the following value:

   ```
   <queryResultWindowSize>160</queryResultWindowSize>
   ```

2. We then changed the maximum number of documents that can be cached for a single query to 160, by adding the following property to the `solrconfig.xml` file:

   ```
   <queryResultMaxDocsCached>160</queryResultMaxDocsCached>
   ```

We also modified `queryResultCache`, but that's a discussion for another recipe. To learn how to change that cache, please refer to the *How to configure the query result cache* recipe in this chapter.

How it works...

So how does Solr behave with the changes proposed in the preceding section? First of all, `queryResultWindowSize` tells Solr to store (in `documentCache`) a maximum of the 160 documents IDs with every query. Therefore, after doing the initial query, we gather more documents than we actually need. Because of this we are sure that when a user clicks on the **next page** button, which is present in our application, the results will be taken from the cache. So there won't be a need for intensive I/O operations. You must remember that the 160 documents IDs will be stored in the cache and won't be visible in the results list, as the result size is controlled by the `rows` parameter.

The `queryResultMaxDocsCached` property tells Solr about the maximum number of document IDs that can be cached for a single query (please remember than in this case, the cache stores the document identifiers and not whole documents). We told Solr that we want a maximum of 160 document IDs for a single query, because the statistics showed us that we don't need more, at least for a typical user.

Of course, there is another thing that should be done – setting the query result cache size, but that is discussed in another recipe.

Configuring the document cache

Cache can play a major role in your deployment's performance. One of the caches that you can configure when setting up Solr is the **document** cache. It is responsible for storing the Lucene internal documents that have been fetched from the disk. The proper configuration of this cache can save precious I/O calls and therefore boost the whole deployment performance. This recipe will show you how to properly configure the document cache.

How to do it...

For the purpose of this recipe, I assumed that we are dealing with the deployment of Solr where we have about 100, 000 documents. In our case, a single Solr instance is getting a maximum of 10 concurrent queries and the maximum number of documents that a query can fetch is 256.

With the preceding parameters, our document cache should look similar to the following code snippet (add this code to the `solrconfig.xml` configuration file):

```
<documentCache
    class="solr.LRUCache"
    size="2560"
    initialSize="2560"/>
```

Notice that we didn't specify the `autowarmCount` parameter—this is because the document cache uses Lucene's internal ID to identify documents. These identifiers can't be copied between index changes and thus we can't automatically warm this cache.

How it works...

The document cache configuration is simple. We define it in the `documentCache` XML tag and specify a few parameters that define the document cache's behavior. First of all, the `class` parameter tells Solr which Java class should be used for implementation. In our example, we use `solr.LRUCache` because we will be adding more information into the cache than we will be fetching from it. When you see that you are getting more information than you add, consider using `solr.FastLRUCache`. The next parameter tells Solr the maximum size of the cache (the `size` parameter). As the Solr wiki says, we should always set this value to more than the maximum number of results returned by the query multiplied by the maximum concurrent queries than we think will be sent to the Solr instance. This will ensure that we always have enough place in the cache, so that Solr will not have to fetch the data from the index multiple times during a single query.

The last parameter tells Solr the initial size of the cache (the `initialSize` parameter). I tend to set it to the same value as the `size` parameter to ensure that Solr won't be wasting its resources on cache resizing.

 The more fields marked as stored in the index structure, the higher the memory usage of this cache will be.

Please remember that when using the values shown in this example, you must always observe your Solr instance and act when you see that your cache is acting in the wrong way. Remember that having a very large cache with very low hit rate can be worse than having no cache at all.

Along with everything else, you should pay attention to your cache usage as your Solr instances work. If you see evictions, then this may be a signal that your caches are too small. If you have a very poor hit rate, then it's sometimes better to turn the cache off. Cache setup is one of those things in Apache Solr that is very dependent on your data, queries, and users; so I'll repeat once again—keep an eye on your caches and don't be afraid to react and change them.

Configuring the query result cache

The major Solr role in a typical e-commerce website is handling user queries. Of course, users of the site can type multiple queries in the **Search** box and we can't easily predict how many unique queries there may be. But, using the logs that Solr gives us, we can check how many different queries there were in the last day, week, month, or year. Using this information, we can configure the query result cache to suit our needs in the most optimal way, and this recipe will show you how to do it.

How to do it...

For the purpose of this recipe, let's assume that one Solr instance of our e-commerce website is handling about 10 to 15 queries per second. Each query can be sorted by four different fields (the user can choose by which field). The user can also choose the order of sort. By analyzing the logs for the past three months, we know that there are about 2000 unique queries that users tend to type in the search box of our application. We also noticed that our users don't usually use the paging mechanism.

On the basis of this information, we configure our query results cache as follows (add this code to the `solrconfig.xml` configuration file):

```
<queryResultCache
    class="solr.LRUCache"
    size="16000"
    initialSize="16000"
    autowarmCount="4000"/>
```

How it works...

Adding the query result cache to the `solrconfig.xml` file is a simple task. We define it in the `queryResultCache` XML tag and specify a few parameters that define the query result's cache behavior. First of all, the `class` parameter tells Solr which Java class should be used for implementation. In our example, we use `solr.LRUCache` because we will be adding more information into the cache than we will fetching from it. When you see that you are get more information than you add, consider using `solr.FastLRUCache`. The next parameter tells Solr about the maximum size of the cache (the `size` parameter). This cache should be able to store the ordered identifiers of the objects that were returned by the query with its `sort` parameter and the range of documents requested. This means that we should take the number of unique queries, multiply it by the number of `sort` parameters and the number of possible orders of sort. So in our example, the size should be at least the result of the following equation:

```
size = 2000 * 4 * 2
```

In our case, it is `16,000`.

I tend to set the initial size of this cache to the maximum size; so in our case, I set the `initialSize` parameter to a value of `16000`. This is done to avoid the resizing of the cache.

The last parameter (`autowarmCount`) says how many entries should be copied when Solr invalidates caches (for example, after a `commit` operation). I tend to set this parameter to a quarter of the maximum size of the cache. This is done because I don't want the caches to be warming for too long. However, please remember that the auto-warming time depends on your deployment and the `autowarmCount` parameter should be adjusted if needed.

Please remember that when using the values shown in this example, you must always observe your Solr instance and act when you see that your cache is acting in the wrong way.

Along with everything else, you should pay attention to your cache usage as your Solr instances work. If you see evictions, then this may be a signal that your caches are too small. If you have a very poor hit rate, then it's sometimes better to turn the cache off. Cache setup is one of those things in Apache Solr that is very dependent on your data, queries, and users; so I'll repeat once again—keep an eye on your caches and don't be afraid to react and change them.

Configuring the filter cache

Almost every client of mine who uses Solr, tends to forget or simply doesn't know how to use filter queries or simply filters. People tend to add another clause with a logical operator to the main query—they forget how efficient filters can be, at least when used wisely. And that's why whenever I can, I tell people using Solr to use filter queries. But when using filter queries, it is nice to know how to set up a cache that is responsible for holding the filters results – the **filter cache**. This recipe will show you how to properly set up the filter cache.

How to do it...

For the purpose of this recipe, let's assume that we have a single Solr slave instance to handle all the queries coming from the application. We took the logs from the last three months and analyzed them. From this we know, that our queries are making about 2000 different filter queries. By getting this information, we can set up the filter cache for our instance. This configuration should look similar to the following code snippet (add this code to the `solrconfig.xml` configuration file):

```
<filterCache
    class="solr.FastLRUCache"
    size="2000"
    initialSize="2000"
    autowarmCount="1000"/>
```

That's it. Now let's see what those values mean.

How it works...

As you may have noticed, adding the filter cache to the `solrconfig.xml` file is a simple task; you just need to know how many unique filters your Solr instance is receiving. We define this in the `filterCache` XML tag and specify a few parameters that define the query result cache behavior. First of all, the `class` parameter tells Solr which Java class should be used for implementation. In our example, we use `solr.LRUCache` because we will be adding more information into the cache than we will be fetching from it. When you see that you are getting more information than you add, consider using `solr.FastLRUCache`.

The next parameter tells Solr the maximum size of the cache (the `size` parameter). In our case, we said that we have about 2000 unique filters and we set the maximum size to that value. This is done because each entry of the filter cache stores the unordered sets of Solr document identifiers that match the given filter. In this way, after the first use of the filter, Solr can use the filter cache to apply filtering and thus save the I/O operations.

The next parameter – `initialSize` tells Solr about the initial size of the filter cache. I tend to set it's value to the same as that of the size parameter to avoid cache resizing. So in our example, we set it to the value of `2000`.

The last parameter (`autowarmCount`) says how many entries should be copied when Solr invalidates caches (for example, after a `commit` operation). I tend to set this parameter to a quarter of the maximum size of the cache. This is done because I don't want the caches to be warming for too long. However, please remember that the auto-warming time depends on your deployment and the `autowarmCount` parameter should be adjusted if needed.

Please remember that when using the values shown in this example, you must always observe your Solr instance and act when you see that your cache is acting in the wrong way.

Along with everything, you should pay attention to your cache usage as your Solr instances work. If you see evictions, then this may be a signal that your caches are too small. If you have a very poor hit rate, then it's sometimes better to turn the cache off. Cache setup is one of those things in Apache Solr that is very dependent on your data, queries, and users; so I'll repeat once again—keep an eye on your caches and don't be afraid to react and change them. For example, take a look at the following screenshot that shows that the filter cache is probably too small, because the evictions are happening (this is a screenshot of the Solr administration panel):

Improving Solr performance right after the startup or commit operation

Anyone with some experience with Solr would have noticed that – right after the startup, Solr doesn't have as much of an improved query performance as after running a while. This happens because Solr doesn't have any information stored in caches, the I/O is not optimized, and so on. Can we do something about it? Of course we can, and this recipe will show you how to do it.

How to do it...

The following steps will explain how we can enhance Solr performance right after the startup or commit operation:

1. First of all, we need to identify the most common and the heaviest queries that we send to Solr. I have two ways of doing this—first of all, I analyze the logs that Solr produces and see how queries behave. I tend to choose those queries that are run often and those that run slowly in my opinion. The second way of choosing the right queries is by analyzing the application that use Solr and seeing what queries they produce, which queries will be the most crucial, and so on. Based on my experience, the log-based approach is usually much faster and can be done using self-written scripts.

   But let's assume that we have identified the following queries as good candidates:

   ```
   q=cats&fq=category:1&sort=title+desc,value+desc,score+desc
   q=cars&fq=category:2&sort=title+desc
   q=harry&fq=category:4&sort=score+desc
   ```

2. What we will do next is just add the so called warming queries to the `solrconfig.xml` file. So the `listener` XML tag definition in the `solrconfig.xml` file should look similar to the following code snippet:

   ```
   <listener event="firstSearcher"
     class="solr.QuerySenderListener">
     <arr name="queries">
       <lst>
         <str name="q">cats</str>
         <str name="fq">category:1</str>
         <str name="sort">
           title desc,value desc,score desc
         </str>
         <str name="start">0</str>
   ```

```
            <str name="rows">20</str>
        </lst>
        <lst>
          <str name="q">cars</str>
          <str name="fq">category:2</str>
          <str name="sort">title desc</str>
          <str name="start">0</str>
          <str name="rows">20</str>
        </lst>
        <lst>
          <str name="q">harry</str>
          <str name="fq">category:4</str>
          <str name="sort">score desc</str>
          <str name="start">0</str>
          <str name="rows">20</str>
        </lst>
      </arr>
    </listener>
```

Basically we added the so-called warming queries to the startup of Solr. Now let's see how it works.

How it works...

By adding the preceding fragment of configuration to the `solrconfig.xml` file, we told Solr that we want it to run those queries whenever a `firstSearcher` event occurs. The `firstSearcher` event is fired whenever a new searcher object is prepared and there is no searcher object available in the memory. So basically, the `firstSearcher` event occurs right after Solr startup.

So what happens after Solr startup? After adding the preceding fragment, Solr runs each of the defined queries. By doing this, the caches get populated with the entries that are significant for the queries that we identified. This means that if we did the job right, we have Solr configured and ready to handle the most common and heaviest queries right after its startup.

Let's just go over what all the configuration options mean. The warm up queries are always defined under the `listener` XML tag. The `event` parameter tells Solr what event should trigger the queries; in our case, it is `firstSearcher`. The `class` parameter is the Java class that implements the listener mechanism. Next, we have an array of queries that are bound together by the `array` tag with the `name="queries"` parameter. Each of the warming queries is defined as a list of parameters that are grouped by the `lst` tag.

There's more...

There is one more thing that I would like to mention (in the following section).

Improving Solr performance after commit operations

If you are interested in improving the performance of your Solr instance, you should also look at the `newSearcher` event. This event occurs whenever a `commit` operation is performed by Solr (for example, after replication). Assuming that we identified the same queries as before as good candidates to warm the caches, we should add the following entries to the `solrconfig.xml` file:

```
<listener event="newSearcher" class="solr.QuerySenderListener">
  <arr name="queries">
    <lst>
      <str name="q">cats</str>
      <str name="fq">category:1</str>
      <str name="sort">title desc,value desc,score desc</str>
      <str name="start">0</str>
      <str name="rows">20</str>
    </lst>
    <lst>
      <str name="q">cars</str>
      <str name="fq">category:2</str>
      <str name="sort">title desc</str>
      <str name="start">0</str>
      <str name="rows">20</str>
    </lst>
    <lst>
      <str name="q">harry</str>
      <str name="fq">category:4</str>
      <str name="sort">score desc</str>
      <str name="start">0</str>
      <str name="rows">20</str>
    </lst>
  </arr>
</listener>
```

Please remember that the warming queries are especially important for the caches that can't be automatically warmed.

Caching whole result pages

Imagine a situation where you have an e-commerce library and your data changes rarely. What can you do to take away the stress on your search servers? The first thing that comes to mind is caching; for example, HTTP caching. And yes, that is a good point. But do we have to set up external caches prior to Solr, or can we tell Solr to use its own caching mechanism? We can use Solr to cache whole result pages and this recipe will show you how to do it.

Getting ready

Before you continue to read this recipe, it would be nice for you to know some basics about the HTTP cache headers. To learn something about it, please refer to the RFC document that can be found on the W3 site at `http://www.w3.org/Protocols/rfc2616/rfc2616-sec13.html`.

How to do it...

So let's configure the HTTP cache. To do this, we need to configure the Solr request dispatcher. Let's assume that our index changes every 60 minutes.

1. Let's start by replacing the request dispatcher definition in the `solrconfig.xml` file with the following content:

   ```
   <requestDispatcher handleSelect="true">
     <httpCaching lastModifiedFrom="openTime"
       etagSeed="Solr">
       <cacheControl>max-age=3600, public</cacheControl>
     </httpCaching>
   </requestDispatcher>
   ```

2. Now, let's try sending a query similar to the following to see the HTTP headers:

   ```
   http://localhost:8983/solr/select?q=book
   ```

   We get the following HTTP headers:

   ```
   HTTP/1.1 200 OK
   Cache-Control: max-age=3600, public
   Expires: Tue, 11 Sep 2012 16:44:56 GMT
   Last-Modified: Tue, 11 Sep 2012 15:43:24 GMT
   ETag: "YzAwMDAwMDAwMDAwMDAwMFNvbHI="
   Content-Type: application/xml; charset=UTF-8
   Transfer-Encoding: chunked
   ```

   From this we can tell that cache works.

How it works...

The cache definition is defined inside the `requestDispatcher` XML tag. The `handleSelect="true"` attribute describes error handling and it should be set to `true`. Then, we see the `httpCaching` tag (notice the lack of the `<httpCaching never304="true">` XML tag), which actually configures the HTTP caching in Solr. The `lastModifiedFrom="openTime"` attribute defines that the last modified HTTP header will be relative to when the current searcher object was opened (for example, relative to the last replication execution date). You can also set this parameter value to `dirLastMod` to be relative to when the physical index was modified. Next, we have the `eTagSeed` attribute, which is responsible for generating the ETag HTTP cache header.

The next configuration tag is the `cacheControl` tag, which can be used to specify the generation of the cache control HTTP headers. In our example, adding the `max-age=3600` parameter tells Solr that it should generate an additional HTTP cache header, which will confirm that the cache is valid for a maximum of one hour. The `public` directive means that the response can be cached by any cache type.

As you can see from the response, the headers that we got as a part of the results returned by Solr tell us that we got what we wanted.

Improving faceting performance for low cardinality fields

Let's assume that our data which we use to calculate faceting can be considered to have low distinct values. For example, we have an e-commerce shop with millions of products – clothes. Each document in our index, apart from name and price, is also described by additional information – target size. So, we have values such as XS, S, M, L, XL, and XXL (that is, six distinct values), and each document can only be described with a single value. In addition to this, we run field faceting on that information and it doesn't work fast by default. This recipe will show you how to change that.

How to do it...

The following steps will explain how we can improve faceting performance for low cardinality fields:

1. Let's begin with the following index structure (add the following entries to your `schema.xml` fields section):

    ```
    <field name="id " type="string" indexed="true"
      stored="true" required="true" />
    ```

```
<field name="name " type="text " indexed="true"
  stored="true" />
<field name="size" type="string" indexed="true"
  stored="true" />
```

The `size` field is the one in which we store our XS, S, M, L, XL, and XXL values (remember: one value per document).

2. Assuming that our user typed `black skirt` into the **Search** box, our query would look similar to the following code snippet:

    ```
    q=name:(black+skirt)&q.op=AND&facet=true&facet.field=size
    ```

    Assuming that the query is matching one-fourth of our documents, we can expect the query to be executing longer than usual. This is because the default faceting calculation is optimized for fields that have many unique values in the index and we have the opposite—we have many documents but few unique terms.

3. In order to speed up faceting in our case, let's add the `facet.method=enum` parameter to our query, so that it looks similar to the following code snippet:

    ```
    q=name:(black+skirt)&q.op=AND&facet=true&facet.field=size&facet.
    method=enum
    ```

If you measure the performance before and after the change you will notice the difference; let's discuss why.

How it works...

Let's take a look at the query—we search for the given words in the `name` field using the AND logical operator (`q.op` parameter). As our requirements state, we also run faceting on the `size` field (`facet=true` and `facet.field=size` parameters).

We know that our fields have only six distinct values, and we also assumed that our queries can return vast amount of documents. To handle such faceting calculation faster than the default method, we decided to use the `enum` method of facet calculation. The default faceting calculation method (`facet.method=fc`) iterates over documents that match the query and sums the terms that appear in the field that we are calculating faceting on. The `enum` method does the other thing – it enumerates all the terms in the field that we want to calculate faceting on, and intersects the documents that match the query with the documents that match the enumerated terms. In this way, less time and processing is needed to calculate field faceting for low cardinality fields, such as size in our case, and thus we see faster query execution.

It is good to know that for field faceting on Boolean fields, Solr uses the `enum` faceting method by default.

There's more...

You can also use the faceting method for each field you perform faceting upon.

Specifying faceting method per field

If you have multiple fields on which you run faceting, then you may only want to change the method for one of them (or more than one, but not all). To do that, instead of adding the `facet.method=enum` parameter, you can add the `facet.FIELD_NAME.method=enum` parameter for each field whose faceting calculation method you would want to change. For example, if you would like to change the faceting method for the `size` field, you can add the following parameter:

```
facet.size.method=enum
```

What to do when Solr slows down during indexing

One of the most common problems when indexing a vast amount of data is the indexing time. Some of the problems with indexing time are not easily resolvable, but others are. Imagine that you need to index about 300,000 documents that are in a single XML file. You run the `post.sh` bash script that is provided with Solr and you wait, wait, and wait. Something is wrong – when you index 10,000 documents you need about a minute, but now you are waiting about an hour and the `commit` operation didn't take place. Is there something we can do to speed it up? Sure, and this recipe will tell you how to.

How to do it...

The solution to the situation is very simple – just add the `commit` operation every now and then. But as you may have noticed, I mentioned that our data is written in a single XML file. So, how do we add the `commit` operation to that kind of data? Send it in parallel to the indexing process? No, we need to enable the auto commit mechanism. To do that, let's modify the `solrconfig.xml` file, and change the update handler definition to the following one:

```
<updateHandler class="solr.DirectUpdateHandler2">
  <autoCommit>
    <maxTime>60000</maxTime>
    <openSearcher>true</openSearcher>
  </autoCommit>
</updateHandler>
```

If you start the indexing described in the indexing process, you will notice that a `commit` command will be sent once a minute while the indexing process is takes place. Now, let's see how it works.

How it works...

Solr tends to slow down the indexing process when indexing a vast amount of data without the commit commands being sent once in a while. This behavior is completely understandable and is bound to the memory and how much of it Solr can use.

We can avoid the slowing down behavior by adding the `commit` command after the set amount of time or set amount of data. In this recipe, we choose the first approach.

We assumed that it would be good to send the `commit` command once every minute. So we add the `<autoCommit>` section with the `<maxTime>` XML tag set to a value of `60000`. This value is specified in milliseconds. We've also specified that we want the search to be reopened after the commit and thus the data available for search (the `<openSearcher>true</openSearcher>` option). If you would only like to write the data to the index and not have it available for search, just change the `<openSearcher>true</openSearcher>` option to `false`. That's all we need to do. After this change, Solr will send a `commit` command after every minute passes during the indexing operation, and we don't have to worry that Solr indexing speed will decrease over time.

There's more...

There are two more things about automatic commits that should be mentioned.

Commit after a set amount of documents

Sometimes, there is a need to rely not on the time between commit operations, but on the amount of documents that were indexed. If this is the case, we can choose to automatically send the `commit` command after a set amount of documents are processed. To do this, we add the `<maxDocs>` XML tag with the appropriate amount. For example, if we want to send the `commit` command after every 50000 documents, the update handler configuration should look similar to the following code snippet:

```
<updateHandler class="solr.DirectUpdateHandler2">
  <autoCommit>
    <maxDocs>50000</maxDocs>
    <openSearcher>true</openSearcher>
  </autoCommit>
</updateHandler>
```

Commit within a set amount of time

There may be situations when you want some of the document to be committed faster than the auto commit settings. In order to do that, you can add the `commitWithin` attribute to the `<add>` tag of your data XML time. This attribute will tell Solr to commit the documents within the specified time (specified in milliseconds). For example, if we want the portion of documents to be indexed within 100 milliseconds, our data file would look similar to the following code snippet:

```
<add commitWithin="100">
  <doc>
    <field name="id">1</field>
    <field name="title">Book 1</field>
  </doc>
</add>
```

Analyzing query performance

Somewhere along the experience with Apache Solr (and not only Solr), you'll end up at a point where some of your queries are not running as you would like them to run – some of them are just slow. Of course, such a situation is not desirable and we have to do something to make those queries run faster. But how do we know which part of the query is the one we should look at ? This recipe will tell you what information you can get from Solr.

How to do it...

The following steps will help you analyze query performance:

1. Let's start with the assumption that we have a query that has parts that are not as fast as we would like it to be. The query is as follows:

   ```
   http://localhost:8983/solr/select?q=metal&facet=true&facet.
   field=date&facet.query=from:[10+TO+2000]
   ```

2. In order to get the information we want, we need to add the `debugQuery=true` parameter to our query, so that it looks similar to the following code snippet:

   `http://localhost:8983/solr/select?q=metal&facet=true&facet.field=date&facet.query=from:[10+TO+2000]&debugQuery=true`

   The response from Solr is as follows (I've cut some parts of the response, because it is quite large and we are only interested in the last section):

   ```
   <?xml version="1.0" encoding="UTF-8"?>
     <response>
       <lst name="responseHeader">
         <int name="status">0</int>
         <int name="QTime">427</int>
   ```

```
    </lst>
    <result name="response" numFound="61553" start="0">
      <doc>
(...)
      </doc>
    </result>
    <lst name="facet_counts">
      <lst name="facet_queries">
        <int name="from:[10 TO 2000]">50820</int>
      </lst>
      <lst name="facet_fields">
        <lst name="date">
          <int name="0">61553</int>
        </lst>
      </lst>
      <lst name="facet_dates"/>
      <lst name="facet_ranges"/>
    </lst>
    <lst name="debug">
      <str name="rawquerystring">metal</str>
      <str name="querystring">metal</str>
      <str name="parsedquery">Body:metal</str>
      <str name="parsedquery_toString">Body:metal</str>
      <lst name="explain">
(...)
      </lst>
      <str name="QParser">LuceneQParser</str>
      <lst name="timing">
        <double name="time">426.0</double>
        <lst name="prepare">
          <double name="time">15.0</double>
          <lst name="org.apache.solr
            .handler.component.QueryComponent">
            <double name="time">14.0</double>
          </lst>
          <lst name="org.apache.
            solr.handler.component.FacetComponent">
            <double name="time">0.0</double>
          </lst>
          <lst name="org.apache.solr
            .handler.component.MoreLikeThisComponent">
            <double name="time">0.0</double>
          </lst>
          <lst name="org.apache.solr
            .handler.component.HighlightComponent">
            <double name="time">0.0</double>
          </lst>
```

```
        <lst name="org.apache.solr
          .handler.component.StatsComponent">
          <double name="time">0.0</double>
        </lst>
        <lst name="org.apache.solr
          .handler.component.DebugComponent">
          <double name="time">0.0</double>
        </lst>
      </lst>
      <lst name="process">
        <double name="time">411.0</double>
        <lst name="org.apache.solr
          .handler.component.QueryComponent">
          <double name="time">43.0</double>
        </lst>
        <lst name="org.apache.solr
          .handler.component.FacetComponent">
          <double name="time">360.0</double>
        </lst>
        <lst name="org.apache.solr
          .handler.component.MoreLikeThisComponent">
          <double name="time">0.0</double>
        </lst>
        <lst name="org.apache.solr
          .handler.component.HighlightComponent">
          <double name="time">0.0</double>
        </lst>
          <lst name="org.apache.solr
            .handler.component.StatsComponent">
            <double name="time">0.0</double>
          </lst>
          <lst name="org.apache.solr
            .handler.component.DebugComponent">
            <double name="time">8.0</double>
          </lst>
        </lst>
      </lst>
    </lst>
  </response>
```

As you can see in the preceding response, there is some information about query time. So let's see what it means.

How it works...

Let's not concentrate on the query, because it is only an example that allows us to discuss what we want to achieve. We've added a single parameter to the query – `debugQuery=true`. This parameter turns on the `debug` mode in Solr, as you can see in the response.

The `debug` mode is divided into few categories. All these categories are nested inside the `<lst name="debug">` XML tag. The first few entries let you see how the query parser parses your query and how it is passed to Lucene, but it's beyond the scope of this chapter to explain this. Similar information is nested inside the `<lst name="explain">` XML tag; we will talk about it in *Chapter 9, Dealing with Problems*.

What we are interested in is the information nested inside the `<lst name="timing">` XML tag. The first information you see under this tag is the total time of your query, which in our case is 426 milliseconds (`<double name="time">426.0</double>`). We have the following two lists:

- ▶ `<lst name="prepare">` holds information regarding the query preparation time
- ▶ `<lst name="process">` holds information regarding the query execution time

You can see that nested inside those lists are components and their time.

The `prepare` list tells us how much time each component spends during the query preparation phase. For example, we can see that `org.apache.solr.handler.component.QueryComponent` spent 14.0 milliseconds during preparation time.

The process list tells us how much time was spent during the query processing phase, which is the phase that is usually the longest one, because of all the computation and I/O operations needed to execute the query. You can see that in our case, there were three components that were working for longer than 0 milliseconds. The last one (`org.apache.solr.handler.component.DebugComponent`) is the component that we added with the `query` parameter, and we can skip it as it won't be used during production queries. The second component, which was running for 43 milliseconds, was `org.apache.solr.handler.component.QueryComponent`, which is responsible for parsing the query and running it. It still takes about 10 percent time of the whole query, which is not what we are looking for. The component that took the most amount of the query execution time is `org.apache.solr.handler.component.FacetComponent`; it was working for 360 milliseconds, so for almost 90 percent of the query execution time.

As you can see, with the use of the `debugQuery` parameter, we identified which part of the query is problematic and we can start optimizing it; But it's beyond the scope of this recipe.

Avoiding filter caching

Imagine that some of the filters you use in your queries are not good candidates for caching. You may wonder why, for example, those filters have a date and time with seconds or are spatial filters scattered all over the world. Such filters are quite unique and when added to the cache, their entries can't be reused much. Thus they are more or less useless. Caching such filters is a waste of memory and CPU cycles. Is there something you can do to avoid filter queries caching? Yes, there is a way and this recipe will show you how to do it.

How to do it...

Let's assume we have the following query being used to get the information we need:

```
q=solr+cookbook&fq=category:books&fq=date:2012-06-12T13:22:12Z
```

The filter query we don't want to cache is the one filtering our documents on the basis of the `date` field. Of course, we still want the filtering to be done. In order to turn off caching, we need to add `{!cache=false}` to our filter with the `date` field, so that our query should look similar to the following code snippet:

```
q=solr+cookbook&fq=category:books&fq={!cache=false}date:2012-06-
12T13:22:12Z
```

Now let's take a look at how this works.

How it works...

The first query is very simple; we just search for the words `solr cookbook` and we want the result set to be narrowed in the `books` category. We also want to narrow the results further to only those that have `2012-06-12T13:22:12Z` in the `date` field.

As you can imagine, if we have many filters with such dates as the one in the query, the filter cache can be filled very fast. In addition to this, if you don't reuse the same value for that field, the entry in the field cache becomes pretty useless. That's why, by adding the `{!cache=false}` part to the filter query, we tell Solr that we don't want the filter query results to be put into the filter cache. With such an approach we won't pollute the filter cache and thus save some CPU cycles and memory. There is one more thing – the filters that are not cached will be executed in parallel with the query, so this may be an improvement to your query execution time.

Controlling the order of execution of filter queries

If you use filter queries extensively, which isn't a bad thing at all, you may be wondering if there is something you can do to improve the execution time of some of your filter queries. For example, if you have some filter queries that use heavy function queries, you may want to have them executed only on the documents that passed all the other filters. Let's see how we can do this.

Getting ready

Before continuing reading please read the *Avoiding filter caching* recipe in this chapter.

How to do it...

The following steps will explain how we can control the order of execution of filter queries:

1. Let's assume we have the following query being used to get the information we need:

    ```
    q=solr+cookbook&fq=category:books&fq={!frange l=10 u=100}log(sum(s
    qrt(popularity),100))&fq={!frange l=0 u=10}if(exists(price_a),sum(
    0,price_a),sum(0,price))
    ```

2. For the purpose of this recipe, let's also assume that `fq={!frange l=10 u=100}` `log(sum(sqrt(popularity),100))` and `fq={!frange l=0 u=10}if(exis` `ts(price_a),sum(0,price_a),sum(0,price))` are the filter queries that are heavy and we would like those filters to be executed as the previous ones. We would also like the second filter to execute only on the documents that were narrowed by other filters. In order to do this, we need to modify our query so that it looks similar to the following code snippet:

    ```
    q=solr+cookbook&fq=category:books&fq={!frange l=10 u=100
    cache=false cost=50}log(sum(sqrt(popularity),100))&fq={!frange l=0
    u=10 cache=false cost=150}if(exists(price_promotion),sum(0,price_
    promotion),sum(0,price))
    ```

As you can see, we've added other two attributes: `cache=false` and `cost` having values as `50` and `150`. Let's see what they mean.

How it works...

As you can see, we search for the words `solr cookbook` in the first query and we want the result set to be narrowed by book category. We also want the documents to be narrowed to only those that have a value of the `log(sum(sqrt(popularity),100))` function between 10 and 100. In addition to this, the last filter query specifies that we want our documents to be filtered to only those that have a `price_promotion` field (`price` if `price_promotion` isn't filled) value between 0 and 10.

Our requirements are such that the second filter query (the one with `log` function query) should be executed after the `fq=category:books` filter query and the last filter should be executed in the end, only on the documents narrowed by other filters. To do this, we set those two filters to not cache and we introduced the `cost` parameter. The `cost` parameter in filter queries specifies the order in which non-cached filter queries are executed; the higher the cost value, the later the filter query will be executed. So our second filter (the one with `cost=50`) should be executed after the `fq=category:books` filter query and the last filter query (the one with `cost=150`) are executed. In addition to this, because the cost of the second non-cached filter query is higher or equal to 100, this filter will be executed only on the documents that matched the main query and all the other filters. So our requirements have been completed.

Forgive me, but I have to say it once again—please remember that the `cost` attribute only works when the filter query is not cached.

Improving the performance of numerical range queries

Let's assume we have the Apache Solr 4.0 deployment where we use range queries. Some of those are run against string fields, while others are run against numerical fields. Using different techniques, we identified that our numerical range queries execute slower than we would like. The usual question arises – is there something that we can do ? Of course, and this recipe will show you what.

How to do it...

The following steps will explain how we can control the order of execution of numerical range queries:

1. Let's begin with the definition of a field that we use to run our numerical range queries:

   ```
   <field name="price" type="float" indexed="true" stored="true"/>
   ```

2. The second step is to define the float field type:

    ```
    <fieldType name="float" class="solr.TrieFloatField"
    precisionStep="8" positionIncrementGap="0"/>
    ```

3. Now the usual query that is run against the preceding field is as follows:

    ```
    q=*:*&fq=price:[10.0+TO+59.00]&facet=true&facet.field=price
    ```

4. In order to have your numerical range queries performance improved, there is just a single thing you need to do – decrease the `precisionStep` attribute of the `float` field type; for example, from `8` to `4`. So, our field type definition would look similar to the following code snippet:

    ```
    <fieldType name="float" class="solr.TrieFloatField"
    precisionStep="4" positionIncrementGap="0"/>
    ```

    After the preceding change, you will have to re-index your data and your numerical queries should be run faster. How faster, depends on your setup. Now let's take a look at how it works.

How it works...

As you can see, in the preceding examples, we used a simple float-based field to run numerical range queries. Before the changes, we specified `precisionStep` on our field type as `8`. This attribute (specified in bits) tells Lucene (which Solr is built on top of) how many tokens should be indexed for a single value in such a field. Smaller `precisionStep` values (when `precisionStep` > 0) will lead to more tokens being generated by a single value and thus make range queries faster. Because of this, when we decreased the `precisionStep` value from `8` to `4`, we saw a performance increase.

However, please remember that decreasing the `precisionStep` value will lead to slightly larger indices. Also, setting the `precisionStep` value to `0` turns off indexing of multiple tokens per value, so don't use that value if you want your range queries to perform faster.

7
In the Cloud

In this chapter we will cover:

- ▶ Creating a new SolrCloud cluster
- ▶ Setting up two collections inside a single cluster
- ▶ Managing your SolrCloud cluster
- ▶ Understanding the SolrCloud cluster administration GUI
- ▶ Distributed indexing and searching
- ▶ Increasing the number of replicas on an already live cluster
- ▶ Stopping automatic document distribution among shards

Introduction

As you know, Apache Solr 4.0 introduced the new SolrCloud feature that allows us to use distributed indexing and searching on a full scale. We can have automatic index distribution across multiple machines, without having to think about doing it in our application. In this chapter, we'll learn how to manage our SolrCloud instances, how to increase the number of replicas, and have multiple collections inside the same cluster.

Creating a new SolrCloud cluster

Imagine a situation where one day you have to set up a distributed cluster with the use of Solr. The amount of data is just too much for a single server to handle. Of course, only you can set up a second server or go for another master database with another set of data. But before Solr 4.0, you would have to take care of the data distribution yourself. In addition to this, you would also have to take care of setting up replication, thinking about data duplication, and so on. You don't have to do this now because Solr 4.0 can do it for you. Let's see how.

Getting ready

Before continuing, I advise you to read the *Installing standalone ZooKeeper* recipe in *Chapter 1, Apache Solr Configuration*. This recipe shows how to set up a **ZooKeeper cluster** ready for production use. However, if you already have ZooKeeper running, you can skip that recipe.

How to do it...

Let's assume we want to create a cluster that will have four Solr servers. We would also like to have our data divided between four Solr servers in such a way that we would have the original data sharded to two machines. In addition to this we would also have a copy of each shard available, in case something happens with one of the Solr instances. I also assume that we already have our ZooKeeper cluster setup, ready, and available at the `192.168.0.10` address on port `9983`.

1. Let's start with populating our cluster configuration into the ZooKeeper cluster. In order to do this, you need to run the following command:

   ```
   java -Dbootstrap_confdir=./solr/collection1/conf -Dcollection.
   configName=twoShardsTwoReplicasConf -DnumShards=2
   -DzkHost=192.168.0.10:9983 -jar start.jar
   ```

2. Now that we have our configuration populated, let's start the second node with the following command:

   ```
   java -DzkHost=192.168.0.10:9983 -jar start.jar
   ```

3. We now have our two shards created and want to create replicas. This is very simple since we have already created the configuration. We just need to start two additional servers with the following command run on each of them:

   ```
   java -DzkHost=192.168.0.10:9983 -jar start.jar
   ```

If you look at the cloud configuration of the Solr administration panel, you will see that you have a cluster that has four nodes, where the first two nodes act as leaders for the shards and the other two nodes act as their replicas. You can start indexing your data to one of the servers now, and Solr will take care of data distribution and will also automatically copy the data to the replicas. Let's see how this works.

How it works...

What we need to do first is send all the configuration files to ZooKeeper in order for the Solr servers to be able to fetch it from there. That's why, when running the first server (only during the first start of it), we add the `-Dboostrap_confdir` and `-Dcollection.configName` parameters. The first parameter specifies the location of the directory with the configuration files that we would like to put into ZooKeeper. The second parameter specifies the name of your configuration. During the first start, we also need to specify the number of shards that should be available in our cluster, and in this example we set it to 2 (the `-DnumShards` parameter). The `-DzkHost` parameter is used to tell Solr about the location and the port used by the Zookeeper cluster.

As you can see, all the other commands are similar to the ones you used while running the Solr instances. The only difference is that we specify one additional parameter, `-DzkHost`, which tells Solr where to look for the ZooKeeper server on the cluster.

When setting up the SolrCloud cluster, please remember to choose the number of shards wisely, because you can't change that for your existing cluster, at least not right now. You can add replicas to an already created cluster, but the number of shards will remain constant.

There's more...

There is one more thing that I would like to mention – the possibility of running a ZooKeeper server embedded into Apache Solr 4.0.

Starting the embedded ZooKeeper server

You can also start an embedded ZooKeeper server shipped with Solr for your test environment. In order to do this, you should pass the `-DzkRun` parameter instead of `-DzkHost=192.168.0.10:9983`, but only in the command that sends our configuration to the ZooKeeper cluster. So the final command should look similar to the following code snippet:

```
java -Dboostrap_confdir=./solr/collection1/conf -Dcollection.configName
=twoShardsTwoReplicasConf -DzkHost=192.168.0.10:9983 -DnumShards=2 -jar
start.jar
```

Setting up two collections inside a single cluster

Imagine that you would like to have more than a single collection inside the same Apache Solr 4.0 cluster. For example, you would like to store books in one collection and users in the second one. SolrCloud allows that, and this recipe will show you how to do it.

Getting ready

Before continuing, I advise you to read the *Installing standalone ZooKeeper* recipe in *Chapter 1, Apache Solr Configuration*, because this recipe assumes that we already have ZooKeeper up and running. We assume that ZooKeeper is running on localhost and is listening on port `2181`.

How to do it...

1. Since we want to start a new SolrCloud cluster that doesn't have any collections defined, we should start with the `solr.xml` file. On both instances of Solr, the `solr.xml` file should look similar to the following code snippet:

```xml
<?xml version="1.0" encoding="UTF-8" ?>
<solr persistent="true">
  <cores adminPath="/admin/cores"
    defaultCoreName="collection1" host="${host:}"
    hostPort="${jetty.port:}"
    hostContext="${hostContext:}"
    zkClientTimeout="${zkClientTimeout:15000}">
  </cores>
</solr>
```

2. Let's assume that we have two SolrCloud instances that form a cluster, both running on the same physical server, one on port `8983` and the second one on `9983`. They are started with the following commands:

```
java -Djetty.port=8983 -DzkHost=localhost:2181 -jar start.jar
java -Djetty.port=9983 -DzkHost=localhost:2181 -jar start.jar
```

3. Now, we need to add the configuration files, which we want to create collections with, to ZooKeeper. Let's assume that we have all the configuration files stored in `/usr/share/config/books/conf` for the books collection, and the configuration files for the users collection stored in `/usr/share/config/users/conf`. To send these files to ZooKeeper, we should run the following commands from our `$SOLR_HOME` directory:

```
cloud-scripts/zkcli.sh -cmdupconfig -zkhost localhost:2181
-confdir /usr/share/config/books/conf -confnamebookscollection
```

And:

```
cloud-scripts/zkcli.sh -cmdupconfig -zkhost localhost:2181
-confdir /usr/share/config/users/conf -confnameuserscollection
```

4. We have pushed our configurations into the ZooKeeper, so we can now create the collections we want. In order to do this, we use the following commands:

```
curl 'http://localhost:8983/solr/admin/collections?action=CREATE&n
ame=bookscollection&numShards=
2&replicationFactor=0'
```

And:

```
curl 'http://localhost:8983/solr/admin/collections?action=CREATE&n
ame=userscollection&numShards=
2&replicationFactor=0'
```

5. Now, just to test if everything went well, we will query the newly created collections as follows:

```
curl 'http://localhost:8983/solr/bookscollection/select?q=*:*'
```

The response to the preceding command will be as follows:

```xml
<?xml version="1.0" encoding="UTF-8"?>
<response>
  <lst name="responseHeader">
    <int name="status">0</int>
    <int name="QTime">39</int>
    <lst name="params">
    <str name="q">*:*</str>
  </lst>
  </lst>
    <result name="response" numFound="0" start="0"
      maxScore="0.0">
  </result>
</response>
```

As you can see, Solr responded correctly. But as we don't have any data indexed, we got 0 documents.

How it works...

As you can see, our `solr.xml` file on both the instances is the same and it doesn't contain any information about the cores. This is done on purpose, since we want to have a clean cluster – one without any collections present.

The mentioned configuration directories should store all the files (`solrconfig.xml`, `schema.xml`, and `stopwords.txt`) that are needed for your Solr instance to work, if you use one. Please remember this before sending them to ZooKeeper or else Solr will fetch those files from ZooKeeper and create collections using them.

Now, let's look at the most interesting aspect – the scripts used to upload the configuration files to ZooKeeper. We used the `zkcli.sh` script provided with the standard Solr 4.0 distribution and placedit in the `cloud-scripts` directory by default. The first thing is the `cmd` parameter, which specifies what we want to do – in this case `upconfig` means that we want to upload the configuration files. The `zkhost` parameter allows us to specify the host and port of the ZooKeeper instance we want to put the configuration to. `confdir` is one of the most crucial parameters and it specifies the directory in which the Solr configuration files are stored – the ones that should be sent to ZooKeeper (in our case, `/usr/share/config/users/conf` and `/usr/share/config/books/conf`). Finally the last parameter, `confname`, specifies the name of the collection we will use the configuration with.

The command in the fourth step lets us create the actual collection in the cluster. In order to do this, we send a request to the `/admin/collections` handler, which uses the newly introduced `collections` API. We tell Solr that we want to create a new collection (the `action=CREATE` parameter) with the name of `bookscollection` (`name=bookscollection`). Please note that the name specified in the `name` parameter is the same as the `confname` parameter value used during configuration files upload. The last two parameters specify the number of shards and replicas that the collection should be created with. The number of shards is the initial number of cores that will be used to hold the data in the collection (`numShards`). The number of replicas (`replicationFactor`) is the exact number of copies of the shards that can be distributed among many servers, and may increase query throughput and reliability.

Managing your SolrCloud cluster

In addition to creating a new collection with the API exposed by SolrCloud, we are also allowed to use two additional operations. The first is to delete our collection and the second one is to reload the whole collection. Along with the ability to create new collections, we are able to dynamically manage our cluster. This recipe will show you how to use the `delete` and `reload` operations and where they can be useful.

Getting ready

The content of this recipe is based on the *Setting up two collections inside a single cluster* recipe in this chapter. Please read it before continuing.

How to do it...

I assume that we already have two collection deployed on our cluster –`bookscollection` and `userscollection` – the same ones that we configured in the *Setting up two collections inside a single cluster* recipe in this chapter. So our cluster view looks similar to the following screenshot:

1. First, let's delete one of the collections – `userscollection`. To do this, we send the following command:

   ```
   curl 'http://localhost:8983/solr/admin/collections?action=DELETE&n
   ame=userscollection'
   ```

2. Now, let's look at our cluster view once again:

As you can see, the `userscollection` collection was deleted.

3. Now, let's see how the reloading of collections works. In order to test it, let's update the `spellings.txt` file located at `/usr/share/config/books/conf` directory. The original file looks similar to the following code snippet:

```
pizza
history
```

After the update, it will look similar to the following code snippet:

```
after
update
```

4. Now, we need to update the `collection` configuration in ZooKeeper. To do this we use the following command, which is run from our Solr instance's `home` directory:

```
cloud-scripts/zkcli.sh -cmdupconfig -zkhost localhost:2181
-confdir /usr/share/config/books/conf -confnamebookscollection
```

5. Now that we have the updated version of our configuration files to `bookscollection` in ZooKeeper, we can send the `reload` command to Solr:

```
curl 'http://localhost:8983/solr/admin/collections?action=RELOAD&n
ame=bookscollection'
```

6. First, let's check if the Solr administration panel sees the changes in ZooKeeper. To do this, we'll use the tree view of the cloud section and navigate to `/configs/bookscollection/spellings.txt`. We should be able to see something similar to the following screenshot:

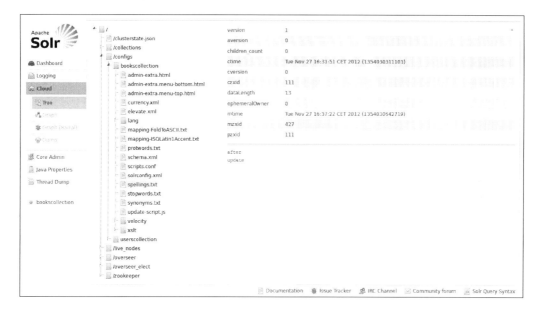

7. In the final check, let's see if Solr itself sees the update. In order to do this we run the following command:

```
curl 'http://localhost:8983/solr/bookscollection/admin/
file?file=spellings.txt'
```

The response of the preceding command would be as follows:

```
after
update
```

So it seems like everything is working as it should. Now let's see how it works.

How it works...

We begin with a cluster that contains two collections. But we want to delete one of them and update the second one. In order to do this we use the `collections` API provided by Solr 4.0.

We start by sending the `delete` action (`action=DELETE`) to the `/solr/admin/` `collections` URL, which is the default address that the `collections` API is available at. In addition to this, we need to provide the name of the collection we want to delete – to do this, we use the `name` parameter with the name of the collection that we want to delete. After sending the command and refreshing the Solr administration panel, we see that the second collection was deleted just as we wanted.

Now, let's discuss the process of updating the second collection. First of all, we've changed the contents of the `spellings.txt` file in order to see how it works. However, be careful when updating collections, because some changes may force you to re-index your data; but let's get back to our update. So after we update the file, we use one of the scripts provided with Solr 4.0 in order to upload all the configuration files that belong to this collection into the ZooKeeper ensemble (if you are not familiar with that command, please see the *Setting up two collections inside a single cluster* recipe, later in this chapter). Now, we needed to tell Solr to reload our collection by sending the `reload` command (`action=RELOAD`) to the same URL as the `delete` command. Of course, just like with the `delete` command, we needed to provide the name of the collection we want to reload using the `name` parameter.

As you can see, on the previous screenshot, the collection was updated at least in the ZooKeeper ensemble. However, we want to be sure that Solr sees those changes, so we use the `/admin/file` handler to get the contents of the `spellings.txt` file. In order to do this, we pass the `file=spellings.txt` parameter to that handler. As you can see, Solr returned the changed contents, so the collection was updated and reloaded successfully.

Understanding the SolrCloud cluster administration GUI

With the release of Solr 4.0, we've got the ability to use a fully-distributed Solr cluster with fully-distributed indexing and searching. Along with this comes the reworked Solr administration panel with parts concentrated on Cloud functionalities. This recipe will show you how to use this part of the administration panel; for example, how to see your cluster distribution and detailed information about shards and replicas.

Getting ready

This recipe assumes that the SolrCloud cluster is up and running. If you are not familiar with setting up the SolrCloud cluster, please refer to the *Creating a new SolrCloud cluster* recipe in this chapter.

How to do it...

1. First of all, let's see how we can check how our cluster distribution looks. In order to do this, let's open our web browser to `http://localhost:8983/solr/` (or the address of the host and port of any of the Solr instances that form the cluster) and open the Cloud graph view. We should be able to see something similar to the following screenshot:

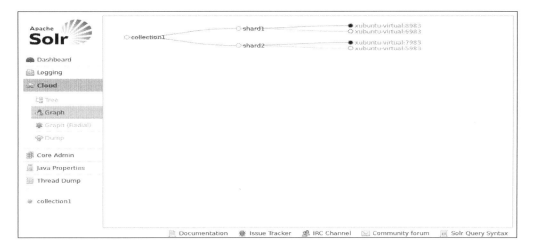

2. There is also a second view of the same information that can be accessed by viewing the **Graph (Radial)** section, and it should look similar to the following screenshot:

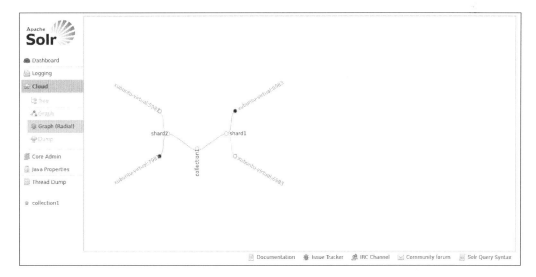

3. Looks nice, doesn't it? However, there is some additional information that can be retrieved. So now, let's look at the **Tree** section of the Cloud administration panel:

As you can see, there is some very detailed information available. So now, let's look at what it means.

How it works...

First of all, remember that the best way to get used to the new administration panel is to just run a simple SolrCloud cluster by yourself and play with it. However, let's look at the provided examples to see what information we have there.

As you can see, in the first two screenshots provided, our cluster consists of a single collection named `collection1`. It consists of two shards (`shard1` and `shard2`) and each shard lives on a single node. One of each shards is the primary one (the ones at `gr0-vaio:8983` and `gr0-vaio:7983`), and each of them has a replica (the ones at `gr0-vaio:6983` and `gr0-vaio:5983`). Both diagrams shown in the screenshots provide the same amount of information and they only differ in the way they present the data.

Now, let's look and discuss the last screenshot – the **Tree** view of the **Cloud** section of the Solr administration panel. As you can see, there is much more information available there. The tree presented in the administration panel is what your ZooKeeper ensemble sees. The first thing is `clusterstate.json`, which holds detailed information about the current state of the cluster.

Next, you can see the `collections` section, which holds information about each collection deployed in the cluster – you can see the information about each shard and its replicas, such as leaders, and some detailed information needed by the Solr and ZooKeeper.

In addition to the preceding information, you can also see the configuration files (the `/configs` section) that were sent to the ZooKeeper and are used as the configuration files for your collection or collections.

Not visible in the screenshot is the additional information connected to ZooKeeper, which is not needed during the usual work with Solr, so I decided to omit discussing it.

Distributed indexing and searching

Having a distributed SolrCloud cluster is very useful; you can have multiple shards and replicas, which are automatically handled by Solr itself. This means that your data will be automatically distributed among shards and replicated between replicas. However, if you have your data spread among multiple shards, you probably want them to be queried while you send the query. With earlier versions of Solr before 4.0, you had to manually specify the list of shards that should be queried. Now you don't need to do that, and this recipe will show you how to make your queries distributed.

Getting ready

If you are not familiar with setting up the SolrCloud cluster, please refer to the *Creating a new SolrCloud cluster* recipe in this chapter. If you are not familiar with how to modify the returned documents using the `fl` parameter, please read the *Modifying returned documents* recipe in *Chapter 4*, *Querying Solr*.

How to do it...

1. First of all, let's assume we have a cluster that consist of three nodes and we have a single collection deployed on that cluster; a collection with three shards. For the purpose of this recipe, I'm using the example configuration files provided with Solr and the example documents stored in the XML files in the `exampledocs` directory of the Solr distribution package. If we look at the Solr administration panel, this is what the Cloud graph will show:

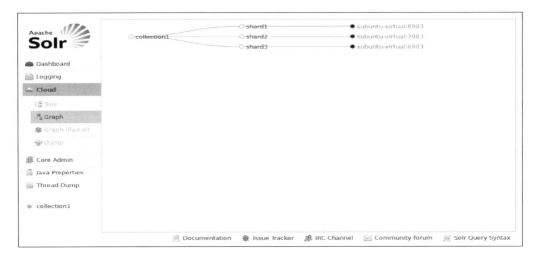

2. Now, the best thing about distributed indexing and searching—if you are using Solr 4.0 and its distributed searching and indexing capabilities—is that you don't need to do anything in addition to sending the proper indexing and searching requests to one of the shards. So, in order to have the example files indexed, I've run the following command from the `exampledocs` directory of the Solr instance running on port `8983`:

```
java -jar post.jar *.xml
```

3. Now, let's use the non-distributed queries to check if the documents were sent to all the shards. In order to do this, we run three queries. The first query is run to the Solr instance holding the first shard:

```
curl 'http://localhost:8983/solr/select?q=*:*&rows=0&distrib=false'
```

Its response will be as follows:

```
<?xml version="1.0" encoding="UTF-8"?>
  <response>
    <lst name="responseHeader">
      <int name="status">0</int>
      <int name="QTime">0</int>
      <lst name="params">
```

```
        <str name="distrib">false</str>
        <str name="q">*:*</str>
        <str name="rows">0</str>
      </lst>
    </lst>
    <result name="response" numFound="8" start="0">
    </result>
</response>
```

4. The second query is run to the Solr instance holding the second shard:

   `curl 'http://localhost:7983/solr/select?q=*:*&rows=0&distrib=false'`

   Its response will be as follows:

```
<?xml version="1.0" encoding="UTF-8"?>
  <response>
    <lst name="responseHeader">
      <int name="status">0</int>
      <int name="QTime">0</int>
      <lst name="params">
      <str name="distrib">false</str>
      <str name="q">*:*</str>
      <str name="rows">0</str>
    </lst>
  </lst>
  <result name="response" numFound="10" start="0">
  </result>
</response>
```

5. The third query is run to the Solr instance holding the last shard:

   `curl 'http://localhost:6983/solr/select?q=*:*&rows=0&distrib=false'`

   Its response will be as follows:

```
<?xml version="1.0" encoding="UTF-8"?>
  <response>
    <lst name="responseHeader">
      <int name="status">0</int>
      <int name="QTime">0</int>
      <lst name="params">
      <str name="distrib">false</str>
      <str name="q">*:*</str>
      <str name="rows">0</str>
    </lst>
  </lst>
  <result name="response" numFound="14" start="0">
  </result>
</response>
```

6. Everything seems to be in the perfect order now, at least by judging the number of documents. So now, let's run the default distributed query to see if all the shards were queried. In order to do this we run the following query:

```
curl 'http://localhost:8983/solr/select?q=*:*&fl=id,[shard]&ro
ws=50'
```

Since the response was quite big, I decided to cut it a bit and show only a single document from each shard:

```xml
<?xml version="1.0" encoding="UTF-8"?>
  <response>
    <lst name="responseHeader">
      <int name="status">0</int>
      <int name="QTime">58</int>
      <lst name="params">
      <str name="fl">id,[shard]</str>
      <str name="q">*:*</str>
      <str name="rows">50</str>
    </lst>
  </lst>
  <result name="response" numFound="32" start="0"
    maxScore="1.0">
    <doc>
      <str name="id">SP2514N</str>
      <str name="[shard]">gr0-vaio:6983/solr/collection1/
      </str>
    </doc>
    ...
    <doc>
      <str name="id">GB18030TEST</str>
      <str name="[shard]">gr0-vaio:7983/solr/collection1/
      </str>
    </doc>
    ...
    <doc>
      <str name="id">IW-02</str>
      <str name="[shard]">gr0-vaio:8983/solr/collection1/
      </str>
    </doc>
    ...
  </result>
</response>
```

As you can see, we got documents from each shard that builds our cluster, so it works as intended. Now, let's look at exactly how it works.

How it works...

As you can see, as shown in the previous screenshot, our test cluster created for the purpose of this recipe contains thee Solr instances, where each of them contains a single shard of the collection deployed on the cluster. This means that the data indexed to any of the shards will be automatically divided and distributed among the shards. In order to choose which shard the document should go to, Solr uses a **hash value** of the identifier of the document.

During indexing, we sent the documents to the Solr instance that is working on port `8983`. However, as our example queries show, when querying only a particular shard (the `distrib=false` parameter), each of them hosts different amount of documents, which is expected. If we had many more documents, the amount of documents on each shard would be probably almost the same if not equal. As you must have guessed by now, the `distrib=false` parameter forces the query to be run on the Solr server that it was sent to in a non-distributed manner, and we want such behavior to see how many documents are hosted on each of the shards.

Let's now focus on the query that was used to fetch all the documents in the cluster. It's a query that you are probably used to – fetching all the documents (`q=*:*`) and returning a maximum of 50 documents (`rows=50`). In addition, we specify the `fl` parameter in such a way that the returned document contains the `id` field and the information about the shard the document was fetched from (`fl=id, [shard]`). As you can see, we got documents coming from all the shards that build the collection in the response. This is because when using the SolrCloud deployment, Solr automatically queries all the relevant shards that are needed to be queried in order to query the whole collection. The information about shards (and replicas, if they exist) is fetched from ZooKeeper, so we don't need to specify it.

Increasing the number of replicas on an already live cluster

If you used Solr before the release of the 4.0 version, you are probably familiar with **replication**. The way deployments usually worked is that there was a single master server and multiple slave servers that were pulling the index from the master server. In Solr 4.0, we don't have to worry about replication and pulling interval – it's done automatically. We can also set up our instances in a way to achieve a similar setup as that of multiple replicas of a single shard where data is stored. This recipe will show you how to do it.

Getting ready

If you are not familiar with setting up a SolrCloud cluster, please refer to the *Creating a new SolrCloud cluster* recipe in this chapter.

How to do it...

For the purpose of this recipe, I'll assume that we want to have a cluster with a single shard running just like the usual Solr deployment, and we want to add two additional replicas to that shard. So, we have more servers to handle the queries.

1. The first step is starting a new Solr 4.0 server. We will use the configuration provided with the example Solr server, but you can use your own if you want. We will also use the ZooKeeper server embedded into Solr, but again, you can use the standalone one. So finally, the command that we use for starting the first instance of Solr is as follows:

    ```
    java -Dbootstrap_confdir=solr/collection1/conf -Dcollection.
    configName=collection1 -DzkRun -DnumShards=1 -jar start.jar
    ```

2. Now, let's take a look at the Solr administration panel to see how our cluster state looks:

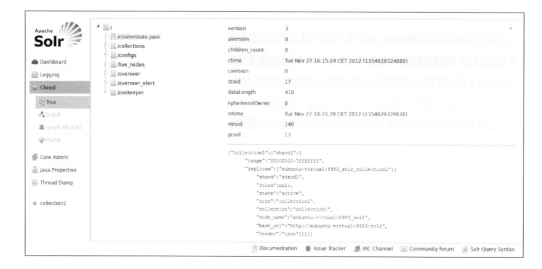

As you can see, we have a single shard in our collection that has a single replica. This can be a bit misleading, because the single replica is actually the initial shard we've created. So we actually have a single shard and zero copies of it. As we said earlier, we want to change that in order to have two additional replicas of our shard. In order to do this, we need to run two additional Solr instances. I'll run them on the same machine as the first one on ports 7893 and 6893. But in a real life situation, you'd probably want to have them on different servers.

3. In order to run these two additional Solr servers, we use the following commands:

```
java -Djetty.port=7983 -DzkHost=localhost:9983 -jar start.jar
java -Djetty.port=6983 -DzkHost=localhost:9983 -jar start.jar
```

4. Now, let's see how our cluster state changes, by looking at the cluster state in the Solr administration panel again. The cluster state information looks similar to the following screenshot after we start the two additional instances of Solr:

```
{"collection1":{"shard1":{
      "range":"80000000-7fffffff",
      "replicas":{
        "xubuntu-virtual:8983_solr_collection1":{
          "shard":"shard1",
          "roles":null,
          "state":"active",
          "core":"collection1",
          "collection":"collection1",
          "node_name":"xubuntu-virtual:8983_solr",
          "base_url":"http://xubuntu-virtual:8983/solr",
          "leader":"true"},
        "xubuntu-virtual:7983_solr_collection1":{
          "shard":"shard1",
          "roles":null,
          "state":"active",
          "core":"collection1",
          "collection":"collection1",
          "node_name":"xubuntu-virtual:7983_solr",
          "base_url":"http://xubuntu-virtual:7983/solr"},
        "xubuntu-virtual:6983_solr_collection1":{
          "shard":"shard1",
          "roles":null,
          "state":"active",
          "core":"collection1",
          "collection":"collection1",
          "node_name":"xubuntu-virtual:6983_solr",
          "base_url":"http://xubuntu-virtual:6983/solr"}}}}}
```

As you see, we still have our initial shard. But right now, we also have two additional replicas present that will be automatically updated and will hold the same data as the primary shard that we created in the beginning.

How it works...

We start our single shard instance with the command that allows us to run the embedded ZooKeeper server along with Solr. The embedded ZooKeeper server is started at the port whose number is the **Solr port + 1000**, which in our case if `9983`. `bootstrap_confdir` specifies the directory where the Solr configuration files are stored, which will be sent to the ZooKeeper. `collection.configName` specifies the name of the collection, `numShards` specifies the amount of shards the collection should have, and `zkRun` tells Solr that we want the embedded ZooKeeper to be run. Of course, this was only used as an example, and in a production environment you should set up a standalone ZooKeeper server.

As shown in the previous screenshot, you can see that our collection consists of a single shard and the only replica we have is this shard. So, we have a single primary shard with no data replication at all. In order to create two replicas that will be automatically populated with exactly the same data as the primary shard, we just need to start the two additional Solr servers. For the purpose of the recipe, we started these new instances on the same machine, but usually in a production environment you would set them up on separate machines.

As you can see in the second screenshot, after adding these two new Solr instances, our cluster is composed of a primary shard and two replicas, which will have their contents updated automatically. So we've got what we wanted.

Stopping automatic document distribution among shards

In most cases, the standard distribution of documents between your SolrCloud instances will be enough, and what's more, it will be the right way to go. However, there are situations where controlling the documents distribution outside of Solr (that is, in your application) may be better. For example, imagine that you'll only allow your users to search in the data they indexed. In such situations, it would be good to have documents for a single client stored in a single shard (if that's possible). In such cases, automatic documents distribution based on the documents identifier may not be the best way. Solr allows us to turn off automatic document distribution and this recipe will show you how to do that.

Getting ready

If you are not familiar with setting up the SolrCloud cluster, please refer to the *Creating a new SolrCloud cluster* recipe in this chapter. If you are not familiar with how to modify the returned documents using the `fl` parameter, please read the *Modifying the returned documents* recipe in *Chapter 4, Querying Solr*.

How to do it...

1. Let's assume that we have the following index structure (`schema.xml`) defined, and that we already have it stored in ZooKeeper:

```
<fields>
  <field name="id" type="string" indexed="true"
    stored="true" required="true" />
  <field name="userName" type="string" indexed="true"
    stored="true" />
  <field name="data" type="text" indexed="true"
    stored="true" />
  <field name="_version_" type="long" indexed="true"
    stored="true"/>
</fields>
```

2. We have two files that contain user data. One is called `data1.xml`, and it holds the data for `user1` and looks similar to the following code snippet:

```
<add>
  <doc>
    <field name="id">1</field>
    <field name="userName">user1</field>
    <field name="data">Data of user1</field>
  </doc>
</add>
```

The second one is called `data2.xml`, and it holds the data for `user2`:

```
<add>
  <doc>
    <field name="id">2</field>
    <field name="userName">user2</field>
    <field name="data">Data of user2</field>
  </doc>
  <doc>
    <field name="id">3</field>
    <field name="userName">user2</field>
    <field name="data">Another data of user2</field>
  </doc>
</add>
```

3. In order to be able to stop the automatic document distribution between shards, we need the following update request processor chain to be defined in the `solrconfig.xml` file:

```
<updateRequestProcessorChain>
  <processor class="solr.LogUpdateProcessorFactory" />
```

```
<processor class="solr.RunUpdateProcessorFactory" />
<processor class="
  solr.NoOpDistributingUpdateProcessorFactory" />
</updateRequestProcessorChain>
```

4. I assume that we already have a cluster containing at least two nodes up and running, these nodes use the preceding configuration files, and that our collection name is `collection1`. One of the nodes is running on a server with the IP address as `192.168.1.1` and the second one is running on a server with the IP address as `192.168.1.2`.

5. As we discussed earlier, we want to manually distribute the data to Solr instances. In our case, we would like the data from the `data1.xml` file to be indexed on the Solr server running at `192.168.1.1`, and the data from `data2.xml` to be indexed on the Solr instance running on `192.168.1.2`. So, we use the following commands to index the data:

```
java -Durl=http://192.168.1.1:8983/solr/collection1/update -jar
post.jar data1.xml
```

```
java -Durl=http://192.168.1.2:8983/solr/collection1/update -jar
post.jar data2.xml
```

6. Now, let's test if it works. In order to do this, we will use the Solr functionality that enables us to see which shard the document is stored at. In our case, it will be the following query:

```
curl http://localhost:7983/solr/select?q=*:*&fl=*,[shard]
```

The response will be as follows:

```
<?xml version="1.0" encoding="UTF-8"?>
  <response>
    <lst name="responseHeader">
      <int name="status">0</int>
      <int name="QTime">24</int>
      <lst name="params">
        <str name="q">*:*</str>
        <str name="fl">*,[shard]</str>
      </lst>
    </lst>
    <result name="response" numFound="3" start="0"
      maxScore="1.0">
      <doc>
        <str name="id">2</str>
```

```
        <str name="userName">user2</str>
        <str name="data">Data of user2</str>
        <str name="[shard]">
          192.168.1.2:8983/solr/collection1/
        </str>
      </doc>
      <doc>
        <str name="id">3</str>
        <str name="userName">user2</str>
        <str name="data">Another data of user2</str>
        <str name="[shard]">
          192.168.1.2:8983/solr/collection1/
        </str>
      </doc>
      <doc>
        <str name="id">1</str>
        <str name="userName">user1</str>
        <str name="data">Data of user1</str>
        <str name="[shard]">
          192.168.1.1:8983/solr/collection1/
        </str>
      </doc>
    </result>
  </response>
```

It seems that we have achieved what we wanted, so let's see how it works.

How it works...

Our `schema.xml` file is very simple. It contains three fields that are used by our data files at the `_version_` field used internally by Solr. The actual data is nothing new as well, so I'll skip discussing it.

The thing we want to look at is the update request processor chain definition. As you can see, apart from the standard `solr.LogUpdateProcessorFactory` and `solr.RunUpdateProcessorFactory` processors, it contains a `solr.NoOpDistributingUpdateProcessorFactory` processor. You can think of this additional processor as the one that forces the `update` command to be indexed on the node it was sent to.

We used the standard `post.jar` library distributed with Solr in order to index the data. In order to specify which server the data should be sent to, we use the `-Durl` parameter. We use two available servers to send the data to – the one running at `192.168.1.1` that should contain one document after indexing, and the one running at `192.168.1.2` that should contain two documents. In order to check this, we use a query that returns all the documents (`q=*:*`). In addition, we specify the `fl` parameter in such a way that the returned document contains not only all the stored fields, but also the shard the document was fetched from (`fl=*,[shard]`).

As you can see, in the results returned by Solr, the documents that belong to `user2` (the ones with `id` field equal to `2` and `3`) were fetched from the Solr server running at `192.168.1.2` (`<str name="[shard]">192.168.1.2:8983/solr/collection1/</str>`), and the one belonging to `user1` came from the Solr instance running at `192.168.1.1` (`<str name="[shard]">192.168.1.1:8983/solr/collection1/</str>`). So, everything is just as we wanted it to be.

One more thing: please remember that when turning off automatic documents distribution, you may end up with shards being uneven. This is because of the different number of documents being stored in each of them. So, you have to carefully plan your distribution.

8
Using Additional Solr Functionalities

In this chapter we will cover:

- ▸ Getting more documents similar to those returned in the results list
- ▸ Highlighting matched words
- ▸ How to highlight long text fields and get good performance
- ▸ Sorting results by a function value
- ▸ Searching words by how they sound
- ▸ Ignoring defined words
- ▸ Computing statistics for the search results
- ▸ Checking the user's spelling mistakes
- ▸ Using field values to group results
- ▸ Using queries to group results
- ▸ Using function queries to group results

Introduction

There are many features of Solr that we don't use every day. You may not encounter highlighting words, ignoring words, or statistics computation in everyday use, but they can come in handy in many situations. In this chapter, I'll try to show how to overcome some typical problems that can be fixed by using some of the Solr functionalities. In addition to that we will see how to use the Solr grouping mechanism in order to get documents that have some fields in common.

Getting more documents similar to those returned in the results list

Imagine a situation where you want to show similar documents to those returned by Solr. Let's imagine a situation where you have an e-commerce library shop, and you want to show users the books similar to the ones they found while using your application. This recipe will show you how to do that.

How to do it...

1. Let's start with the following index structure (just add this to your `schema.xml` file, to the `field` section):

```
<field name="id" type="string" indexed="true" stored="true"
required="true" />
<field name="name" type="text" indexed="true" stored="true"
termVectors="true" />
```

2. Next, let's use the following test data:

```
<add>
 <doc>
  <field name="id">1</field>
  <field name="name">Solr Cookbook first edition</field>
 </doc>
 <doc>
  <field name="id">2</field>
  <field name="name">Solr Cookbook second edition</field>
 </doc>
 <doc>
  <field name="id">3</field>
  <field name="name">Solr by example first edition</field>
 </doc>
 <doc>
  <field name="id">4</field>
  <field name="name">My book second edition</field>
 </doc>
</add>
```

3. Let's assume that our hypothetical user wants to find books that have `cookbook` and `second` in their names. But, we also want to show him/her similar books. To do that we send the following query:

```
http://localhost:8983/solr/select?q=cookbook+second&mm=2&qf=name&d
efType=edismax&mlt=true&mlt.fl=name&mlt.mintf=1&mlt.mindf=1
```

The results returned by Solr for the preceding query are as follows:

```xml
<?xml version="1.0" encoding="UTF-8"?>
<response>
  <lst name="responseHeader">
   <int name="status">0</int>
   <int name="QTime">2</int>
   <lst name="params">
    <str name="mm">2</str>
    <str name="mlt.mindf">1</str>
    <str name="mlt.fl">name</str>
    <str name="q">cookbook second</str>
    <str name="mlt.mintf">1</str>
    <str name="qf">name</str>
    <str name="mlt">true</str>
    <str name="defType">edismax</str>
   </lst>
  </lst>
  <result name="response" numFound="1" start="0">
   <doc>
    <str name="id">2</str>
    <str name="name">Solr Cookbook second edition</str>
    <long name="_version_">1415606105364496384</long>
   </doc>
  </result>
  <lst name="moreLikeThis">
   <result name="2" numFound="3" start="0">
    <doc>
     <str name="id">1</str>
     <str name="name">Solr Cookbook first edition</str>
     <long name="_version_">1415606105279561728</long>
    </doc>
    <doc>
     <str name="id">4</str>
     <str name="name">My book second edition</str>
     <long name="_version_">1415606105366593536</long>
    </doc>
    <doc>
     <str name="id">3</str>
     <str name="name">Solr by example first edition</str>
     <long name="_version_">1415606105365544960</long>
    </doc>
   </result>
  </lst>
</response>
```

Now let's see how it works.

How it works...

As you can see the index structure and the data are really simple. One thing to note is the `termVectors` attribute set to `true` in the `name` field definition. It is a good thing to have when using the `more like this` component, and should be used whenever possible in the fields on which we plan to use this component.

Now let's take a look at the query. As you can see, we added some additional parameters besides the standard `q` one (and the ones such as `mm` and `defType` which specify how our query should be handled). The parameter `mlt=true` says that we want to add the `more like this` component to the result processing. The `mlt.fl` parameter specifies which fields we want to use with the `more like this` component. In our case we will use the `name` field. The `mlt.mintf` parameter asks Solr to ignore terms from the source document (the ones from the original result list) with the term frequency below the given value. In our case we don't want to include the terms that will have a frequency lower than 1. The last parameter, `mlt.mindf`, tells Solr that words appearing less than the value of the parameter documents should be ignored. In our case we want to consider words that appear in at least one document.

Last is the search results. As you can see, there is an additional section (`<lst name="moreLikeThis">`) that is responsible for showing us the `more like this` component results. For each document in the results there is one `more like this` section added to the response. In our case, Solr added a section for the document with the unique identifier 3 (`<result name="3" numFound="3" start="0">`), and there were three similar documents found. The value of the `id` attribute is assigned the value of the unique identifier of the document for which the similar documents are calculated for.

Highlighting matched words

Imagine a situation where you want to show your users which words were matched in the document shown in the results list. For example, you want to show which words in the book name were matched and display that to the user. Do you have to store the documents and do the matching on the application side? The answer is no. We can force Solr to do that for us and this recipe will show you how to do that.

How to do it...

1. We begin by creating the following index structure (just add this to your `schema.xml` file, to the `field` section):

```
<field name="id" type="string" indexed="true" stored="true"
required="true" />
<field name="name" type="text" indexed="true" stored="true" />
```

2. Our test data looks like the following code:

```
<add>
 <doc>
  <field name="id">1</field>
  <field name="name">Solr Cookbook first edition</field>
 </doc>
 <doc>
  <field name="id">2</field>
  <field name="name">Solr Cookbook second edition</field>
 </doc>
 <doc>
  <field name="id">3</field>
  <field name="name">Solr by example first edition</field>
 </doc>
 <doc>
  <field name="id">4</field>
  <field name="name">My book second edition</field>
 </doc>
</add>
```

3. Let's assume that our user is searching for the word book. To tell Solr that we want to highlight the matches, we send the following query:

```
http://localhost:8983/solr/select?q=name:book&hl=true
```

The response from Solr should be as follows:

```
<?xml version="1.0" encoding="UTF-8"?>
 <response>
  <lst name="responseHeader">
   <int name="status">0</int>
   <int name="QTime">2</int>
   <lst name="params">
    <str name="hl">true</str>
    <str name="q">name:book</str>
   </lst>
  </lst>
  <result name="response" numFound="1" start="0">
   <doc>
    <str name="id">4</str>
    <str name="name">My book second edition</str>
   </doc>
  </result>
```

```
<lst name="highlighting">
 <lst name="4">
  <arr name="name">
   <str>My &lt;em&gt;book&lt;/em&gt; second edition</str>
  </arr>
 </lst>
</lst>
</response>
```

As you can see, besides the normal results list we got the highlighting results (the highlighting results are grouped by the `<lst name="highlighting">` XML tag). The word `book` is surrounded by the `<em>` and `</em>` HTML tags. So everything is working as intended. Now let's see how it works.

How it works...

As you can see the index structure and the data are really simple, so I'll skip discussing this part of the recipe. Please note that in order to use the highlighting mechanism, your fields should be stored and not analysed by aggressive filters (such as stemming). Otherwise the highlighting results can be misleading to the users. Let's think of a simple example of such behavior – imagine the user types the word `bought` in the search but Solr highlighted the word `buy` because of the stemming algorithm.

The query is also not complicated. We can see the standard `q` parameter that passes the query to Solr. But there is also one additional parameter, the `hl` parameter set to `true`. This parameter tells Solr to include the highlighting component results to the results list. As you can see in the results list, in addition to the standard results, there is a new section `<lst name="highlighting">`, which contains the highlighting results. For every document, in our case the only one found (`<lst name="4">` means that the highlighting result is presented for the document with the unique identifier value of `4`), there is a list of fields that contain the sample data with the matched words (or words) highlighted. By highlighted I mean surrounded by the HTML tag, in this case the `<em>` tag.

You should also remember one other thing: if you are using the standard `LuceneQParser` query parser then the default field used for highlighting will be the one set in the `schema.xml` file. If you are using `DismaxQParser` then the default fields used for highlighting are the ones specified by the `qf` parameter.

There's more...

There are a few things that can be useful when using the highlighting mechanism.

Specifying the fields for highlighting

In many real life situations we want to decide what fields we would want to show the highlighting for. To do that, you must add an additional parameter – `hl.fl` with the list of fields separated by the comma character. For example, if we would like to show the highlighting for the fields `name` and `description`, our query should look as follows:

```
http://localhost:8983/solr/select?q=name:book&hl=true&hl.
fl=name,description
```

Changing the default HTML tags that surround the matched word

There are situations where you would like to change the default `<em>` and `</em>` HTML tags to the ones of your choice. To do that you should add the `hl.simple.pre` and `hl.simple.post` parameters. The first one specifies the prefix that will be added in front of the matched word and the second one specifies the postfix that will be added after the matched word. For example, if you would like to surround the matched word with the `<b>` and `</b>` HTML tags the query would look like this:

```
http://localhost:8983/solr/select?q=name:book&hl=true&hl.simple.
pre=<b>&hl.simple.post=</b>
```

How to highlight long text fields and get good performance

In certain situations, the standard highlighting mechanism may not be performing as well as you would like it to be. For example, you may have long text fields and you want the highlighting mechanism to work with them. This recipe will show you how to do that.

How to do it...

1. We begin the index structure configuration which looks as follows (just add this to your `schema.xml` file, to the `field` section):

```
<field name="id" type="string" indexed="true" stored="true"
required="true" />
<field name="name" type="text" indexed="true" stored="true"
termVectors="true" termPositions="true" termOffsets="true" />
```

2. The next step is to index the data. We will use the test data which looks like the following code:

```
<add>
 <doc>
  <field name="id">1</field>
```

```
  <field name="name">Solr Cookbook first edition</field>
 </doc>
 <doc>
  <field name="id">2</field>
  <field name="name">Solr Cookbook second edition</field>
 </doc>
 <doc>
  <field name="id">3</field>
  <field name="name">Solr by example first edition</field>
 </doc>
 <doc>
  <field name="id">4</field>
  <field name="name">My book second edition</field>
 </doc>
</add>
```

3. Let's assume that our user is searching for the word `book`. To tell Solr that we want to highlight the matches, we send the following query:

```
http://localhost:8983/solr/select?q=name:book&hl=true&hl.
useFastVectorHighlighter=true
```

The response from Solr should be as follows:

```
<?xml version="1.0" encoding="UTF-8"?>
 <response>
  <lst name="responseHeader">
   <int name="status">0</int>
   <int name="QTime">15</int>
   <lst name="params">
    <str name="hl">true</str>
    <str name="q">name:book</str>
   </lst>
  </lst>
  <result name="response" numFound="1" start="0">
   <doc>
    <str name="id">4</str>
    <str name="name">My book second edition</str>
   </doc>
  </result>
  <lst name="highlighting">
   <lst name="4">
    <arr name="name">
     <str>My &lt;em&gt;book&lt;/em&gt; second edition</str>
    </arr>
   </lst>
  </lst>
</response>
```

As you can see everything is working as intended. Now let's see how.

How it works...

As you can see the index structure and the data are really simple, but there is a difference between using the standard highlighter and the new `FastVectorHighlighting` feature. To be able to use the new highlighting mechanism, you need to store the information about term vectors, position, and offsets. This is done by adding the following attributes to the field definition or to the type definition: `termVectors="true"` `termPositions="true"` `termOffsets="true"`.

Please note that in order to use the highlighting mechanism, your fields should be stored and not analysed by aggressive filters (such as stemming). Otherwise the highlighting results can be misleading to the users. An example of such a behavior is simple – imagine that the user types the word `bought` in the search box but Solr highlighted the word `buy` because of the stemming algorithm.

The query is also not complicated. We can see the standard `q` parameter that passes the query to Solr. But there is also one additional parameter, the `hl` parameter set to `true`. This parameter tells Solr to include the highlighting component results to the results list. In addition we add the parameter to tell Solr to use the `FastVectorHighlighting` feature: `hl.useFastVectorHighlighter=true`.

As you can see in the results list, in addition to the standard results, there is a new section called `<lst name="highlighting">` that contains the highlighting results. For every document, in our case the only one found (`<lst name="4">` means that the highlighting result is presented for the document with the unique identifier value of `4`), there is a list of fields that contain the sample data with the matched words (or words) highlighted. By highlighted I mean surrounded by the HTML tag, in this case the `<em>` tag.

Sorting results by a function value

Let's imagine that you have an application that allows the user to search through the companies that are stored in the index. You would like to add an additional feature to your application to sort the results on the basis of the distance of a certain geographical point. Is this possible with Solr? Yes, and this recipe will show you how to do that.

Getting ready

The following recipe uses spatial search. If you are not familiar with geographical search in Solr please read the *Storing geographical points in the index* recipe in *Chapter 3, Analyzing Your Text Data*.

How to do it...

1. Let's start with the following index structure (just add this to your `schema.xml` file, to the `field` section):

```
<field name="id" type="string" indexed="true" stored="true"
required="true" />
<field name="name" type="text" indexed="true" stored="true" />
<field name="geo" type="location" indexed="true" stored="true" />
<dynamicField name="*_coordinate"  type="tdouble" indexed="true"
stored="false" />
```

2. Our test data that we want to index looks like the following code:

```
<add>
 <doc>
  <field name="id">1</field>
  <field name="name">Company one</field>
  <field name="geo">10.1,10.1</field>
 </doc>
 <doc>
  <field name="id">2</field>
  <field name="name">Company two</field>
  <field name="geo">11.1,11.1</field>
 </doc>
 <doc>
  <field name="id">3</field>
  <field name="name">Company three</field>
  <field name="geo">12.2,12.2</field>
 </doc>
</add>
```

3. In addition to that we also need to define the following field type in the `schema.xml` file in the `types` section:

```
<fieldType name="location" class="solr.LatLonType"
subFieldSuffix="_coordinate"/>
```

4. Let's assume that our hypothetical user searches for the word `company` and the user is in the location with the geographical point of `(13, 13)`. So, in order to show the results of the query and sort them by the distance from the given point, we send the following query to Solr:

```
http://localhost:8983/solr/select?q=name:company&sort=geodist(geo,
13,13)+asc
```

The results list returned by the query is as follows:

```
<?xml version="1.0" encoding="UTF-8"?>
 <response>
```

```
<lst name="responseHeader">
 <int name="status">0</int>
 <int name="QTime">2</int>
 <lst name="params">
  <str name="q">name:company</str>
  <str name="sort">geodist(geo,13,13) asc</str>
 </lst>
</lst>
<result name="response" numFound="3" start="0">
 <doc>
  <str name="id">3</str>
  <str name="name">Company three</str>
  <str name="geo">12.2,12.2</str>
 </doc>
 <doc>
  <str name="id">2</str>
  <str name="name">Company two</str>
  <str name="geo">11.1,11.1</str>
 </doc>
 <doc>
  <str name="id">1</str>
  <str name="name">Company one</str>
  <str name="geo">10.1,10.1</str>
 </doc>
</result>
</response>
```

As you can see, everything is working as it should be. So now let's see exactly how this works.

How it works...

Let's start from the index structure. We have four fields – one for holding the unique identifier (the id field), one for holding the name of the company (the name field), and one field responsible for the geographical location of the company (the geo field). The last field, the dynamic one, is needed for the location type to work. The data is pretty simple so let's just skip discussing that.

Besides the standard q parameter responsible for the user query, you can see the sort parameter. But the sort is a bit different from the ones you are probably used to. It uses the geodist function to calculate the distance from the given point, and the value returned by the function is then used to sort the documents in the results list. The first argument of the geodist function (the geo value) tells Solr which field to use to calculate the distance. The next two arguments specify the point from which the distance should be calculated. Of course as with every sort we specify the order in which we want the sort to take place. In our case we want to sort from the nearest to the furthest company (the asc value).

As you can see in the results, the documents were sorted as they should be.

Searching words by how they sound

One day your boss comes to your office and says "Hey, I want our search engine to be able to find the same documents when I enter `phone` or `fone` into the search box". You tried to say something, but your boss is already at the other side of the door to your office. So, you wonder if this kind of functionality is available in Solr. I think you already know the answer – yes it is, and this recipe will show you how to configure it and use with Solr.

How to do it...

1. We start with the following index structure (just add this to your `schema.xml` file, to the `field` section):

   ```
   <field name="id" type="string" indexed="true" stored="true"
   required="true" />
   <field name="name" type="phonetic" indexed="true" stored="true" />
   ```

2. Next we define the `phonetic` type, which looks like the following code (paste it into the `schema.xml` file):

   ```
   <fieldtype name="phonetic" stored="false" indexed="true"
   class="solr.TextField" >
     <analyzer>
       <tokenizer class="solr.StandardTokenizerFactory"/>
       <filter class="solr.DoubleMetaphoneFilterFactory" inject="false"/>
     </analyzer>
   </fieldtype>
   ```

3. Now we need to index our test data, which looks like the following code:

   ```
   <add>
     <doc>
       <field name="id">1</field>
       <field name="name">Phone</field>
     </doc>
     <doc>
       <field name="id">2</field>
       <field name="name">Fone</field>
     </doc>
   </add>
   ```

4. Now let's assume that our user wants to find documents that have the word that sounds like `fon`. So, we send the following query to Solr:

   ```
   http://localhost:8983/solr/select?q=name:fon
   ```

The result list returned by the query is as follows:

```xml
<?xml version="1.0" encoding="UTF-8"?>
 <response>
  <lst name="responseHeader">
   <int name="status">0</int>
   <int name="QTime">1</int>
   <lst name="params">
    <str name="q">name:fon</str>
   </lst>
  </lst>
  <result name="response" numFound="2" start="0">
   <doc>
    <str name="id">1</str>
    <str name="name">Phone</str>
   </doc>
   <doc>
    <str name="id">2</str>
    <str name="name">Fone</str>
   </doc>
  </result>
 </response>
```

So, the filter worked! We got two documents in the results list. Now let's see how it worked.

How it works...

Let's start with the index structure. As you can see we have two fields, the id field responsible for holding the unique identifier of the product and the name field responsible for holding the name of the product.

The name field is the one that will be used for phonetic search. For that we defined a new field type named phonetic. Besides the standard parts (such as class among many others) we defined a new filter: DoubleMetaphoneFilterFactory. It is responsible for analysis and checking how the words sound. This filter uses an algorithm named double metaphone to analyse the phonetics of the words. The additional attribute inject="false" tells Solr to replace the existing tokens instead of inserting additional ones, which mean that the original tokens will be replaced by the ones that the filter produces.

As you can see from the query and the data, the fon word was matched to the word phone and also to the word fone, which means that the algorithm (and thus the filter) works quite well. But take into consideration that this is only an algorithm, so some words that you think should be matched will not match.

See also

If you would like to know other phonetic algorithms, please take a look at the Solr Wiki page that can be found at the following URL address: `http://wiki.apache.org/solr/AnalyzersTokenizersTokenFilters`.

Ignoring defined words

Imagine a situation where you would like to filter the words that are considered vulgar from the data we are indexing. Of course, by accident, such words can be found in your data and you don't want them to be searchable thus you want to ignore them. Can we do that with Solr? Of course we can, and this recipe will show you how to do that.

How to do it...

1. Let's start with the following index structure (just add this to your `schema.xml` file, to the `field` section):

```
<field name="id" type="string" indexed="true" stored="true"
required="true" />
<field name="name" type="text_ignored" indexed="true"
stored="true" />
```

2. The second step is to define the `text_ignored` type, which looks like the following code:

```
<fieldType name="text_ignored" class="solr.TextField"
positionIncrementGap="100">
  <analyzer>
    <tokenizer class="solr.WhitespaceTokenizerFactory"/>
    <filter class="solr.StopFilterFactory" ignoreCase="true"
    words="ignored.txt" enablePositionIncrements="true" />
  </analyzer>
</fieldType>
```

3. Now we create the `ignored.txt` file, whose contents looks as follows:

```
vulgar
vulgar2
vulgar3
```

4. The next step is to index our test data, which looks as follows:

```
<add>
  <doc>
    <field name="id">1</field>
    <field name="name">Company name</field>
  </doc>
</add>
```

5. Now let's assume that our user wants to find the documents that have the words `Company` and `vulgar`. So, we send the following query to Solr:

   ```
   http://localhost:8983/solr/select?q=name:(Company+AND+vulgar)
   ```

   In the standard situation there shouldn't be any results because we don't have a document that matches the two given words. But let's look at what Solr returned to us as the preceding query's result:

   ```xml
   <?xml version="1.0" encoding="UTF-8"?>
     <response>
       <lst name="responseHeader">
         <int name="status">0</int>
         <int name="QTime">1</int>
         <lst name="params">
           <str name="q">name:(Company AND vulgar)</str>
         </lst>
       </lst>
       <result name="response" numFound="1" start="0">
         <doc>
           <str name="id">1</str>
           <str name="name">Company name</str>
         </doc>
       </result>
     </response>
   ```

6. Hmm... it works. To be perfectly sure, let's look at the analysis page found at the administration interface, as shown in the following screenshot:

   As you can see the word `vulgar` was cut and thus ignored.

How it works...

Let's start with the index structure. As you can see we have two fields, the `id` field responsible for holding the unique identifier of the product and the `name` field responsible for holding the name of the product.

The `name` field is the one we will use to mention the ignoring functionalities of Solr – `StopFilterFactory`. As you can see the `text_ignored` type definition is analysed the same way both in the query and index time. The unusual thing is the new filter – `StopFilterFactory`. The `words` attribute of the filter definition specifies the name of the file, encoded in UTF-8, which consists of words (a new word at every file line) that should be ignored. The defined file should be placed in the same directory in which we placed the `schema.xml` file. The `ignoreCase` attribute set to `true` tells the filter to ignore the case of the tokens and the words defined in the file. The last attribute, `enablePositionIncrements=true`, tells Solr to increment the position of the tokens in the token stream. The `enablePositionIncrements` parameter should be set to `true` if you want to preserve the next token after the discarded one to increment its position in the token stream.

As you can see in the query, our hypothetical user queried Solr for two words with the logical operator `AND`, which means that both words must be present in the document. But, the filter we added cut the word `vulgar` and thus the results list consists of the document that has only one of the words. The same situation occurs when you are indexing your data. The words defined in the `ignored.txt` file will not be indexed.

If you look at the provided screenshot from the analysis page of the Solr administration interface (refer to step 6 of the *How to do it...* section), you can see that the word `vulgar` was cut during the processing of the token stream in the `StopFilterFactory` filter.

Computing statistics for the search results

Imagine a situation where you want to compute some basic statistics about the documents in the results list. For example, you have an e-commerce shop where you want to show the minimum and the maximum price of the documents that were found for a given query. Of course you could fetch all the documents and count them by yourself, but imagine Solr doing it for you. Yes, it can! And this recipe will show you how to use that functionality.

How to do it...

1. Let's start with the index structure (just add this to your `schema.xml` file, to the `field` section):

    ```
    <field name="id" type="string" indexed="true" stored="true"
    required="true" />
    <field name="name" type="text" indexed="true" stored="true" />
    <field name="price" type="float" indexed="true" stored="true" />
    ```

2. The example data that we index looks like the following code:

```
<add>
 <doc>
  <field name="id">1</field>
  <field name="name">Book 1</field>
  <field name="price">39.99</field>
 </doc>
 <doc>
  <field name="id">2</field>
  <field name="name">Book 2</field>
  <field name="price">30.11</field>
 </doc>
 <doc>
  <field name="id">3</field>
  <field name="name">Book 3</field>
  <field name="price">27.77</field>
 </doc>
</add>
```

3. Let's assume that we want our statistics to be computed for the `price` field. To do that, we send the following query to Solr:

```
http://localhost:8983/solr/select?q=name:book&stats=true&stats.
field=price
```

The response Solr returned should be as follows:

```
<?xml version="1.0" encoding="UTF-8"?>
 <response>
  <lst name="responseHeader">
   <int name="status">0</int>
   <int name="QTime">1</int>
   <lst name="params">
    <str name="q">name:book</str>
    <str name="stats">true</str>
    <str name="stats.field">price</str>
   </lst>
  </lst>
  <result name="response" numFound="3" start="0">
   <doc>
    <str name="id">1</str>
    <str name="name">Book 1</str>
    <float name="price">39.99</float>
   </doc>
   <doc>
```

```
        <str name="id">2</str>
        <str name="name">Book 2</str>
        <float name="price">30.11</float>
       </doc>
       <doc>
        <str name="id">3</str>
        <str name="name">Book 3</str>
        <float name="price">27.77</float>
       </doc>
      </result>
      <lst name="stats">
       <lst name="stats_fields">
        <lst name="price">
         <double name="min">27.770000457763672</double>
         <double name="max">39.9900016784668</double>
         <long name="count">3</long>
         <long name="missing">0</long>
         <double name="sum">97.87000274658203</double>
         <double name="sumOfSquares">3276.9852964233432</double>
         <double name="mean">32.62333424886068</double>
         <double name="stddev">6.486119174232198</double>
        <lst name="facets"/>
       </lst>
      </lst>
     </response>
```

As you can see, in addition to the standard results list, there was an additional section available. Now let's see how it worked.

How it works...

The index structure is pretty straightforward. It contains three fields – one for holding the unique identifier (the id field), one for holding the name (the name field), and one for holding the price (the price field).

The file that contains the example data is simple, so I'll skip discussing it.

The query is interesting. In addition to the q parameter we have two new parameters. The first one, stats=true, tells Solr that we want to use StatsComponent – the component which will calculate the statistics for us. The second parameter, stats.field=price tells StatsComponent which field to use for the calculation. In our case, we told Solr to use the price field.

Now let's look at the result returned by Solr. As you can see, `StatsComponent`, added an additional section to the results. The section contains the statistics generated for the field that we told Solr we wanted the statistics for. The following statistics are available:

- `min`: This is the minimum value that was found in the field, for the documents that matched the query
- `max`: This is the maximum value that was found in the field, for the documents that matched the query
- `sum`: This is the sum of all values in the field, for the documents that matched the query
- `count`: This specifies how many non-null values were found in the field for the documents that matched the query
- `missing`: This specifies the number of documents that matched the query but didn't have any value in the specified field
- `sumOfSquares`: This specifies the sum of all values squared in the field, for the documents that matched the query
- `mean`: This specifies the average for the values in the field, for the documents that matched the query
- `stddev`: This specifies the standard deviation for the values in the field, for the documents that matched the query

You should also remember that you can specify a number of the `stats.field` parameters to calculate the statistics for the different fields in a single query.

Please be careful when using this component on the multivalued fields as it can be a performance bottleneck.

Checking the user's spelling mistakes

Most modern search sites have some kind of user spelling mistakes correction mechanism. Some of those sites have a sophisticated mechanism, while others just have a basic one. But actually that doesn't matter. If all search engines have it then there is a high probability that your client or boss will want one too. Is there a way to integrate such a functionality into Solr? Yes there is, and this recipe will show you how to do it.

Getting ready

In this recipe we'll learn how to use the Solr spellchecker component. The detailed information about setting up the spellchecker component can be found in the *Configuring spellchecker to not use its own index* recipe in *Chapter 1, Apache Solr Configuration*.

How to do it...

1. Let's begin with the index structure (just add this to your `schema.xml` file, to the `field` section):

```
<field name="id" type="string" indexed="true" stored="true"
required="true" />
<field name="name" type="text" indexed="true" stored="true" />
```

2. The data that we are going to index looks like the following code:

```
<add>
 <doc>
  <field name="id">1</field>
  <field name="name">Solr cookbook</field>
 </doc>
 <doc>
  <field name="id">2</field>
  <field name="name">Mechanics cookbook</field>
 </doc>
 <doc>
  <field name="id">3</field>
  <field name="name">Other book</field>
 </doc>
</add>
```

3. Our spell checking mechanism will work on the basis of the `name` field. Now, let's add the appropriate search component to the `solrconfig.xml` file:

```
<searchComponent name="spellcheck" class="solr.
SpellCheckComponent">
  <str name="queryAnalyzerFieldType">name</str>
  <lst name="spellchecker">
    <str name="name">direct</str>
    <str name="field">name</str>
    <str name="classname">solr.DirectSolrSpellChecker</str>
    <str name="buildOnCommit">true</str>
  </lst>
</searchComponent>
```

4. In addition to that we would like to have it integrated into our search handler, so we make the default search handler definition the same as in the following code (add this to your `solrconfig.xml` file):

```
<requestHandler name="/spell" class="solr.SearchHandler"
startup="lazy">
 <lst name="defaults">
  <str name="df">name</str>
  <str name="spellcheck.dictionary">direct</str>
  <str name="spellcheck">on</str>
```

```
   <str name="spellcheck.collate">true</str>
  </lst>
  <arr name="last-components">
   <str>spellcheck</str>
  </arr>
 </requestHandler>
```

5. Now let's check how it works. To do that we will send a query that contains a spelling mistake. We will send the words `other boak` instead of `other book`. The query doing that should look like as follows:

```
http://localhost:8983/solr/spell?q=name:(othar boak)
```

The Solr response for that query looks like the following response:

```
<?xml version="1.0" encoding="UTF-8"?>
 <response>
  <lst name="responseHeader">
   <int name="status">0</int>
   <int name="QTime">3</int>
  </lst>
  <result name="response" numFound="0" start="0">
  </result>
  <lst name="spellcheck">
   <lst name="suggestions">
    <lst name="other">
     <int name="numFound">1</int>
     <int name="startOffset">6</int>
     <int name="endOffset">11</int>
     <arr name="suggestion">
      <str>other</str>
     </arr>
    </lst>
    <lst name="boak">
     <int name="numFound">1</int>
     <int name="startOffset">12</int>
     <int name="endOffset">16</int>
     <arr name="suggestion">
      <str>book</str>
     </arr>
    </lst>
    <str name="collation">name:(other book)</str>
   </lst>
  </lst>
 </response>
```

As you can see for the preceding response, Solr corrected the spelling mistake we made. Now let's see how that happened.

How it works...

The index structure is pretty straightforward. It contains two fields, one for holding the unique identifier (the `id` field), one for holding the name (the `name` field). The file that contains the example data is simple, so I'll skip discussing it.

The spellchecker component configuration is something we discussed already in the *Configuring spellchecker to not use its own index* recipe in the first chapter. So again, I'll look at only the most important fragments.

As you can see in the configuration, we've defined a spellchecker component that will use Solr `DirectSolrSpellChecker` in order to not store its index on the hard disk drive. In addition to that, we configured it to use the `name` field for spellchecking and also to use that field analyzer to process queries. Our `/spell` handler is configured to automatically include spellchecking results (`<str name="spellcheck">on</str>`), to create collation (`<str name="spellcheck.collate">true</str>`), and to use direct dictionary (`<str name="spellcheck.dictionary">direct</str>`). All those properties were already discussed in the previously mentioned recipe.

Now let's look at the query. We send the `boak` and `othar` words in the query parameter (`q`). The spellchecker component will be activated automatically because of the configuration of our `/spell` handler, and that's actually all there is to it when it comes to the query.

Finally we come to the results returned by Solr. As you can see there were no documents found for the word `boak` and the word `other`, that's what we actually were expecting. But as you can see there is a spellchecker component section added to the results list (the `<lst name="spellcheck">` tag). For each word there is a suggestion returned by Solr (the tag `<lst name="boak">` is the suggestion for the word `boak`). As you can see, the spellchecker component informed us about the number of suggestions found (`<int name="numFound">`), about the start and end offset of the suggestion (`<int name="startOffset">`and `<int name="endOffset">`), and about the actual suggestions (the `<arr name="suggestion">` array). The only suggestion that Solr returned was the book word (`<str>book</str>` under the suggestion array). The same goes for the second word.

There is an additional section in the spellchecker component results generated by the `spellcheck.collate=true` parameter, `<str name="collation">name:(other book)</str>`. This tells us what query Solr suggested to us. We can either show the query to the user or send it automatically to Solr and show to the user the corrected results list and this one is up to you.

Using field values to group results

Imagine a situation where your data set is divided into different categories, subcategories, price ranges, and things like that. What if you would like to not only get information about counts in such a group (with the use of faceting), but would also like to show the most relevant documents in each of the groups? Is there a grouping mechanism of some kind in Solr? Yes there is, and this recipe will show you how to use this functionality in order to divide documents into groups on the basis of field values.

How to do it...

1. Let's start with the index structure. Let's assume that we have the following fields in our index (just add this to the `schema.xml` file to the `field` section):

```
<field name="id" type="string" indexed="true" stored="true"
required="true" />
<field name="name" type="text" indexed="true" stored="true" />
<field name="category" type="string" indexed="true" stored="true"
/>
<field name="price" type="tfloat" indexed="true" stored="true" />
```

2. The example data, which we are going to index, looks like the following code:

```
<add>
 <doc>
  <field name="id">1</field>
  <field name="name">Solr cookbook</field>
  <field name="category">it</field>
  <field name="price">39.99</field>
 </doc>
 <doc>
  <field name="id">2</field>
  <field name="name">Mechanics cookbook</field>
  <field name="category">mechanics</field>
  <field name="price">19.99</field>
 </doc>
 <doc>
  <field name="id">3</field>
  <field name="name">ElasticSearch book</field>
  <field name="category">it</field>
  <field name="price">49.99</field>
 </doc>
</add>
```

3. Let's assume that we would like to get our data divided into groups on the basis of their category. In order to do that we send the following query to Solr:

```
http://localhost:8983/solr/select?q=*:*&group=true&group.
field=category
```

The results returned by the preceding query are as follows:

```
<?xml version="1.0" encoding="UTF-8"?>
 <response>
  <lst name="responseHeader">
   <int name="status">0</int>
   <int name="QTime">1</int>
   <lst name="params">
    <str name="group.field">category</str>
    <str name="group">true</str>
    <str name="q">*:*</str>
   </lst>
  </lst>
  <lst name="grouped">
   <lst name="category">
    <int name="matches">3</int>
    <arr name="groups">
     <lst>
      <str name="groupValue">it</str>
      <result name="doclist" numFound="2" start="0">
       <doc>
        <str name="id">1</str>
        <str name="name">Solr cookbook</str>
        <str name="category">it</str>
        <float name="price">39.99</float>
       </doc>
      </result>
     </lst>
     <lst>
      <str name="groupValue">mechanics</str>
      <result name="doclist" numFound="1" start="0">
       <doc>
        <str name="id">2</str>
        <str name="name">Mechanics cookbook</str>
        <str name="category">mechanics</str>
        <float name="price">19.99</float>
       </doc>
      </result>
```

```
        </lst>
      </arr>
     </lst>
    </lst>
  </response>
```

As you can see the grouped results are different from the ones returned during a usual search. But as you can see we got a single document per group which means it worked. So now let's see how.

How it works...

Our index structure is very simple. It consist four fields – one responsible for the document identifier (the `id` field), one used for holding the name of the book (the `name` field), its category (the `category` field), and the last one used to hold the price of the book (the `price` field). Our example data is also very simple, but please know that the first and second book belongs to the same `it` category and the second book belongs to another category.

Let's look at our query now. We said that we want to have our documents divided on the basis of contents of the `category` field. In order to do that, we've added a new parameter called `group`, which is set to `true`. This tells Solr that we want to enable the grouping functionality. And similar to faceting, we've added a second parameter we are not familiar with. The `group.field` parameter is set to the name of the field holding books category, and that's all we need.

If we look at the results returned by Solr, they are a bit different than the usual results. You can see the usual response header, however, the resulting groups are returned in the `<lst name="grouped">` tag. The `<lst name="category">` tag is generated for each `group.field` parameter passed in the query; this time it tells us that the following results will be for the `category` field. The `<int name="matches">3</int>` tag informs us how many documents were found for our query. This is the same as the `numFound` value during our usual query.

Next we have the `groups` array, which holds the information about the groups that were created by Solr in the results. Each group is described by the `it` value, that is, the `<str name="groupValue">it</str>` section for the first group, which means that all documents in that group have the `it` value in the field used for grouping. In the `result` tag we can see the documents returned for the group. By default Solr will return the most relevant document for each group. I'll skip commenting on the `result` tag as it is almost identical to the results Solr returns for a non-grouped query and we are familiar with those, right?

One last thing – you can specify multiple `group.field` parameters with different fields in a single query in order to get multiple grouping.

There's more...

There is one more thing about grouping on the basis of field values and I would like to share a few thoughts about that.

More than a single document in a group

Sometimes you may need to return more than a single document in a group. In order to do that you will need to use the `group.limit` parameter and set it to the maximum number of documents you want to have. For example, if we would like to have 10 documents per group of results, we would send the following query:

```
http://localhost:8983/solr/select?q=*:*&group=true&group.
field=category&group.limit=10
```

Using queries to group results

Sometimes grouping results on the basis of field values is not enough. For example, imagine that we would like to group documents in price brackets, that is, we would like to show the most relevant document for documents with price range of 1.0 to 19.99, a document for documents with price range of 20.00 to 50.0, and so on. Solr allows us to group results on the basis of query results. This recipe will show you how to do that.

Getting ready

In this chapter we will use the same index structure and test data as we used in the *Using field values to group results* recipe in this chapter. Please read it before continuing.

How to do it...

As we are reusing the data and index structure from the *Using field values to group results* recipe, we can start with the query. In order to group our documents on the basis of query results, we can send the following query:

```
http://localhost:8983/solr/select?q=*:*&group=true&group.query=price:
[20.0+TO+50.0]&group.query=price:[1.0+TO+19.99]
```

The results of the preceding query look as follows:

```
<?xml version="1.0" encoding="UTF-8"?>
 <response>
  <lst name="responseHeader">
    <int name="status">0</int>
    <int name="QTime">2</int>
    <lst name="params">
```

```
        <arr name="group.query">
         <str>price:[20.0 TO 50.0]</str>
         <str>price:[1.0 TO 19.99]</str>
        </arr>
        <str name="group">true</str>
        <str name="q">*:*</str>
       </lst>
      </lst>
      <lst name="grouped">
       <lst name="price:[20.0 TO 50.0]">
        <int name="matches">3</int>
        <result name="doclist" numFound="2" start="0">
         <doc>
          <str name="id">1</str>
          <str name="name">Solr cookbook</str>
          <str name="category">it</str>
          <float name="price">39.99</float>
         </doc>
        </result>
       </lst>
       <lst name="price:[1.0 TO 19.99]">
        <int name="matches">3</int>
        <result name="doclist" numFound="1" start="0">
         <doc>
          <str name="id">2</str>
          <str name="name">Mechanics cookbook</str>
          <str name="category">mechanics</str>
          <float name="price">19.99</float>
         </doc>
        </result>
       </lst>
      </lst>
     </response>
```

So now let's look at how it works.

How it works...

As you can see in the query we told Solr that we want to use the grouping functionality by using the group=true parameter. In addition to that we specify that we want to have two groups calculated on the basis of the queries. The first group should contain the documents that match the following range query price=[20.0+TO+50.00] (the group.query=price:[1.0+TO+19.99] parameter), and the second group should contain documents that match the following range query price=[1.0+TO+19.99] (the group.query=price:[1.0+TO+19.99] parameter).

If you look at the results, they are very similar to the ones for grouping on the basis of field values. The only difference is in the name of the groups. When using the field values for grouping, groups were named after the used field names. However, when using queries to group documents, groups are named as our grouping queries. So in our case, we have two groups – one named `price:[1.0+TO+19.99]` (the `<lst name="price:[1.0 TO 19.99]">` tag) and a second one named `price:[20.0 TO 50.0]` (the `<lst name="price:[20.0 TO 50.0]">` tag).

Using function queries to group results

Imagine that you would like to group results not by using queries or field contents, but instead you would like to use a value returned by a function query. Imagine you could group documents on the basis of their distance from a point. Sounds good, Solr allows that and in the following recipe we will see how we can use a simple function query to group results.

Getting ready

In this chapter we will use the same index structure and test data we used in the *Sorting results by a function value* recipe in this chapter. We will also use some knowledge that we gained in the *Using field values to group results* recipe in this chapter. Please read them before continuing.

How to do it...

I assume that we would like to have our documents grouped on the basis of the distance from a given point (in real life we would probably like to have some kind of bracket calculated, but let's skip that for now).

As we are using the same index structure and test data as we used in the *Sorting results by a function value* recipe in this chapter, we'll start with the query. In order to achieve what we want we send the following query:

```
http://localhost:8983/solr/select?q=*:*&group=true&group.
func=geodist(geo,0.0,0.0)
```

The following results were returned by Solr after running the preceding query:

```
<?xml version="1.0" encoding="UTF-8"?>
 <response>
  <lst name="responseHeader">
   <int name="status">0</int>
   <int name="QTime">2</int>
   <lst name="params">
    <str name="group.func">geodist(geo,0.0,0.0)</str>
```

```
            <str name="group">true</str>
            <str name="q">*:*</str>
         </lst>
      </lst>
      <lst name="grouped">
       <lst name="geodist(geo,0.0,0.0)">
         <int name="matches">3</int>
         <arr name="groups">
          <lst>
            <double name="groupValue">1584.126028923632</double>
            <result name="doclist" numFound="1" start="0">
             <doc>
               <str name="id">1</str>
               <str name="name">Company one</str>
               <str name="geo">10.1,10.1</str>
             </doc>
            </result>
          </lst>
          <lst>
            <double name="groupValue">1740.0195023531824</double>
            <result name="doclist" numFound="1" start="0">
             <doc>
               <str name="id">2</str>
               <str name="name">Company two</str>
               <str name="geo">11.1,11.1</str>
             </doc>
            </result>
          </lst>
          <lst>
            <double name="groupValue">1911.187477467305</double>
            <result name="doclist" numFound="1" start="0">
             <doc>
               <str name="id">3</str>
               <str name="name">Company three</str>
               <str name="geo">12.2,12.2</str>
             </doc>
            </result>
          </lst>
         </arr>
       </lst>
      </lst>
   </response>
```

Everything worked as it should have, so now let's see how it worked.

How it works...

As you can see, the query is very similar to the one we used when grouping our documents on the basis of field values. So, we again pass the `group=true` parameter to enable grouping, but this time in addition to that we pass the `group.func` parameter with the value, that is, our function query based on whose results Solr should group our documents.

If you look at the results, they are again very similar to the ones seen in grouping on the basis of field values. The only difference is in the names of the groups. When using the field values for grouping, groups were named after the used field names. However, when using function queries to group documents, groups are named by the result of the function query. So in our case, we have three groups because our function query returned three different results, as illustrated in the following list:

- The group named 1584.126028923632 (the `<double name="groupVal ue">1584.126028923632</double>` tag)

- The group named 1740.0195023531824 (the `<double name="groupVal ue">1740.0195023531824</double>` tag)

- The group named 1911.187477467305 (the `<double name="groupVal ue">1911.187477467305</double>` tag)

9
Dealing with Problems

In this chapter we will cover:

- ▸ How to deal with too many opened files
- ▸ How to deal with out-of-memory problems
- ▸ How to sort non-English languages properly
- ▸ How to make your index smaller
- ▸ Diagnosing Solr problems
- ▸ How to avoid swapping

Introduction

Every Solr deployment will, sooner or later, have some kind of problem. It doesn't matter if the deployment is small and simple or if it's a big and complicated deployment containing multiple servers and shards. In this chapter I'll try to help you with some of the problems you can run into when running Solr. I hope this will help you and make your task easier.

How to deal with too many opened files

Sometimes you might encounter a strange error, something that lies on the edge between Lucene and the operating system—the "too many files opened" exception. Is there something we can do about it? Yes, we can, and this recipe will show you how.

How to do it...

The following steps show how to deal with too many opened files:

1. So, for the purpose of the recipe let's assume that the header of the exception thrown by Solr looks like this:

   ```
   java.io.FileNotFoundException: /use/share/solr/data/index/_1.fdx
   (Too many open files)
   ```

2. What can you do instead of pulling your hair out? First of all, this probably occurred on a Unix-/Linux-based operating system. So, let's start with setting the opened files' limit higher. To do that, you need to edit the `/etc/security/limits.conf` file of your operating system and set the following values (I assume Solr is running as `solr` user):

   ```
   solr soft nofile 32000
   solr hard nofile 32000
   ```

3. Now let's add the following line to the `.bash_profile` file in the `solr` user home directory:

   ```
   ulimit -n 32000
   ```

   The probable cause of the "too many files opened" exception is the number of files the index is built of. The more segments the index is built of, the more files will be used.

4. The next thing sometimes worth considering is lowering the `mergeFactor` parameter. To make things simple, the lower the `mergeFactor` setting, the fewer files will be used to construct the index (please read the *How it works...* section that follows, about the dangers of having a very low merge factor). So, let's set `mergeFactor` to 2. We modify the following line in the `solrconfig.xml` file and set it with the appropriate value (2 in our case):

   ```
   <mergeFactor>2</mergeFactor>
   ```

After we set that configuration value, we need to run the optimization of the index. Now let's see what the options mean.

How it works...

We don't discuss the operating system's internal working in this book, but in this section we will make an exception. The mentioned `limits.conf` file in the `/etc/security` directory lets you specify the opened files limit for the users of your system. In the example shown earlier, we set the two necessary limits to `32000` for the user `solr`, so if you had problems with the number of opened files in the default setup you should see the difference after restarting Solr. However, remember that if you are working as the user and you change the limits then you may need to log out and log in again to see those changes.

Next, we have the `mergeFactor` parameter. This configuration parameter lets you determine how often Lucene segments will be merged. The lower the value of `mergeFactor`, the smaller the number of index files will be. However, you have to remember that having a small `mergeFactor` value will lead to more background merges being done by Lucene, and thus the indexing speed will be lower compared to the ones with a higher `mergeFactor` value and your node's I/O system will be used more extensively. On the other hand, lower values of `mergeFactor` will speed up searching.

How to deal with out-of-memory problems

As with every application written in Java, sometimes memory problems happen. When talking about Solr, those problems are usually related to heap size. They usually happen when the heap size is too low. This recipe will show you how to deal with those problems and what to do to avoid them.

How to do it...

Let's consider what to do when we see an exception like this:

```
SEVERE: java.lang.OutOfMemoryError: Java heap space
```

Firstly, you can do something to make your task easier. You can add more memory that the Java virtual machine can use if you have some free physical memory available in your system. To do that, you need to add the `Xmx` and, preferably, the `Xms` parameter to the start-up script of your servlet container (Apache Tomcat or Jetty). To do that, I used the default Solr deployment and modified the parameters. This is how Solr was run with more than the default heap size:

```
java –Xmx1024M –Xms512m –jar start.jar
```

How it works...

So what do the `Xmx` and `Xms` Java virtual machine parameters do? The `Xms` parameter specifies how much heap memory should be assigned by the virtual machine at the start and thus this is the minimal size of the heap memory that will be assigned by the virtual machine. The `Xmx` parameter specifies the maximum size of the heap. The Java virtual machine will not be able to assign more memory for the heap than the `Xmx` parameter.

You should remember one thing—sometimes it's good to set the `Xmx` and `Xms` parameters to the same values. It will ensure that the virtual machine won't be resizing the heap size during application execution and thus won't lose precious time in heap resizing.

One additional thing—be careful when setting the heap size to be too big. It is usually not advised to give the heap size more than 60 percent of your total memory available in the system, because your operating system's I/O cache will suffer.

There are a few more things I would like to discuss when it comes to memory issues.

Monitoring heap when an out-of-memory error occurs

If the out-of-memory errors occurs even after the actions you've done, you should start monitoring your heap. One of the easiest ways to do that is to add the appropriate Java virtual machine parameters. Those parameters are `XX:+HeapDumpOnOutOfMemory` and `XX:HeapDumpPath`. Those two parameters tell the virtual machine to dump the heap on the out-of-memory error and write it to a file created in the specified directory. So the default Solr deployment's `start` command would look like this:

```
java -jar -XX:+HeapDumpOnOutOfMemoryError -XX:HeapDumpPath=/var/log/dump/
start.jar
```

Reducing the amount of memory needed by Solr

However there are times (even if your system has a large amount of memory available), when you may be forced to think about Solr memory consumption reduction. In such cases there is no general advice, but these are a few things that you can keep in mind:

- Look at your queries and consider how they are built
- How you use the faceting mechanism and so on (`facet.method=fc` tends to use less memory when the field has many unique terms in the index)
- Remember that fetching too many documents at a time may cause Solr to run out of heap memory (for example, when setting a large value for the query result window)
- Reduce the number of calculated faceting results (`facet.limit` parameter)
- Check the memory usage of your caches—this can also be one of the reasons for the problems with memory
- If you don't need to use the normalization factor for text fields, you can set `omitNorms="true"` for such fields and save some additional memory too
- Remember that grouping mechanisms requires memory; for big result sets and high numbers of groups, a vast amount of memory may be needed

How to sort non-English languages properly

As you probably already know, Solr supports UTF-8 encoding and thus can handle data in many languages. But, if you ever needed to sort some languages that have characters specific to them you probably know that it doesn't work well on a standard Solr `string` type. This recipe will show you how to deal with sorting in Solr.

How to do it...

These steps tell us how to sort non-English languages properly:

1. For the purpose of this recipe, I have assumed that we will have to sort text that contains Polish characters. To show the good and bad sorting behaviour we need to create the following index structure (add this to your `schema.xml` file):

```
<field name="id" type="string" indexed="true" stored="true"
required="true" />
<field name="name" type="text" indexed="true" stored="true" />
<field name="name_sort_bad" type="string" indexed="true"
stored="true" />
<field name="name_sort_good" type="text_sort" indexed="true"
stored="true" />
```

2. Now let's define some copy fields to automatically fill the `name_sort_bad` and `name_sort_good` fields. Here is how they are defined (add this after the fields section in the `schema.xml` file):

```
<copyField source="name" dest="name_sort_bad" />
<copyField source="name" dest="name_sort_good" />
```

3. The last thing about the `schema.xml` file is the new type. So the `text_sort` definition looks like this:

```
<fieldType name="text_sort" class="solr.TextField">
 <analyzer>
  <tokenizer class="solr.KeywordTokenizerFactory" />
    <filter class="solr.CollationKeyFilterFactory" language="pl"
country="PL" strength="primary" />
 </analyzer>
</fieldType>
```

4. The test we need to index looks like this:

```
<add>
 <doc>
  <field name="id">1</field>
  <field name="name">Łąka</field>
 </doc>
 <doc>
  <field name="id">2</field>
  <field name="name">Lalka</field>
 </doc>
 <doc>
  <field name="id">3</field>
  <field name="name">Ząb</field>
 </doc>
</add>
```

5. First, let's take a look at how the incorrect sorting order looks. To do this, we send the following query to Solr:

```
http://localhost:8983/solr/select?q=*:*&sort=name_sort_bad+asc
```

And now the response that was returned for the query is as follows:

```xml
<?xml version="1.0" encoding="UTF-8"?>
<response>
<lst name="responseHeader">
  <int name="status">0</int>
  <int name="QTime">1</int>
  <lst name="params">
    <str name="q">*:*</str>
    <str name="sort">name_sort_bad asc</str>
  </lst>
</lst>
<result name="response" numFound="3" start="0">
  <doc>
    <str name="id">2</str>
    <str name="name">Lalka</str>
    <str name="name_sort_bad">Lalka</str>
    <str name="name_sort_good">Lalka</str>
  </doc>
  <doc>
    <str name="id">3</str>
    <str name="name">Ząb</str>
    <str name="name_sort_bad">Ząb</str>
    <str name="name_sort_good">Ząb</str>
  </doc>
  <doc>
    <str name="id">1</str>
    <str name="name">Łąka</str>
    <str name="name_sort_bad">Łąka</str>
    <str name="name_sort_good">Łąka</str>
  </doc>
</result>
</response>
```

6. Now let's send the query that should return the documents sorted in the correct order. The query looks like this:

```
http://localhost:8983/solr/select?q=*:*&sort=name_sort_good+asc
```

And the results returned by Solr are as follows:

```xml
<?xml version="1.0" encoding="UTF-8"?>
<response>
<lst name="responseHeader">
  <int name="status">0</int>
  <int name="QTime">6</int>
  <lst name="params">
    <str name="q">*:*</str>
    <str name="sort">name_sort_good asc</str>
  </lst>
</lst>
<result name="response" numFound="3" start="0">
  <doc>
    <str name="id">2</str>
    <str name="name">Lalka</str>
    <str name="name_sort_bad">Lalka</str>
    <str name="name_sort_good">Lalka</str>
  </doc>
  <doc>
    <str name="id">1</str>
    <str name="name">Łąka</str>
    <str name="name_sort_bad">Łąka</str>
    <str name="name_sort_good">Łąka</str>
  </doc>
  <doc>
    <str name="id">3</str>
    <str name="name">Ząb</str>
    <str name="name_sort_bad">Ząb</str>
    <str name="name_sort_good">Ząb</str>
  </doc>
</result>
</response>
```

As you can see the order is different and believe me it's correct. Now let's see how it works.

How it works...

Every document in the index is built on four fields. The id field is responsible for holding the unique identifier of the document. The name field is responsible for holding the name of the document. The last two fields are used for sorting.

The name_sort_bad field is nothing new; it's just a field based on string, which is used to perform sorting. The name_sort_good field is based on a new type, the text_sort field type. The field is based on the solr.TextField type and on solr.KeywordTokenizerFactory, which basically means that our text won't be tokenized. We used this trick because we want to sort on that field and thus we don't want the data in it to be tokenized, but we want to use a special filter on that field. The filter that allows Solr to sort correctly is the solr.CollationKeyFilterFactory filter. We used three attributes of this filter. First, the language attribute, which tells Solr about the language of the field. The second attribute is country which tells Solr about the country variant (this can be skipped if necessary). The strength attribute informs Solr about the collation strength used. More information about those parameters can be found in the JDK documentation. One thing that is crucial is that you need to create an appropriate field and set the appropriate attribute's value for every non-English language you want to sort on.

The two queries you can see in the examples differ in only one thing, the field used for sorting. The first query uses the string-based field, name_sort_bad. When sorting on this field, the document order will be incorrect when there are non-English characters present. However, when sorting on the name_sort_good field everything will be in the correct order as shown in the example.

How to make your index smaller

There may be situations where you would like to make your index smaller. The reasons may be different—you may want to have a smaller index so that it would fit into the operating system's I/O cache or you want to store your index in RAMDirectory. This recipe will try to help you with the process of index slimming.

How to do it...

The following steps tell us how to make your index smaller:

1. For the purpose of this recipe, I assumed that we will have four fields that describe the document. I created the following index structure (add this to your schema.xml file):

```
<field name="id" type="string" indexed="true" stored="true"
required="true" />
<field name="name" type="text" indexed="true" stored="true" />
<field name="description" type="text" indexed="true" stored="true"
/>
<field name="price" type="string" indexed="true" stored="true" />
```

   Let's assume that our application has the following requirements:

   - We need to search on name and description fields
   - We need to show two fields in the results: id and price
   - We don't use highlighting and spellchecker

2. So the first thing we should do is set the `stored="false"` attribute for the `name` and `description` fields.

3. Next, we set the `indexed="false"` attribute for the `price` field.

4. Now, the last thing to do is add the term options. We add the `termVectors="false"`, `termPositions="false"`, and `termOffsets="false"` attributes to the `name` and `description` fields. The modified schema looks like this:

```
<field name="id" type="string" indexed="true" stored="true"
required="true" />
<field name="name" type="text" indexed="true" stored="false"
termVectors="false" termPositions="false" termOffsets="false"/>
<field name="description" type="text" indexed="true"
stored="false" termVectors="false" termPositions="false"
termOffsets="false"/>
<field name="price" type="string" indexed="false" stored="true" />
```

Let's check the index size now. I've indexed 1,000,000 sample documents with the use of the original `schema.xml` file. The index size was 329,237,331 bytes. After changing the `schema.xml` file and indexing the same data the index size was 84,301,603 bytes. So as you can see, the index size was reduced.

Now let's see why we see this reduction in the index size.

How it works...

The first `schema.xml` file you see is the standard index structure provided with Solr example deployment, at least when talking about the types. We have four fields, all of them indexed and stored, which means all of them are searchable and are shown in the result list.

Now let's look at the requirements. First of all we only need to search on the `name` and `description` fields, which mean that the rest of the fields can be set up as not indexed (`indexed="false"` attribute). We set that for the `price` field, while we set the `id` field to be searchable, as we need that to avoid duplicates. When the `indexed` attribute is set to `false`, the information in that field is not indexed which basically means that it isn't written into the Lucene-inverted index and thus it is not available; this saves index space. Of course you can't set this attribute to `false` if you need this field to be searchable.

The second requirement tells us what fields we are obligated to show in the search results. Those field are the ones that need the `stored` attribute set to `true`, and the rest can have this attribute set to `false`. When we set this attribute to `false`, we tell Solr that we don't want to store the original value—the one before analysis—thus we don't want this field to be included in the search results. Setting this attribute to `true` on many fields will increase the index size substantially.

The last requirement is actually information; we don't need to worry about highlighting functionality so we can reduce the index size in a greater way. To do that we add the `termVectors="false"`, `termPositions="false"`, and `termOffsets="false"` attributes to the `name` and `description` fields. By doing that we tell Solr not to store any information about terms in the index. This basically means that we can't use the highlighting functionalities of Solr, but we have reduced our index size substantially and we don't need highlighting.

If we don't need index time boosting and we do not care about length normalization, we could also turn on the omitting of that factor (the `omitNorms="true"` attribute) for the fields based on the `text` type (for primitive types such as `string`, `integer`, and so on it's turned on by default in Solr 4.0). This would shrink the index a bit more and in addition to that save us some memory during queries.

Last few words. Every time you think about reducing the index size, first do the optimization, then look at your `schema.xml` file and see if you need all those fields. Then check which fields shouldn't be stored and which you can omit when indexing. The last thing should be removing the information about terms, because there may come a time when you will need this information and the only thing you will be able to do is a full indexation of millions of documents.

There's more...

There is one additional thing I would like to mention.

Estimating your index size and memory usage

Sometimes it's necessary to have a rough estimate of the index size and the memory usage of your Solr instance. Currently there is a draft of the Microsoft Excel spreadsheet that lets you do that kind of estimation. If you are interested in it, download the following file: `http://svn.apache.org/repos/asf/lucene/dev/trunk/dev-tools/size-estimator-lucene-solr.xls`.

Diagnosing Solr problems

There are many tools out there that can help you diagnose problems with Solr. You can monitor your operating system by yourself by using different operating system commands such as `vmstat`, `dstat`, and `iostat`. You can use different Java tools such as `jconsole` and `jvisualvm` to look at the JMX mbeans, you can monitor your garbage collector work, and so on. However in order to properly diagnose what's happening with your Apache Solr cluster you'll need to see the whole view as well as the specifics. There are different tools out there that you can use, however this recipe will show you what you can find in one of them—Scalable Performance Monitoring.

Getting ready

This recipe assumes that you have Scalable Performance Monitoring installed and running. If you don't, please go to `http://sematext.com/spm/index.html`, create a free account, and download the client that's suitable for you. The installation is very simple and you'll be guided by the Scalable Performance Monitoring installer from the beginning to the end.

How to do it...

1. Let's assume that we want to check our Solr instance health by looking at the GUI of Scalable Performance Monitoring. After logging we would get the following view:

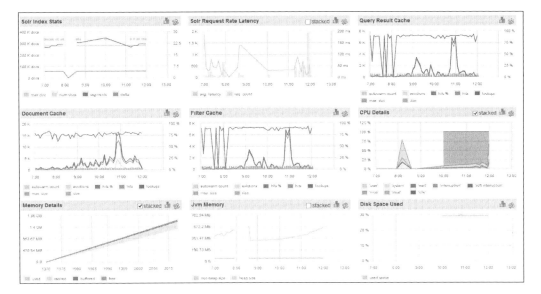

This is an overview of the system, however we would like to see some details.

2. Let's start with the information about indices.

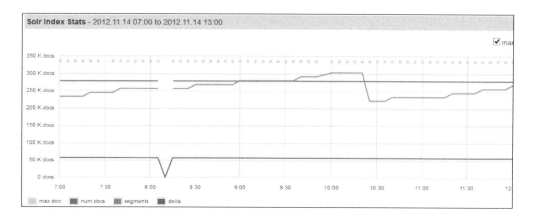

3. Now let's have a look at the cache usage:

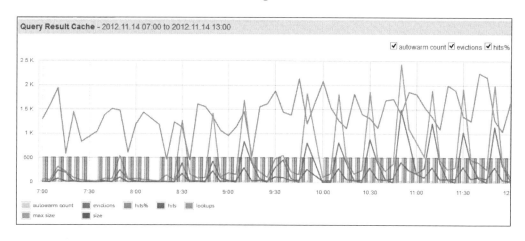

4. By now we know what our index and Solr caches' usage looks like and we know if we need to tune them or not, so now let's look at the query rate and its latency:

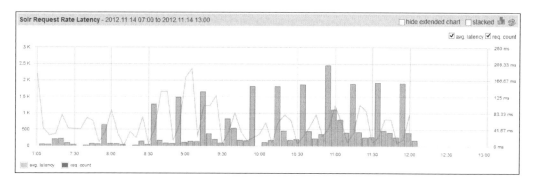

5. Here we can see the warm-up queries' time and execution:

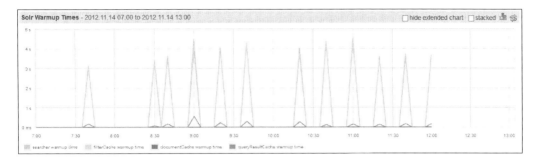

We've got all the information that is connected to queries, so now we can go and see the other crucial information such as memory and CPU usage, Java heap usage, and how Java garbage collector works.

6. Let's start with the memory and CPU usage:

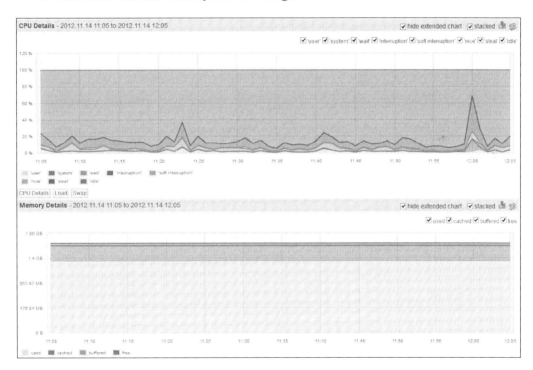

7. And now we can see the JVM heap statistics:

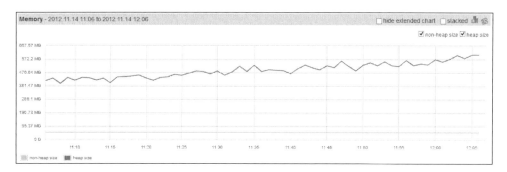

8. And finally we can see how the garbage collector works:

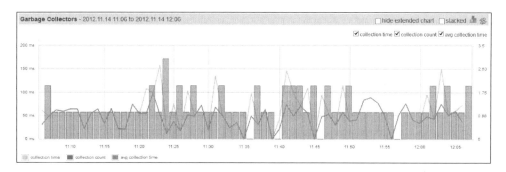

That's all we need during the usual work when we want to see how different parts of Solr work. If we would like to go in depth and see how the I/O subsystem works or the swap usage we can use other aggregated reports available in any of the monitoring systems, or you could just use the appropriate system commands like the ones mentioned in the introduction to the recipe.

How it works...

Let's discuss the provided statistics in a bit more dtail. On the first screenshot provided you can see the overview of the system. This part of Scalable Performance Monitoring will be shown to you as soon as you log in to the system. You'll usually use it to get the whole idea about the system, but you'll want to look at the detailed reports in order to see a higher granularity of your data.

On the second screenshot you can see the index statistics (or indices depending on the options you've chosen). You can see the information about the number of documents in the index, the maximum size of the index, the number of segments, and the **delta**, which is calculated as *the maximum number of documents minus the current number of documents*. Not shown on the screenshot are the filesystem statistics which tell you about the size of the index on the disk. With the use of this data you can see the complete information about your core's or collection's disk drive usage.

The third screenshot is one of the most important ones—the information about Apache Solr caches. Although I haven't shown all the information here, you can see a single cache on the screenshot—the query result cache (we didn't show the document cache and the filter cache). You can see information about the size of the cache, the maximum size of the cache, the number of evictions, and so on. Remember, if your cache is too low, its size will be equal to the maximum size and you'll start seeing evictions, which is not good and you'll probably want to change the cache configuration.

The query rate and latency report shown in the fourth screenshot provides information about the number of queries and their average latency. You can see how your queries were executed and if you need to start thinking about the optimization of your system.

In order to check how your warm-up queries were executed you can look at the fifth of the provided screenshots. You can see the amount of time for which your warm-up queries were executed and how long it took to auto-warm your query result cache and your filter cache. This information can be valuable when dealing with problems such as Solr hanging during the opening of new or first searches.

The last three screenshots provide the information that is not directly connected to Apache Solr, but very valuable from our point of view, when we have to see what is happening with our Solr instance. So let's discuss them.

The sixth screenshot shows information about the CPU and memory usage. For the CPU information you can see how it works; the percent of time spent idling, working on user-run software, working with operating system software, handling interruptions, and so on. If you look at the memory graph you will find the total, used, free, cached, and buffered statistics. That's basically all you need in order to see if your CPU is 100 percent utilized and how your system memory is utilized. This is crucial when your system is not working in the way that you would like it to.

The seventh screenshot provides information about the Java virtual machine. You can see the heap memory statistics and the threading information (which is not shown in the screenshot). The heap usage graph allows us to see if the amount of memory we specified for our Solr instance is enough to handle all the operations that need to be done.

The final screenshot provides information about how your JVM garbage collector works. In most situations you will want it to run more frequently, but for a shorter period of time stop the world events which may cause your Solr instances to stop handling queries or indexing for a short period of time.

To sum up, all the information can be gathered manually by using different system and Java tools. The crucial part of every monitoring system is the ability to show you graphs that will let you point to a certain event in time. We looked at a single monitoring solution, but there are many more available and if you don't like Scalable Performance Monitoring you can use any available. One more thing; please remember that we only scraped the surface in this recipe and the book (or e-book) you are holding in your hands doesn't describe all the information regarding monitoring and dealing with problems. However I hope that this recipe will help you at least start with this topic.

If you don't want to use Scalable Performance Monitoring, you can choose some other technology that is available like Ganglia (`http://ganglia.sourceforge.net/`), Mumin (`http://munin-monitoring.org/`), Zabix (`http://www.zabbix.com/`), Cacti (`http://www.cacti.net/`), or any commercial ones like New Relic (`http://newrelic.com/`).

How to avoid swapping

One of the crucial things when running your Solr instance in production is performance. What you want is to give your clients relevant results in the blink of an eye. If your clients have to wait for results for too long, some of them may choose other vendors or sites that provide similar services. One of the things to remember when running a Java application such as Apache Solr is to ensure that the operating system won't write the heap to disk. This ensures that the part of the memory used by Solr won't be swapped at all. This recipe will show you how to achieve that on a Linux operating system.

Getting ready

Please note that the following recipe is only valid when running Apache Solr on a Linux operating system. In addition to that, please be advised that turning off swapping should only be done when you have enough memory to handle all the necessary application in your system and you want to be sure that there won't be any swapping.

How to do it...

1. Before turning off swapping let's look at the amount of swap memory used by our operating system. In order to do that let's look at the main page of the Solr administration panel:

2. As you can see some swap memory is being used. In order to demonstrate how to turn off swap usage I've freed some memory on the virtual machine I was using for tests and after that I've run the following commands:

```
sudo sysctl -w vm.swappiness=0
sudo /sbin/swapoff -a
```

3. After the second command is done running, refresh the main page of the Solr admin instance and this is what it will show:

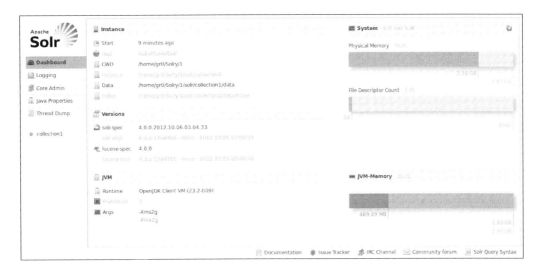

4. It seems like it is working, but in order to be sure I've run the following command:

```
free -m
```

And the response of it was:

	total	used	free	shared	buffers	cached
Mem:	3001	2326	675	0	3	97
-/+ buffers/cache:		2226	775			
Swap:	0	0	0			

And again we can see that there is no swap usage. Now let's see how this works.

How it works...

On the first provided screenshot you can see that there is a bit more than 183 MB of swap memory being used. This is not good; in a production environment you want to avoid swapping, of course, if you have the necessary amount of memory. Swapping will make the contents of the memory to be written onto the hard disk drive, thus making your operating system and applications execute slower. This can also affect Solr.

So, in order to turn off swapping in a Linux operating system, we've run two commands. The first one sets the `vm.swappiness` operating system property to `0`, which means that we want to avoid swapping. We needed to use `sudo`, because in order to set that property with the use of the `sysctl` command we need administration privileges. The second command (the `/sbin/swapoff -a` one) disables swapping on all known devices.

As you can see on the second screenshot, the Solr administration panel didn't even include the swapping information so we may suspect that it was turned off. However in order to be sure, we've used another Linux command, the `free` command with the `-m` switch, in order to see the memory usage on our system. As you can see, the `Swap` section shows `0`, so we can now be sure that swapping was turned off.

Real-life Situations

In this chapter we will cover:

- How to implement a product's autocomplete functionality
- How to implement a category's autocomplete functionality
- How to use different query parsers in a single query
- How to get documents right after they were sent for indexation
- How to search your data in a near real-time manner
- How to get documents with all the query words at the top of the results set
- How to boost documents based on their publication date

Introduction

In the previous nine chapters, we discussed about the different Apache Solr functionalities and how to overcome some common problems and situations. However, I decided that we will describe a few of the most common problems that arise on the Apache Solr mailing list and during our work with our clients. This chapter is dedicated to describing how to handle such situations, and I hope that you'll find it useful.

How to implement a product's autocomplete functionality

The autocomplete functionality is very popular now. You can find it in most e-commerce sites, on Google, Bing, and so on. It enables your users or clients to find what they want and do it fast. In most cases, the autocomplete functionality also increases the relevance of your search by pointing to the right author, title, and so on, right away without looking at the search results. What's more, sites that use autocomplete report higher revenue after deploying it in comparison to the situation before implementing it. Seems like a win-win situation, both for you and your clients. So, let's look at how we can implement a product's autocomplete functionality in Solr.

How to do it...

Let's assume that we want to show the full product name whenever our users enter a part of the word that the product name is made up of. In addition to this, we want to show the number of documents with the same names.

1. Let's start with an example data that is going to be indexed:

```
<add>
  <doc>
    <field name="id">1</field>
    <field name="name">First Solr 4.0 CookBook</field>
  </doc>
  <doc>
    <field name="id">2</field>
    <field name="name">Second Solr 4.0 CookBook</field>
  </doc>
</add>
```

2. We will need two main fields in the index – one for the document identifier and one for the name. We will need two additional fields – one for autocomplete and one for faceting that we will use. So, our index structure will look similar to the following code snippet (we should add it to the schema.xml fields section):

```
<field name="id" type="string" indexed="true"
  stored="true" required="true" />
<field name="name" type="text" indexed="true"
  stored="true" />
<field name="name_autocomplete" type="text_autocomplete"
  indexed="true" stored="false" />
<field name="name_show" type="string" indexed="true"
  stored="false" />
```

3.   In addition to this, we want Solr to automatically copy the data from the `name` field to the `name_autocomplete` and `name_show` fields. So, we should add the following `copy` fields section to the `schema.xml` file:

```
<copyField source="name" dest="name_autocomplete"/>
<copyField source="name" dest="name_show"/>
```

4.   Now, the final thing about the `schema.xml` file — that is, the `text_autocomplete` field type — it should look similar to the following code snippet (place it in the `types` section of the `schema.xml` file):

```
<fieldType name="text_autocomplete"
   class="solr.TextField" positionIncrementGap="100">
   <analyzer type="index">
     <tokenizer class="solr.WhitespaceTokenizerFactory"/>
     <filter class="solr.LowerCaseFilterFactory"/>
     <filter class="solr.EdgeNGramFilterFactory"
       minGramSize="1" maxGramSize="25" />
   </analyzer>
   <analyzer type="query">
     <tokenizer class="solr.WhitespaceTokenizerFactory"/>
     <filter class="solr.LowerCaseFilterFactory"/>
   </analyzer>
</fieldType>
```

5.   That's all. Now, if we would like to show all the products that start with the word `sol` to our users, we would send the following query:

```
curl 'http://localhost:8983/solr/select?q=name_autocomplete:sol&q.
op=AND&rows=0&&facet=true&facet.field=name_show&facet.
mincount=1&facet.limit=5'
```

The response returned by Solr would be as follows:

```
<?xml version="1.0" encoding="UTF-8"?>
<response>
  <lst name="responseHeader">
    <int name="status">0</int>
    <int name="QTime">1</int>
    <lst name="params">
      <str name="facet">true</str>
      <str name="fl">name</str>
      <str name="facet.mincount">1</str>
      <str name="q">name_autocomplete:sol</str>
      <str name="facet.limit">5</str>
      <str name="q.op">AND</str>
      <str name="facet.field">name_show</str>
```

```
            <str name="rows">0</str>
        </lst>
    </lst>
        <result name="response" numFound="2" start="0">
        </result>
        <lst name="facet_counts">
        <lst name="facet_queries"/>
        <lst name="facet_fields">
          <lst name="name_show">
            <int name="First Solr 4.0 CookBook">1</int>
            <int name="Second Solr 4.0 CookBook">1</int>
          </lst>
        </lst>
        <lst name="facet_dates"/>
        <lst name="facet_ranges"/>
    </lst>
</response>
```

As you can see, the faceting results returned by Solr are exactly what we were looking for. So now, let's see how it works.

How it works...

Our example documents are pretty simple – they are only built of an identifier and a name that we will use to make autocomplete. The index structure is where things are getting interesting. The first two fields are the ones that you would have expected – they are used to hold the identifier of the document and its name. However, we have two additional fields available; the `name_autocomplete` field that will be used for querying and `name_show` that will be used for faceting. The `name_show` field is based on a string type, because we want to have a single token per name when using faceting.

With the use of the copy field sections, we can let Solr automatically copy the values of the fields defined by the `source` attribute to the field defined by the `dest` field. Copying is done before any analysis.

The `name_autocomplete` field is based on the `text_autocomplete` field type, which is defined differently for indexing and querying. During query time, we divide the entered query on the basis of white space characters using `solr.WhitespaceTokenizerFactory`, and we lowercase the tokens with the use of `solr.LowerCaseFilterFactory`. For query time, this is what we want because we don't want any more processing. For index time, we not only use the same tokenizer and filter, but also `solr.NGramFilterFactory`. This is because we want to allow our users to efficiently search for prefixes, so that when someone enters the word `sol`, we would like to show all the products that have a word starting with that prefix, and `solr.NGramFilterFactory` allows us to do that. For the word `solr`, it will produce the tokens `s`, `so`, `sol`, and `solr`.

We've also said that we are interested in grams starting from a single character (the `minGramsSize` property) and the maximum size of grams allowed is 25 (the `maxGramSize` property).

Now comes the query. As you can see, we've sent the prefix of the word that the users have entered to the `name_autocomplete` field (`q=name_autocomplete:sol`). In addition to this, we've also said that we want words in our query to be connected with the logical AND operator (the `q.op` parameter), and that we are not interested in the search results (the `rows=0` parameter). As we said, we will use faceting for our autocomplete functionality, because we need the information about the number of documents with the same titles, so we've turned faceting on (the `facet=true` parameter). We said that we want to calculate the faceting on our `name_show` field (the `facet.field=name_show` parameter). We are also only interested in faceting a calculation for the values that have at least one document in them (`facet.mincount=1`), and we want the top five results (`facet.limit=5`).

As you can see, we've got two distinct values in the faceting results; both with a single document with the same title, which matches our sample data.

How to implement a category's autocomplete functionality

Sometimes we are not just interested in our product's name for autocomplete. Imagine that we want to show the category of our products in the autocomplete box along with the number of products in each category. Let's see how we can use faceting to do that.

How to do it...

This recipe will show how we can implement a category's autocomplete functionality.

1. Let's start with the example data, which is going to be indexed and which looks similar to the following code snippet:

```
<add>
  <doc>
    <field name="id">1</field>
    <field name="name">First Solr 4.0 CookBook</field>
    <field name="category">Books</field>
  </doc>
  <doc>
    <field name="id">2</field>
    <field name="name">Second Solr 4.0 CookBook</field>
    <field name="category">Books And Tutorials</field>
  </doc>
</add>
```

2. The `fields` section of the `schema.xml` configuration file that can handle the preceding data should look similar to the following code snippet:

```
<field name="id" type="string" indexed="true"
  stored="true" required="true" />
<field name="name" type="text" indexed="true"
  stored="true" />
<field name="category" type="text_lowercase"
  indexed="true" stored="true" />
```

3. One final thing is the `text_lowercase` type definition, which should be placed in the `types` section of the `schema.xml` file. It should look similar to the following code snippet:

```
<fieldType name="text_lowercase" class="solr.TextField"
  positionIncrementGap="100">
  <analyzer>
    <tokenizer class="solr.KeywordTokenizerFactory"/>
    <filter class="solr.LowerCaseFilterFactory"/>
  </analyzer>
</fieldType>
```

4. So now, if we would like to get all the categories that start with `boo`, along with the number of products in those categories, we would send the following query:

```
curl 'http://localhost:8983/solr/select?q=*:*&rows=0&facet=tr
ue&facet.field=category&facet.mincount=1&facet.limit=5&facet.
prefix=boo'
```

The following response will be returned by Solr:

```
<?xml version="1.0" encoding="UTF-8"?>
<response>
  <lst name="responseHeader">
    <int name="status">0</int>
    <int name="QTime">1</int>
    <lst name="params">
      <str name="facet">true</str>
      <str name="facet.mincount">1</str>
      <str name="indent">true</str>
      <str name="q">*:* </str>
      <str name="facet.limit">5</str>
      <str name="facet.prefix">boo</str>
      <str name="facet.field">category</str>
      <str name="rows">0</str>
```

```
        </lst>
      </lst>

      <result name="response" numFound="2" start="0">
      </result>
        <lst name="facet_counts">
          <lst name="facet_queries"/>
          <lst name="facet_fields">
          <lst name="category">
            <int name="books">1</int>
            <int name="books and tutorials">1</int>
          </lst>
        </lst>
        <lst name="facet_dates"/>
        <lst name="facet_ranges"/>
      </lst>
</response>
```

As you can see, we have two categories, each containing a single product. So this is what matches our example data. Let's now see how it works.

How it works...

Our data is very simple. We have three fields for each of our documents – one for the `identifier` fields, one for holding the name of the document, and one for its category. We will use the `category` field to do the autocomplete functionality, and we will use faceting for it.

If you look at the index structure, for the `category` field, we use a special type – the `text_lowercase` one. What it does is that it stores the category as a single token in the index because of `solr.KeywordTokenizerFactory`. We also lowercase with the appropriate filter. This is because we want to send the lowercased queries while using faceting.

The query is quite simple – we query for all the documents (`q=*:*` parameter), and we don't want any results returned (the `rows=0` parameter). We will use faceting for autocomplete, so we turn it on (`facet=true`) and we specify the `category` field to calculate the faceting (`facet.field=category`). We are also only interested in faceting a calculation for the values that have at least one document in them (`facet.mincount=1`), and we want the top five results (`facet.limit=5`). One of of the most important parameters in the query is `facet.prefix` – using it we can return on those results in faceting that start with the prefix defined by the mentioned parameter, which can be seen in the results.

How to use different query parsers in a single query

Sometimes, it is good to be able to choose different query parsers in the same query. For example, imagine that you would like to use the Extended DisMax query parser for the main query, but in addition to this, we would like to use the field query parser for filter queries. This recipe will show you how to do it.

How to do it...

This recipe will show how we can use different query parsers in a single query.

1. Let's start with the following index structure (this should go to the `field` section in the `schema.xml` file):

```
<field name="id" type="string" indexed="true"
  stored="true" required="true" />
<field name="name" type="text" indexed="true"
  stored="true" />
<field name="category" type="string" indexed="true"
  stored="true" />
```

2. Now, let's index the following data:

```
<add>
  <doc>
    <field name="id">1</field>
    <field name="name">First Solr 4.0 CookBook</field>
    <field name="category">Books</field>
  </doc>
  <doc>
    <field name="id">2</field>
    <field name="name">Second Solr 4.0 CookBook</field>
    <field name="category">Books And Tutorials</field>
  </doc>
</add>
```

3. So, if we search for all the documents using the Extended DisMax query parser and want to narrow our results to the **Books And Tutorials** category, then we can send the following query:

```
curl 'http://localhost:8983/solr/select?q=*:*&defType=edismax&fq={
!term f=category}Books And Tutorials'
```

The results returned by Solr would be as follows:

```xml
<?xml version="1.0" encoding="UTF-8"?>
<response>
  <lst name="responseHeader">
    <int name="status">0</int>
    <int name="QTime">1</int>
    <lst name="params">
      <str name="fq">
        {!term f=category}Books And Tutorials
      </str>
      <str name="q">*:*</str>
      <str name="defType">edismax</str>
    </lst>
  </lst>
  <result name="response" numFound="1" start="0">
    <doc>
      <str name="id">2</str>
      <str name="name">Second Solr 4.0 CookBook</str>
      <str name="category">Books And Tutorials</str>
    </doc>
  </result>
</response>
```

As you can see, we got what we expected. So let's see how it works.

How it works...

Our index structure and example data are not that relevant for this recipe, so I'll skip discussing them.

What we want to achieve is be sure that the data we filter will be properly processed, and we want to avoid thinking about any kind of query parsing and Lucene special characters escaping. In order to do this, we use the term **query parser**. To inform Solr that we want to use this query parser in the filter query (the `fq` parameter), we use local parameter syntax and send this filter query: `{!term f=category}Books And Tutorials`. The `!term` part of the filter query says which query parser we want to use, and the `f` property specifies the field to which we want to send the provided `Books And Tutorials` value.

That's all; as you can see in the provided results, everything works as intended.

How to get documents right after they were sent for indexation

Let's say that we would like to get our documents as soon as they were sent for indexing, but without any commit (both hard and soft) operation occurring. Solr 4.0 comes with a special functionality called **real-time get**, which uses the information of uncommitted documents and can return them as documents. Let's see how we can use it.

How to do it...

This recipe will show how we can get documents right after they were sent for indexation.

1. Let's begin with defining the following index structure (add it to the field section in your `schema.xml` file):

```
<field name="id" type="string" indexed="true"
  stored="true" required="true" />
<field name="name" type="text" indexed="true"
  stored="true" />
```

2. In addition to this, we need the `_version_` field to be present, so let's also add the following field to our `schema.xml` file in its `field` section:

```
<field name="_version_" type="long" indexed="true"
  stored="true"/>
```

3. The third step is to turn on the transaction log functionality in Solr. In order to do this, we should add the following section to the `updateHandler` configuration section (in the `solrconfig.xml` file):

```
<updateLog>
  <str name="dir">${solr.data.dir:}</str>
</updateLog>
```

4. The last thing we need to do is add a proper request handler configuration to our `solrconfig.xml` file:

```
<requestHandler name="/get"
  class="solr.RealTimeGetHandler">
  <lst name="defaults">
    <str name="omitHeader">true</str>
    <str name="indent">true</str>
    <str name="wt">xml</str>
  </lst>
</requestHandler>
```

5. Now, we can test how the handler works. In order to do this, let's index the following document (which we've stored in the `data.xml` file):

```
<add>
  <doc>
    <field name="id">1</field>
    <field name="name">Solr 4.0 CookBook</field>
  </doc>
</add>
```

6. In order to index it, we use the following command:

```
curl 'http://localhost:8983/solr/update' --data-binary @data.xml
-H 'Content-type:application/xml'
```

7. Now, let's try two things. First, let's search for the document we've just added. In order to do this, we run the following query:

```
curl 'http://localhost:8983/solr/select?q=id:1'
```

8. As you can imagine, we didn't get any documents returned, because we didn't send any `commit` command – not even the soft commit one. So now, let's use our defined handler:

```
curl 'http://localhost:8983/solr/get?id=1'
```

The following response will be returned by Solr:

```
<?xml version="1.0" encoding="UTF-8"?>
<response>
  <doc name="doc">
    <str name="id">1</str>
    <str name="name">Solr 4.0 CookBook</str>
    <long name="_version_">1418467767663722496</long>
  </doc>
</response>
```

As you can see, our document is returned by our `get` handler. Let's see how it works now.

How it works...

Our index structure is simple, and there is only one relevant piece of information there – the `_version_` field. The real-time `get` functionality needs that field to be present in our documents, because the transaction log relies on it. However, as you can see in the provided example data, we don't need to worry about this field, because its filled and updated automatically by Solr.

But let's backtrack a bit and discuss the changes made to the `solrconfig.xml` file. There are two things there. The first one is the update log (the `updateLog` section), which Solr uses to store the so-called transaction log. Solr stores recent index changes there (until hard commit), in order to provide write durability, consistency, and the ability to provide the real-time get functionality.

The second thing is the handler we defined under the name of `/get` with the use of the `solr.RealTimeGetHandler` class. It uses the information in the transaction log to get the documents we want by using their identifier. It can even retrieve the documents that weren't committed and are only stored in the transaction log. So, if we want to get the newest version of the document, we can use it. The other configuration parameters are the same as with the usual request handler, so I'll skip commenting them.

The next thing we do is send the `update` command without adding the `commit` command, so that we shouldn't be able to see the document during a standard search. If you look at the results returned by the first query, you'll notice that we didn't get that document. However, when using the `/get` handler that we previously defined, we get the document we requested. This is because Solr uses the transaction log in order to even the uncommitted document.

How to search your data in a near real-time manner

Sometimes, we need our data to be available as soon as possible. Imagine that we have a SolrCloud cluster up and running, and we want to have our documents available for searching with only a slight delay. For example, our application can be a content management system where it would be very weird if a user adds a new document, and it would take some time for it to be searchable. In order to achieve this, Solr exposes the soft commit functionality, and this recipe will show you how to set it up.

How to do it...

This recipe will show how we can search for data in a near real-time manner.

1. For the purpose of this recipe, let's assume that we have the following index structure (add it to the `field` section in your `schema.xml` file):

   ```
   <field name="id" type="string" indexed="true"
     stored="true" required="true" />
   <field name="name" type="text" indexed="true"
     stored="true" />
   ```

2. In addition to this, we need to set up the hard and soft automatic commits, for which we will need to add the following section to the `updateHandler` section in the `solrconfig.xml` file:

```
<autoCommit>
  <maxTime>60000</maxTime>
  <openSearcher>false</openSearcher>
</autoCommit>

<autoSoftCommit>
  <maxTime>1000</maxTime>
</autoSoftCommit>
```

3. Let's test if that works. In order to do this, let's index the following document (which we've stored in the `data.xml` file):

```
<add>
  <doc>
    <field name="id">1</field>
    <field name="name">Solr 4.0 CookBook</field>
  </doc>
</add>
```

4. In order to index it, we use the following command:

```
curl 'http://localhost:8983/solr/update' --data-binary @data.xml
-H 'Content-type:application/xml'
```

5. We didn't send any `commit` command, so we shouldn't see any documents, right? I think there will be one available – the one we've just send for indexation. But, let's check that out by running the following simple search command:

```
curl 'http://localhost:8983/solr/select?q=id:1'
```

The following response will be returned by Solr:

```
<?xml version="1.0" encoding="UTF-8"?>
<response>
  <lst name="responseHeader">
    <int name="status">0</int>
    <int name="QTime">0</int>
    <lst name="params">
      <str name="q">id:1</str>
    </lst>
  </lst>
  <result name="response" numFound="1" start="0">
    <doc>
      <str name="id">1</str>
      <str name="name">Solr 4.0 CookBook</str>
    </doc>
  </result>
</response>
```

As you can see, our document was returned. So, let's see how it works.

How it works...

As you may know, the standard commit operation is quite resource-intensive – it flushes the changes since the last commit to the disk to the new segment. If you would like to do that every second, we could run into a problem of a very high amount of I/O writes and thus our searches would suffer (of course, this depends on the situation). That's why, with Lucene and Solr 4.0, the new commit type was introduced – the soft commit, which doesn't flush the changes to disk, but just reopens the searcher object and allows us to search the data that is stored in the memory.

As we are usually lazy and don't want to remember when it's time to send the commit and when to use soft commit, we'll let Solr manage that so we properly need to configure the update handler. First, we add the standard auto commit by adding the `autoCommit` section and saying that we want to commit after every 60 seconds (the `maxTime` property is specified in milliseconds), and that we don't want to reopen the searcher after the standard commit (the `openSearcher` property is set to `false`).

The next thing is to configure the soft auto commit functionality by adding the `softAutoCommit` section to the `update` handler configuration. We've specified that we want the soft commit to be fired every second (the `maxTime property` is specified in milliseconds), and thus our searcher will be reopened every second if there are changes.

As you can see, even though we didn't specify the commit command after our `update` command, we are still able to find the document we've sent for indexation.

How to get the documents with all the query words to the top of the results set

One of the most common problems that users struggle with when using Apache Solr is how to improve the relevancy of their results. Of course, relevancy tuning is, in most cases, connected to your business needs, but one of the common problems is to have documents that have all the query words in their fields at the top of the results list. You can imagine a situation where you search for all the documents that match at least a single query word, but you would like to show the ones with all the query words first. This recipe will show you how to achieve that.

How to do it...

This recipe will show how we can get the documents with all the query words to the top of the results set.

1. Let's start with the following index structure (add it to the `field` section in your `schema.xml` file):

```
<field name="id" type="string" indexed="true"
  stored="true" required="true" />
<field name="name" type="text" indexed="true"
  stored="true" />
<field name="description" type="text" indexed="true"
  stored="true" />
```

2. The second step is to index the following sample data:

```
<add>
  <doc>
    <field name="id">1</field>
    <field name="name">Solr and all the others</field>
    <field name="description">This is about Solr</field>
  </doc>
  <doc>
    <field name="id">2</field>
    <field name="name">Lucene and all the others</field>
    <field name="description">
      This is a book about Solr and Lucene
    </field>
  </doc>
</add>
```

3. Let's assume that our usual queries look similar to the following code snippet:

```
http://localhost:8983/solr/select?q=solr book&defType=edismax&mm=1
&qf=name^10000+description
```

Nothing complicated; however, the results of such query don't satisfy us, because they look similar to the following code snippet:

```
<?xml version="1.0" encoding="UTF-8"?>
<response>
  <lst name="responseHeader">
    <int name="status">0</int>
    <int name="QTime">1</int>
    <lst name="params">
      <str name="qf">name^10000 description</str>
      <str name="mm">1</str>
      <str name="q">solr book</str>
      <str name="defType">edismax</str>
    </lst>
  </lst>
  <result name="response" numFound="2" start="0">
```

```
      <doc>
        <str name="id">1</str>
        <str name="name">Solr and all the others</str>
        <str name="description">This is about Solr</str>
      </doc>
      <doc>
        <str name="id">2</str>
        <str name="name">Lucene and all the others</str>
       <str name="description">
          This is a book about Solr and Lucene
        </str>
      </doc>
    </result>
</response>
```

4. In order to change this, let's introduce a new handler in our `solrconfig.xml` file:

```
<requestHandler name="/better"
  class="solr.StandardRequestHandler">
  <lst name="defaults">
    <str name="indent">true</str>
    <str name="q">
      _query_:"{!edismaxqf=$qfQuery mm=$mmQuerypf=
        $pfQuerybq=$boostQuery v=$mainQuery}"
    </str>
    <str name="qfQuery">name^100000 description</str>
    <str name="mmQuery">1</str>
    <str name="pfQuery">name description</str>
    <str name="boostQuery">
      _query_:"{!edismaxqf=$boostQueryQf mm=100%
        v=$mainQuery}"^100000
    </str>
    <str name="boostQueryQf">name description</str>
  </lst>
</requestHandler>
```

5. So, let's send a query to our new handler:

    `http://localhost:8983/solr/better?mainQuery=solr book`

    We get the following results:

```
<?xml version="1.0" encoding="UTF-8"?>
<response>
  <lst name="responseHeader">
    <int name="status">0</int>
```

```
    <int name="QTime">2</int>
  </lst>
  <result name="response" numFound="2" start="0">
    <doc>
      <str name="id">2</str>
      <str name="name">Lucene and all the others</str>
      <str name="description">
        This is a book about Solr and Lucene
      </str>
    </doc>
    <doc>
      <str name="id">1</str>
      <str name="name">Solr and all the others</str>
      <str name="description">This is about Solr</str>
    </doc>
  </result>
</response>
```

As you can see, it works. So let's discuss how.

How it works...

For the purpose of the recipe, we've used a simple index structure that consists of a document identifier, its name, and description. Our data is very simple as well; it just contains two documents.

During the first query, the document with the identifier 1 is placed at the top of the query results. However, what we would like to achieve is be able to boost the name. In addition to this, we would like to have the documents with words from the query close to each other at the top of the results.

In order to do this, we've defined a new request handler named /better, which will leverage the local params. The first thing is the defined q parameter, which is the standard query. It uses the Extended DisMax parser (the {!edismax part of the query), and defines several additional parameters:

- qf: This defines the fields against which edismax should send the query. We tell Solr that we will provide the fields by specifying the qfQuery parameter by using the $qfQuery value.

- mm: This is the "minimum should match" parameter, which tells edismax how many words from the query should be found in a document for the document to be considered a match. We tell Solr that we will provide the fields by specifying the mmQuery parameter, by using the $mmQuery value.

- ▶ pf: This is the phrase fields definition which specifies the fields on which Solr should generate phrase queries automatically. Similar to the previous parameters that we've specified, we will provide the fields by specifying the pfQuery parameter, by using the $pfQuery value.

- ▶ bq: This is the boost query that will be used to boost the documents. Again, we use the parameter dereferencing functionality and tell Solr that we will provide the value in the bqQuery parameter, by using the $bqQuery value.

- ▶ v: This is the final parameter which specifies the content of the query; in our case, the user query will be specified in the mainQuery parameter.

Basically, the preceding queries say that we will use the edismax query parser, phrase, and boost queries. Now let's discuss the values of the parameters.

The first thing is the qfQuery parameter, which is exactly the same as the qf parameter in the first query we sent to Solr. Using it, we just specify the fields that we want to be searched and their boosts. Next, we have the mmQuery parameter set to 1 that will be used as mm in edismax, which means that a document will be considered a match when a single word from the query will be found in it. As you will remember, the pfQuery parameter value will be passed to the pf parameter, and thus the phrase query will be automatically made on the fields defined in those fields.

Now, the last and probably the most important part of the query, the boostQuery parameter, specifies the value that will be passed to the bq parameter. Our boost query is very similar to our main query, however, we say that the query should only match the documents that have all the words from the query (the mm=100% parameter). We also specify that the documents that match that query should be boosted by adding the ^100000 part at the end of it.

To sum up all the parameters of our query, they will promote the documents with all the words from the query present in the fields we want to search on. In addition to this, we will promote the documents that have phrases matched. So finally, let's look at how the newly created handler work. As you can see, when providing our query to it with the mainQuery parameter, the previous document is now placed as the first one. So, we have achieved what we wanted.

How to boost documents based on their publishing date

Imagine that you would like to place documents that are newer above the ones that are older. For example, you have a book store and want to promote the books that have been published recently, and place them above the books that have been present in our store for a long time. Solr lets us do this, and this recipe will show you how.

How to do it...

This recipe will show how we can boost documents based on their publishing date.

1. Let's begin with the following index structure (add it to the `field` section in your `schema.xml` file):

```
<field name="id" type="string" indexed="true"
  stored="true" required="true" />
<field name="name" type="text" indexed="true"
  stored="true" />
<field name="published" type="date" indexed="true"
  stored="true" default="NOW" />
```

2. Now, let's index the following sample data:

```
<add>
  <doc>
    <field name="id">1</field>
    <field name="name">Solr 3.1 CookBook</field>
    <field name="published">2011-02-02T12:00:00Z</field>
  </doc>
  <doc>
    <field name="id">2</field>
    <field name="name">Solr 4.0 CookBook</field>
    <field name="published">2012-10-01T12:00:00Z</field>
  </doc>
</add>
```

3. Now, let's run a simple query:

```
curl 'http://localhost:8983/solr/select?q=solr+cookbook&qf=name&de
fType=edismax'
```

For the preceding query, Solr will return the following results:

```
<?xml version="1.0" encoding="UTF-8"?>
<response>
  <lst name="responseHeader">
    <int name="status">0</int>
    <int name="QTime">1</int>
    <lst name="params">
      <str name="qf">name</str>
      <str name="q">solr cookbook</str>
      <str name="defType">edismax</str>
    </lst>
  </lst>
```

```
<result name="response" numFound="2" start="0">
  <doc>
    <str name="id">1</str>
    <str name="name">Solr 3.1 CookBook</str>
    <date name="published">2011-02-02T12:00:00Z</date>
  </doc>
  <doc>
    <str name="id">2</str>
    <str name="name">Solr 4.0 CookBook</str>
    <date name="published">2012-10-01T12:00:00Z</date>
  </doc>
</result>
</response>
```

4. As you can see, the newest document is the second one, which we want to avoid. So, we need to change our query to the following one:

```
curl 'http://localhost:8983/solr/select?q=solr+cookbook&qf=name&bf
=recip(ms(NOW/HOUR,published),3.16e-11,1,1)defType=edismax'
```

Now, the response will be as follows:

```
<?xml version="1.0" encoding="UTF-8"?>
<response>
  <lst name="responseHeader">
    <int name="status">0</int>
    <int name="QTime">2</int>
    <lst name="params">
      <str name="qf">name</str>
      <str name="bf">
        recip(ms(NOW/HOUR,published),3.16e-11,1,1)
      </str>
      <str name="q">solr cookbook</str>
      <str name="defType">edismax</str>
    </lst>
  </lst>
  <result name="response" numFound="2" start="0">
    <doc>
      <str name="id">2</str>
      <str name="name">Solr 4.0 CookBook</str>
      <date name="published">2012-10-01T12:00:00Z</date>
    </doc>
    <doc>
      <str name="id">1</str>
      <str name="name">Solr 3.1 CookBook</str>
```

```
        <date name="published">2011-02-02T12:00:00Z</date>
      </doc>
    </result>
  </response>
```

So, we have achieved what we wanted. Now, let's see how it works.

How it works...

Our index structure consists of three fields; one responsible for holding the identifier of the document, one for the name of the document, and the last one; the one which we will be most interested in, in which we hold the publishing date.

The published field has one nice feature – if we don't define it in the document and send it for indexation, then it will get the value of the date and time when it is processed (the `default="NOW"` attribute).

As you can see, the first query that we sent to Solr returned results not in a way we would like them to be sorted. The most recent document is the second one. Of course, we could have sorted them by date, but we don't want to do that, because we would like to have the most recent and the most relevant documents at the top, not only the newest ones.

In order to achieve this, we use the `bf` (boost function) parameter. We specify the boosting function. At first, it can look very complicated, but it's not. In order to boost our documents, we use the `recip(ms(NOW/HOUR,published),3.16e-11,1,1)` function query. `3.16e10` specifies the number of milliseconds that are in a single year, so we use `3.16e-11` to invert that, and we use the reciprocal function (recip) to calculate the scaling value, which will return values near 1 for recent documents, `1/2` for documents from about a year, `1/3` for documents that are about two years old, `1/4` for documents that are about three years old, and so on.

We've also used `NOW/HOUR` to reduce the precision of the published field, in order for our function query to consume less memory and because we don't need that granularity; our results will be just fine.

As you can see, our query with the `bf` parameter and the time-based function query work as intended.

There's more...

If you want to read more about function queries, please refer to the `http://wiki.apache.org/solr/FunctionQuery` Solr wiki page.

Index

Symbols

A

B

C

Thank you for buying
Apache Solr 4 Cookbook

About Packt Publishing

Packt, pronounced 'packed', published its first book "*Mastering phpMyAdmin for Effective MySQL Management*" in April 2004 and subsequently continued to specialize in publishing highly focused books on specific technologies and solutions.

Our books and publications share the experiences of your fellow IT professionals in adapting and customizing today's systems, applications, and frameworks. Our solution based books give you the knowledge and power to customize the software and technologies you're using to get the job done. Packt books are more specific and less general than the IT books you have seen in the past. Our unique business model allows us to bring you more focused information, giving you more of what you need to know, and less of what you don't.

Packt is a modern, yet unique publishing company, which focuses on producing quality, cutting-edge books for communities of developers, administrators, and newbies alike. For more information, please visit our website: www.packtpub.com.

About Packt Open Source

In 2010, Packt launched two new brands, Packt Open Source and Packt Enterprise, in order to continue its focus on specialization. This book is part of the Packt Open Source brand, home to books published on software built around Open Source licences, and offering information to anybody from advanced developers to budding web designers. The Open Source brand also runs Packt's Open Source Royalty Scheme, by which Packt gives a royalty to each Open Source project about whose software a book is sold.

Writing for Packt

We welcome all inquiries from people who are interested in authoring. Book proposals should be sent to author@packtpub.com. If your book idea is still at an early stage and you would like to discuss it first before writing a formal book proposal, contact us; one of our commissioning editors will get in touch with you.

We're not just looking for published authors; if you have strong technical skills but no writing experience, our experienced editors can help you develop a writing career, or simply get some additional reward for your expertise.

Apache Solr 3 Enterprise Search Server

ISBN: 978-1-84951-606-8   Paperback: 418 pages

Enhance your search with faceted navigation, result highlighting relevancy ranked sorting, and more

1. Comprehensive information on Apache Solr 3 with examples and tips so you can focus on the important parts

2. Integration examples with databases, web-crawlers, XSLT, Java & embedded-Solr, PHP & Drupal, JavaScript, Ruby frameworks

3. Advice on data modeling, deployment considerations to include security, logging, and monitoring, and advice on scaling Solr and measuring performance

HBase Administration Cookbook

ISBN: 978-1-84951-714-0   Paperback: 332 pages

Master HBase configuration and administration for optimum database performance

1. Move large amounts of data into HBase and learn how to manage it efficiently

2. Set up HBase on the cloud, get it ready for production, and run it smoothly with high performance

3. Maximize the ability of HBase with the Hadoop eco-system including HDFS, MapReduce, Zookeeper, and Hive

Please check **www.PacktPub.com** for information on our titles

Hadoop Real World Solutions Cookbook

ISBN: 978-1-84951-912-0   Paperback: 325 pages

Realistic, simple code examples to solve problems at scale with Hadoop and related technologies

1. Solutions to common problems when working in the Hadoop environment

2. Recipes for (un)loading data, analytics, and troubleshooting

3. In depth code examples demonstrating various analytic models, analytic solutions, and common best practices

Cassandra High Performance Cookbook

ISBN: 978-1-84951-512-2   Paperback: 310 pages

Over 150 recipes to design and optimize large-scale Apache Cassandra deployments

1. Get the best out of Cassandra using this efficient recipe bank

2. Configure and tune Cassandra components to enhance performance

3. Deploy Cassandra in various environments and monitor its performance

4. Well illustrated, step-by-step recipes to make all tasks look easy!

Please check **www.PacktPub.com** for information on our titles

Made in the USA
San Bernardino, CA
15 February 2014